Circe's Cup

CRITICAL CONDITIONS: FIELD DAY ESSAYS AND MONOGRAPHS

Edited by Seamus Deane

Critical Conditions: Field Day Essays

Circe's Cup

Cultural Transformations in Early Modern Writing about Ireland

Clare Carroll

UNIVERSITY OF NOTRE DAME PRESS
in association with
FIELD DAY

Published in the United States in 2001 by
University of Notre Dame Press
Notre Dame, IN 46556

All Rights Reserved

And in Ireland by
Cork University Press
University College Cork, Ireland

© Clare Carroll 2001

A record of the Library of Congress Cataloging-in-Publication Data is available upon request.

ISBN 0-268-02274-7

CONTENTS

ACKNOWLEDGEMENTS

Since I first met her in May 1998, Sara Wilbourne of Cork University Press has encouraged me to bring my work together into this collection of essays. In keeping with the design of the Critical Conditions series to make widely scattered articles easily available, this book brings together essays that appeared earlier elsewhere. Thanks are due to the editors of *Albion: A Journal of British History*, *Criticism*, and the *Irish University Review* for permission to reprint the following: 'The Construction of Gender, Class and the Cultural and Political Other in *The Faerie Queene V* and *A View of the Present State of Ireland*', *Criticism* 32, 2 (Spring 1990), pp. 163–92; 'Representations of Women in Some Early Modern English Tracts on the Colonization of Ireland', *Albion* 25, 3 (1993), pp. 379–94; 'Spenser's Relation to the Irish Language: The Sons of Milesio in *A View*, *Faerie Queene V*, and the *Leabhar Gabhála*', *Irish University Review* 26, 2, (Autumn/Winter 1996), pp. 281–90. I am also grateful to Four Courts Press for permission to reprint 'Irish and Spanish Cultural and Political Relations in the Work of O'Sullivan Beare', which was originally published in Hiram Morgan (ed.), *Political Ideology in Ireland 1541–1641* (Dublin, 1999), and 'Custom and Law in the Philosophy of Suárez and in the Histories of O'Sullivan Beare, Céitinn and Ó Cléirigh', which first appeared in Thomas O'Connor (ed.), *The Irish in Europe 1580–1815* (Dublin, 2001). Hiram Morgan and Thomas O'Connor were both careful and challenging editors of my work. And they both deserve credit for encouraging not only me but so many others to do research and publish in early modern Irish history – Hiram through his Folger Institute seminar on political thought in early modern Ireland, and Thomas O'Connor through his ongoing conferences at the National University of Ireland, Maynooth (1999, 2000) on the Irish in Europe.

Many others contributed to my work, foremost among them Vincent Carey, with whom I co-edited Richard Beacon's *Solon His Follie*. Vincent taught me how to read the secretary hand and how to do research in the State Papers, and he gave me invaluable criticism on more than one version of every essay in this volume. Earlier versions of chapter 3 on representations of women in the tracts on Ireland received helpful criticism from Nicholas Canny and from the members of the CUNY Seminar on Women in the Renaissance. Anne Fogarty and Patricia Coughlan responded to earlier versions of chapter 4 on Spenser's relation to the Irish language. Chapter 5 on Ariosto in Ireland is a revised version of papers I originally gave at the annual conference of the Renaissance Society of America in 1995 and 1999; critical comments from fellow ariostisti Daniel Javitch and Dennis Looney gave me insight into the meaning of the allegorization and translation of the *Furioso*. Chapter 7 on O'Sullivan Beare's context in Spain resulted from research that I did in both Hiram

Morgan's and Jane Ohlmeyer's Folger Institute seminars. Both of them provided useful advice on research and turned my attention to sources that I might otherwise have overlooked. At a later stage, conversations on Spanish historiography and humanism with Ottavio di Camillo of the Spanish Department at the CUNY Graduate Center led to further research on the intellectual and political history of early modern Spain. In Jane Ohlmeyer's seminar on seventeenth-century political thought in Ireland, I met Breandán Ó Buachalla, from whose published work and lectures I learned an enormous amount about historiography and politics in Irish language texts. I also had the opportunity to attend his seminar at New York University's Ireland House in fall 1997.

In fall 1996, Patricia King and Bob Scally of Glucksmann Ireland House invited me to give a graduate seminar at New York University sponsored by the English Department on early modern Ireland entitled 'What ish my nation?' The course description for this seminar prompted Kevin Whelan to suggest that I might have a manuscript in the making for the Field Day Critical Conditions series. My initial inquiry to series editor Seamus Deane met with an encouraging response. Since then not only he but also Kevin Whelan and Luke Gibbons of Notre Dame have discussed my work with me in relation to how these debates about early modern Irish culture relate to the longer trajectory of Irish history and its wider relation to the history of colonization around the world.

It was partially out of such discussions that Patricia King and I decided to organize a conference on Ireland and the post-colonial world at New York University in fall 1997. Chapter 1, 'Barbarous Slaves and Civil Cannibals', is a revised version of the paper that I gave at that conference. Reading the work of Walter Mignolo, David Lloyd and Gauri Viswanathan, as well as of my colleagues in the Queens Comparative Literature Department, Ali Jimale Ahmed and Amitav Ghosh, I wanted to make the connection between the origins of colonialism and the critique of colonialism in the early modern period and its nineteenth- and twentieth-century manifestations, both in Ireland and the rest of the world. Another version of this article resulted from the discussions that I had with faculty and graduate students at University of California at Davis, where Seth Schein invited me to address the Comparative Literature Department seminar.

In addition to Glucksman Ireland House of New York University, the institutions I need to thank are: the Professional Staff Congress of the City University of New York, which provided me with grants for research in England and Ireland in summer 1990 and 1991, and 2000; the Folger Institute, which granted me aid to attend seminars on early modern Ireland in fall 1995 and spring 1997, and a short term fellowship in fall 1995; and Queens College, which honoured me with the President's Award for Research in spring 1999. I am also grateful for the invaluable assistance of the librarians at the Folger Shakespeare Library, the New York Public Library, the National Library of Ireland, and the Trinity College Dublin Manuscripts Department.

The Comparative Literature Department of the CUNY Graduate Center and Irish Studies Program at Queens College also gave me the opportunity to teach seminars related to the research of this book. Students whose readings of early modern texts and discussions of the theories of early modern colonization influenced the writing of this book include Monica Calabritto, Tara Helfman, and Cyrus Moore. My research assistant John Pilsner helped me locate books and articles as well as iron out computer problems.

Lastly, I want to thank my friends and family. Anne McCoy and Marilyn Miller, who both happen to be editors as well as friends, advised me on all sorts of details. And Janice Lee encouraged me to finish this book and let go of it. My brother Charles and sisters Dev, Kate and Ann have been a real source of moral support, especially since the death of our mother in 1999. During the entire time that I was writing these essays, my first and most intensely critical and appreciative audience was my husband Daniel Scanlon. This book would not be possible without the years we spent together learning Irish and discussing Irish history.

INTRODUCTION

Both Old and New English early modern writers used the metaphor of 'Circe's cup'[1] to conjure up the bewitching, sexually seductive, and morally debilitating influence that they attributed to Irish culture. This metaphor for the loss of human identity – men turned to swine through intercourse with a corrupting female outsider – works as a part of the ethnographic rhetoric in English writing about Ireland to rationalize political and economic domination that would be best effected by cultural separation. The events through which such domination was achieved and resisted – the plantations, wars, and consequent social upheavals of the late sixteenth and early seventeenth centuries – constitute *the* transformation analysed in this book. The cultural changes negotiated in early modern texts on Ireland both give testimony to these events and provide perspectives on them. In the nine essays that follow, I investigate the role that writing played in transforming early modern Irish culture. The essays describe the trajectory of my own work – from the analysis of ethnography, to translation, to political philosophy. The first three chapters are devoted to the development of a new discourse of barbarity versus civility in early modern English writing about Ireland, one that can be compared to European writing about cultural, political and religious others both inside and outside Europe (chapter 1). In chapters 2 and 3, I examine in particular the expression of that new cultural anthropology with its highly gendered language to portray Irish cultural otherness. The next two chapters take up the relation between antiquarianism and translation as agents of cultural preservation and destruction (chapters 4 and 5). The final four chapters treat the appropriation of Continental political thought in the debate over how to colonize Ireland by English writers and in the critique of colonization by Irish writers (chapters 6–9). Although these essays were not written together as a single book-length narrative, they are printed here in the order in which they were written (with the exception of chapter 1), and they follow the increasingly comparative direction of my research on early modern Ireland. From an initial focus on how early modern English writers represented Ireland in English language texts, the perspective of the essays broadens to consider how both Irish and English writers represented Ireland through the lens of European models in literature, political theory and history, and through the medium of Irish and Latin as well as English. These essays widen the field of inquiry on early modern Ireland both across disciplines (literature, history, and political thought) and across languages (English, Irish, Italian, Latin, and Spanish).

It is necessary to place English and Irish writing about Ireland in a European context for two reasons: first, there are the scholarly responsibilities as well as opportunities such a large, if often overlooked, body of texts presents, and second, because not to do so would be to produce a skewed Anglocentric cultural history. (This skewed perspective derives from the artificial boundaries of the contemporary Anglo-American academy that are the inheritance of a benighted nineteenth-century national division of knowledge.) Analysing English and Irish texts side by side in relation to European sources allows us to move beyond the repetition of dichotomies that are the hallmark of ethnographic and critical binarism (including at times my own). Even criticism that attempts to oppose the Manichean categories of ethnography can be linguistically trapped within them. Ethnography views the colonized culture as primitive, ancient, and outside history, and the culture of the colonizer as progressive and modern. The victor is the writer of history. From the Elizabethan conquest to the defeat of O'Neill at Kinsale and the exile of so many of the Irish intelligentsia in the early seventeenth century, both English and Irish cultures were changing dramatically – cataclysmically in the case of Ireland. And in Ireland, new modes of political, economic, and social practice emerged from the collision between the two cultures. As a consequence of this collision, new strategies of legitimization and resistance were sought in the imitation and interpretation of European models. This is not to say that early modern English and Irish cultures existed in a neutral European continuum, or that their relationships with Europe were identical. A comparative perspective highlights rather than erases the complex differences and inequalities in political and cultural power. Europe is now as contentious an issue in current Irish historiographical debate as it has been in Irish history. While the Kojevian (or, if you prefer, Orwellian) version of integration, globalism, and utopian political economy commands wide assent, the European dimension of the Irish past still provokes spirited and occasionally strident defensive reactions. The husbandman is ever watchful for evidence of continental trysts – especially Catholic ones.

My earlier work on Spenser and the New English is a good illustration of the limitations of the monolingual study of Ireland. Such a metaphor of sexuality for power relations and such a symbol of the feminine for ethnic difference as expressed in the image of Circe's poisoned cup reveals something about early modern English perspectives on Ireland, but very little about Ireland or the Irish. Just as Circe's mirror reveals Ulysses's self-reflection (as in the Waterhouse painting on the cover of this book), so too do the English representations of the Irish reveal an exclusively English subjectivity, however complex its anxiety over cultural dissolution and its self-confidence in its cultural superiority. To gain any sense of the Irish view of the English, such gendered images of sexual licentiousness and corruption from New English writing need to be compared with images of Ireland as a woman in Irish writing.

If I were to rewrite my essay on gender in early modern Ireland now, I would turn to bardic poetry. For example, in Aonghus Ó Dalaigh's 'Ar Éirinn', if Ireland is viewed 'as a harlot by the foreigners' ('meas méirdrughe . . . a-tá ag gach aon d'allmhurchaibh') it is because 'every man is raping her' ('gach éin-fhear dá héignioghadh') and she is left as a 'woman who has children with no father' ('clann gan athair aici-se').[2] Such images of Ireland as a woman violated and defenceless are frequent in bardic poetry in the wake of the Nine Years' War, when this poem appears to have been composed, and even later in the poetry of Aogán Ó Rathaile.[3] The image of Ireland as a woman, especially as a goddess and spouse of the king, dates from ancient times.[4] Within this tradition the lady seated on a throne who offers the king a cup of liquor is allegorized as *Flaith Érenn*, or 'the Sovereignty of Ireland'.[5] Rather than Circe's cup, Ériu's cup, symbolizing the marriage between king and land and his sovereignty over it, would be a fitter title for the final four chapters of this book that deal with native Irish concepts of political jurisdiction. As the proverb goes, Bíonn dhá insint ar gach scéal.

But I had only been trained to see one side of the story when I started to work on Ireland about thirteen years ago. My first intervention into the study of early modern Ireland was through an analysis of 'The Construction of Gender and the Cultural and Political Other in *The Faerie Queene V* and *A View of the Present State of Ireland*', which now forms chapter 2 of this collection. The mouthful of a title marks the article as a product of the late eighties, an attempt to meet the demands of its audience for a study of gender, race, and class. I wrote this essay first as a lecture for colleagues of a conventional American academic leftish bent in the English Department at Wesleyan University. As a PhD in Comparative Literature with an interest in philology and the history of ideas, and having written a dissertation on Stoicism in the *Orlando Furioso* and other Italian Renaiassance texts, I could find little common ground with my colleagues. Given their interest in contextualizing literature and my own interest in the need to further explore the connection between Spenser and Ireland that Stephen Greenblatt had written about in *Renaissance Self-Fashioning*, I thought that I had found a topic sufficiently compelling to interest them as it did me. Their reluctance to grant the importance of the study of Ireland to English literature was summed up sarcastically by Dick Ohmann: 'Yeah, yeah, that's what we should all be working on, Ireland.' It is unlikely that he would have dared to say this to anyone working in African American or Jewish Studies. My audience was typically selective in the way of the American left about its causes – united in supporting sanctions on South Africa (we all marched on the trustees' meeting), divided at best on the issue of Palestine (some would not show at Edward Said's lecture for fear of alienating senior faculty), and completely uninterested in the North of Ireland (I was the sole member of the department to attend a screening of the award-winning feminist documentary 'Mother Ireland' directed by Anne Crilly from Derry). I wanted to speak to these people in terms they would understand,

and partially succeeded, since at least Hazel Carby commented that Spenser's proposal for colonization in Ireland was very much like what the British did in Kenya. In a sense I was translating an argument not unlike Brendan Bradshaw's contribution to the debate over Spenser into the language of feminist analysis.[6] Not that this made many people besides Brendan Bradshaw happy, least of all the guardians of the institution of Spenser criticism, who called me a 'self-righteous British Marxist New Historicist' in their letters of rejection. I still do not think this article will make too many happy because it is about the expression of colonial discourse through gender not only in Spenser's prose tract but also in Spenser criticism. Eleven years after the appearance of my article, Willy Maley's and Andrew Hadfield's books have provided us with thoroughgoing analyses of Spenser's Irish experience, and Sheila Cavanagh and Lauren Silbermann have written the most exhaustive studies of gender in Spenser's work.[7] Rather than update the endnotes to my article, I turn the reader to their books. My own intervention still connects these two topics in a way that offers a different window on to Spenser's representation of Ireland and shows how, whatever we might write about it, our commentary can scarcely escape reproducing the ideologies embedded in it. I was already beginning to see the limits of monolingual research on Ireland.

In my next article, 'Representations of Women in Some Early Modern English Tracts on the Colonization of Ireland', I examined writing by a wide range of English authors other than Spenser. In a sense I was revisiting the seminal work of Nicholas Canny on Anglo-Irish identity, to break up the concept of an univocal New English ideology and to observe the differences among these writers' perspectives.[8] For example, Barnabe Riche displays an obsession with tropes of adultery, sodomy, and prostitution, to represent the recusancy both of English and Irish Catholics, that contrasts with the relatively minor role Spenser assigns to religion. Whereas Spenser is overwhelmingly concerned with language as the source of culture, and the need for the conqueror's language to prevail in order for the conquest to succeed, Riche applauds the Protestant translation of the Bible into Irish. I originally presented this article to a seminar on the Study of Women in the Renaissance run by Betty Travitsky at the CUNY Graduate Center. This group encouraged me in my work despite the fact that it was not really centred on the social history of women. The argument of the article is that gender is not a stable signifier, that gendered representations are not solely or primarily about women but rather make use of a language about women to symbolize relationships of power and to represent other cultural categories such as religion, politics, and language.

In 1991, just a year after the publication of my first article, I began to study the Irish language in classes held by Pádraig Ó Cearúil in a little bookshop in lower Manhattan. In the summers, my husband Daniel Scanlon and I took language courses – at Oideas Gael in 1992 and 1993, and in Gaoth Dobhair, County Donegal, in 1994. I was now working in the linguistically cosmopolitan and intellectually wide-ranging atmosphere of the Comparative Literature Department at Queens and the CUNY Graduate Center, in the company of colleagues who were also learning new languages and encouraged my study of Irish. I was particularly grateful for the intellectual interchange with Joan Dayan and Ali Jimale Ahmed, who were also working on postcolonialism. It was at CUNY that I first had the opportunity to study Old Irish in Catherine McKenna's graduate seminar, and to attend lectures in Irish history in Vincent Carey's undergraduate survey.

When Anne Fogarty asked me to write an article for an issue of the *Irish University Review* devoted to Spenser, I wanted to use my Irish in my research. My topic was the possibility of Spenser's knowledge of Irish. I set about reinterpreting the work of the old philologists who had catalogued his use of Irish words and tracked down possible Irish sources for stories in the *Faerie Queene*. Spenser's Irish vocabulary was a necessary form of intelligence for the daily administration of the plantation of Munster, where he was surrounded by Irish speakers. And in the *Faerie Queene* he reworks a story from Irish mythology into a New English adaptation. Whereas some scholars have argued that mistakes which Spenser made in Irish grammar mean that he did not know the language, I argued simply that he did not know it perfectly or very well; after all it is a difficult language.[9] A presentation of my argument at a Spenser conference at Yale in 1996 prompted the panel respondent to say that I was 'somewhat out on a limb' in this take on Spenser. But Nicholas Canny in the audience agreed that the New English had to have known some Irish just to communicate in a basic way with the majority of Irish people, who were still overwhelmingly Irish-speaking.

Spenser's appropriation of Irish mythology in the *Faerie Queene* raises questions about the consequences of antiquarianism. These are also relevant for the next chapter, which is concerned, among other things, with the uses to which the Welsh antiquarian Edward Lhuyd put an Irish language adaptation of a story from the *Orlando Furioso*. In preserving Irish language material for élite study and for translation, antiquarianism simultaneously destroys Irish as a living language by removing it from the customs and practices embedded within it. At the same time, Lhuyd's philological studies were crucial in the evaluation of Irish as a Celtic and a European language, thus dismantling the myth of its barbaric Scythian origins, and bringing the study of Irish into a comparative European framework.

I had first become interested in Lhuyd when I discovered that one of the manuscripts of the 'Orlando agus Melora' had been copied for his use. My work on the Irish prose romance 'Orlando agus Melora' allowed me for the first time to bring together my interest in Ireland and in Ariosto's epic, on which I had written my dissertation, now revised as a published book. I wanted to see if Sir John Harington's English translation of the *Orlando Furioso*, which circulated in Ireland, had any influence on this Irish prose romance. Mícheál Mac Craith had already argued that Harington influenced

Irish love poetry in the Renaissance, and Harington had himself written of the popularity of his translation of the *Orlando Furioso*.[10] The text of 'Orlando agus Melora' had already appeared in two modern Irish editions; however, the most important connection between the English *Furioso* and this Irish text came in a manuscript copied by Uilliam Ó Loinsigh that contained illustrations closely based on the Porro engravings that accompanied Harington's text. The Irish scribe of this manuscript of 1696 had apparently had his hands on Harington's translation of 1591, and it had formed a filter through which he transcribed the text, already copied earlier in 1679, and possibly written as early as the first half of the seventeenth century. This was a case of two writers – one English (well known and in print), the other Irish (virtually anonymous and in manuscript) – who had rendered versions of the most popular narrative poem of the Renaissance into their own languages and cultures. In my comparative study of these two texts, I show how each is a cultural as well as a linguistic translation. Just as Spenser rewrote Irish sources for a New English audience, so Harington and Ó Loinsigh adapted the *Furioso* for their own contexts. To evaluate the cultural uses to which each translation was put, I examine these texts in relation to their paratexts – the elaborate allegories of Harington's translation, and the detailed lexicon, grammar and pronunciation guide that accompany the 'Orlando agus Melora'. The comparative study of these two adaptations and their paratexts yields the possibility of allegorical interpretation for both texts, as well as their use for either Irish speakers learning English or English speakers learning Irish. Translation from the Italian becomes a medium for interaction between the two traditions, which, as Thomas Kinsella has argued, were more often than not ignorant of each other.

The last four chapters of the book turn from literary translation to the translation of political philosophy and historiography. Through editing Richard Beacon's *Solon His Follie* and participating in two Folger Institute seminars on political ideology in Ireland, I had become aware of the need to set both English and Irish texts in a comparative framework of European political thought. After all, the first English language texts to make extensive use of Machiavelli were Elizabethan texts on the colonization of Ireland. The application of Machiavelli's *Prince* and *Discourses* to the problem of how to maintain power in Ireland by New English writers cried out for an explanation. In the years that followed the debate in Hiram Morgan's seminar between Vincent Carey and Markku Peltonen, these two, along with David Armitage and Andrew Hadfield, weighed in with their versions of why these New English authors turned to Machiavelli.[11] Because I felt each of these analyses of the application of Machiavelli to Ireland was leaving out a crucial element of the relation between republic and empire in the *Discourses*, and because none of them considered the possibility that Irish writers, too, might also have been influenced by Machiavellian strategies for interpreting history, I thought it still worthwhile (four years after I had written on Richard Beacon's indebtedness to Machiavelli in my introduction to *Solon His Follie*) to return to the question of why and how Machiavelli's work crops up in early modern Ireland.

Even more important was the need to respond to John Pocock's challenge, 'Where is the ancient Irish constitution?' Breandán Ó Buachalla's work on both Irish historiography and Jacobite poetry has gone a long way towards answering that crucial question.[12] Bernadette Cunningham, too, has contributed articles on Irish historiography and a book on Keating.[13] I see my own work in part as extending the work begun by Ó Buachalla in his wide-ranging article in Irish on the relation between Irish historiography and European humanism. I initiated some of the ongoing work that is needed to answer Pocock's question in my lecture on natural law theory and seventeenth-century Irish historiography at a conference on the Irish in Europe, organized by Thomas O'Connor at Maynooth in 1999. Appearing here as the eighth chapter of the book, this lecture analyses O'Sullivan Beare's critique of English rule in Ireland. The essay explains the indebtedness of O'Sullivan Beare's use of such concepts as sovereignty, indigenousness, and the law of nations to the natural law theory of the school of Salamanca. Beyond that, the role of custom in the establishment of the law, as argued theoretically by O'Sullivan Beare following Suárez, receives an Irish language translation in the histories of Céitinn and Ó Cléirigh. Whether directly influenced by Suárez or not (and given their wide European learning and Céitinn's study at Bordeaux and Ó Cléirigh's at Louvain they certainly could have been), these Irish historians give an account of Irish custom based on the traditional lore of *senchas*, an account that is in itself part of the record of the ancient Irish constitution. In the early modern period, this is the constitution of a culture with an emerging awareness of itself as a nation, despite the absence of a nation state, and perhaps even more acutely aware of its own status as a nation because of the denial of that status in the English conquest and plantations.

Chapter seven, also on O'Sullivan Beare, places the issue of an emerging national consciousness in relation to the conditions of the Irish exile community in Spain. Educated in Spain, and serving as an officer in the Spanish navy, O'Sullivan Beare wrote his history in Latin for a Spanish audience – most pointedly with the hope of seeking the aid of the Spanish crown for an armed invasion and liberation of Ireland from English rule.[14] In his analysis of the various groups within Ireland, the Irish and Old English, whom he calls Old and New Irish, he stresses the political allegiance to the cause of O'Neill in the Nine Years' War as the most important factor in determining who is trustworthy. O'Sullivan Beare's position as an exile gives him the freedom of having lost everything in Ireland and having nothing to lose. Living in Spain, he did not have to reach an accommodation with the rule of Ireland by the English king, as those in Ireland absolutely had to. His education in Spain and circulation in court circles made him conversant with early modern Spanish historiography. Such Spanish influences as the model of colonial martyrdom in the work of Las Casas (itself having a common model with Foxe's *Book of*

Martyrs in the work of Eusebius) and the critique of tyranny in the work of Juan de Mariana, all impinge upon O'Sullivan Beare's writing of the *Historiae Catholicae Iberniae Compendium*, first printed in Lisbon in 1621.

Taken as a whole these essays argue for the necessity to be able to read Irish, Latin, English, Spanish, and Italian – in that order – in order to do research on early modern Ireland. If the intellectual culture of English writers is not confined to sources in that language, most texts by Irish writers are either in Latin or Irish. These essays also argue for the need to see similarities between Irish and English texts due in part to their common European sources. But what at least one reader of my work has called a 'continuum' of English and Irish cultures in a European framework should not obscure the sharp and often irreconcilable differences between certain interpretations of the intellectual tradition. The questions 'which natural law? whose sovereignty?' yield very different answers from English and Irish writers. For example, Spenser's argument for the subjugation of the Irish, based on the Aristotelian concept of the natural slave, cannot be reconciled with O'Sullivan Beare's principle that 'all peoples even Gentiles and barbarians have the right to their own constitution', based on the natural law philosophy of the school of Salamanca. The English poet's concept of legitimate rule is the Irish historian's tyranny. My first chapter, 'Barbarous Slaves and Civil Cannibals', attempts to explain why the English representation of the Irish as natural slaves was in some respects even more denigrating than certain European representations of the Amerindians. Ironically, the position of the Irish as the proximate 'other' or enemy within Europe makes the English view of them even more intensely alien – combining the sense of cultural, political and religious difference in Spanish views of the Moors.

While the study of early modern Ireland within Europe shares a comparative and multinational approach with the study of Ireland within the British Isles, a very different account of the Irish past and of national identity emerges from the comparison of different nations, different institutions, and different languages. Within the recent practice of the new British history, the comparisons of Ireland with Scotland and Wales have highlighted the unique character of early modern Irish resistance to incorporation within Britain and pointed to sources of that resistance in links with European powers, such as Spain, and European institutions, chief among these the Catholic Church. For example, the failure of the Reformation in Ireland and the triumph of the Counter Reformation have been attributed to the flourishing of the mendicant orders and to the persistence of a papally appointed clergy at both episcopal and parochial levels, alongside the officially sanctioned state clergy.[15] The education of these clergymen took place in Europe. At the colleges the Irish founded in Spain, the Low Countries, France, Rome and Prague, a clerical élite was educated to do missionary work in Ireland. The intellectuals within the colleges also produced saints' lives, catechisms, and devotional works that promoted a highly politicized and nationally conscious form of Catholicism, what Brendan Bradshaw has called religion as ' "ideology", as creed or confession' rather than as ' "practice", as discipline or observance'.[16] The sense of the Irish nation forged in Irish bardic poetry, as well as in Irish histories both in Irish and Latin, was developed within this new and invigorated Roman Catholicism, which included both Anglo-Norman and Gaelic Irish. The Irish Catholic national identity was in turn supported by 'a common Gaelic historical and cultural heritage', as well as by the geopolitical unity in the concept of 'the sovereignty of the island'.[17]

To suggest that the broader more inclusive framework for early modern Irish history is 'its *wider* "Three Kingdoms", imperial and Atlantic contexts', as some of the best new British history does, is to relegate Catholic Europe to the position of a narrower context.[18] This is highly debatable if one thinks of Irish history over a longer stretch of time, since Catholic Europe provides a context for Ireland throughout the greater part of its history, both before the Norman invasion and after independence from the United Kingdom. At the same time, Catholic Europe can provide a fruitful if much overlooked context even for England where, despite the success of the Reformation, Catholicism was not entirely extinguished and continued as an important minority intellectual tradition in the sixteenth and seventeenth centuries.[19] Both Ireland's and Britain's histories are inextricably bound up with the history of Europe. If, in studying the history of Ireland, one focuses on English language institutions, one will necessarily turn to English language documents, the administration of English government and law in sixteenth- and seventeenth-century Ireland as recorded in the State Papers and in numerous other political position papers, pamphlets, and tracts. But there were other sorts of interactions, in education, religion, trade, and military and diplomatic affairs, between Ireland and other parts of Europe, including Louvain, Lisbon, Madrid, Rome, and even Prague.[20] It is not surprising that the study of exclusively English language material and the consideration of history as the history of the state yields what Pocock has defined as 'a settler nationalism' by which he means an Old English nationalism.[21] All institutions within early modern Ireland, however, were not English. The most all-pervasive features of Irish daily life for the vast majority of the people, religion and language, were not English, and certainly did not correspond to 'Anglo-Irish settler nationalism' any more than they did to the term 'British'. For both the seventeenth and the twentieth centuries, if not for the period between 1801 and 1916, the term 'British' is an anachronism.[22] A more accurate description of the nation would be *Éireannaigh,* the term for Irish identity that begins to crop up in the late sixteenth century and which is specifically coined to describe the new alliance between Gaelic Irish and Old English.[23] The new British history is at times not just too narrow for, but simply blind to, whole areas of Irish history. As a model that presupposes the study of English sovereignty, government, and laws, the British history of Ireland will necessarily leave out so much of the history of a nation that had to conceive of itself as a nation without the presence of its own nation state.

A large part of this construction of the nation as a culture in the absence of the nation state was carried out in Europe by aristocrats, diplomats, and soldiers, as well as by learned clerics.[24] Contrary to the notion that nationalism only arose in the late eighteenth century, with the advent of print culture and the enlightenment-inspired movement for popular political enfranchisement, the Irish example shows how the need for nationalism arose when the Irish became more and more conscious of the need to defend their nation as they came under attack from an expanding English nationalism.[25] The complaints against the English for political disenfranchisement and confiscation of land that O'Sullivan Beare makes spurred on the drive to construct a history of Irish politics, religion, and language, to record the culture that identified the people with each other and with the land. Irish intellectuals in exile wrote dictionaries and grammars, poetry, history and moral theology in the Irish language, as well as in Latin, many of which texts were printed on the Continent because they could not be printed in Ireland. Among these texts are O'Sulllivan Beare's *Historiae Catholicae Iberniae Compendium* (Lisbon, 1621) and *Iberni patritiana decas* and *Archicornigeromastix* (Madrid, 1629) as well as Peter Lombard's *De regno Hiberniae sanctorum insula commentarius* (Louvain, 1632).[26] Indeed, such works became important later within the nineteenth-century revival of Irish cultural nationalism.[27] Taken as a whole, these Irish works produced in Europe constitute the creation of a national culture in exile. There is much work to do on this material; many of the works still do not exist in easily available modern editions and remain untranslated.[28] They represent a hidden intellectual history of Ireland. At least it is hidden in the sense that it has been kept separate from the rest of Irish cultural history, in the form of religious history or Irish language literary study. It is to the works of these seventeenth-century Irish intellectuals on the Continent that my current research has taken me.

Early modern Irish intellectuals in Europe were, as the first translator of Keating calls them, 'fugitives' in and from their native land due to the conditions of English rule; at the same time they were heirs to their own as well as Continental traditions of thought from which to critique that domination.[29] My own initial interventions into the history of what role European intellectual traditions played in how the Irish wrote their histories and defended their national culture in such conditions have shown me how much we still need to learn: the specifics of who studied where, what they read, how they related to their audience in Ireland, and to what extent their texts were read in Ireland. While we are amassing the information through research, I believe it is still important to attempt a critical analysis of early modern Irish writing within the context of European literature, politics, and historiography. And that is precisely what I am beginning to do here.

2001

BARBAROUS SLAVES AND CIVIL CANNIBALS
Translating Civility in Early Modern Ireland

If, as Denis Donoghue has claimed, 'the post-colonial vocabularies of Bhabha, Said, and Achebe were designed to deal with historical and political conditions in Africa, India, Algeria, and the Middle East rather than in Ireland', these concepts travel well in Irish history.[1] Even the first text on the English conquest of Ireland, Gerald of Wales's twelfth-century *Topographia Hibernica*, provides an example of what Homi Bhabha calls hybridity or 'the repetition of discriminatory identity . . . in strategies of subversion that turn the gaze of the discriminated back upon the eye of power'.[2] Bhabha's 'sly civility'[3] lurks in the Archbishop of Cashel's response to Gerald's denigration of the Irish for their lack of martyrs: 'although our people are barbarous, uncivilized, and savage, they have always paid great honour and reverence to churchmen . . . But now a people has come to the kingdom which knows how, and is accustomed, to make martyrs. From now on, Ireland will have its martyrs.'[5]

Objections to considering contemporary Ireland as post-colonial follow from a denial of early modern Ireland as colonial. So the sixteenth-century English conquest of Ireland, which set in motion the complete transformation of the culture that the twelfth-century Normans largely assimilated to, is an important place to start a genealogy of post-colonialism. Current historiography that views Ireland as primarily part of British history often denies early modern Ireland's status as a colony. Since Henry VIII was proclaimed King of Ireland in 1542, and since James I claimed *dominium* over the three kingdoms of England, Scotland, and Ireland in 1603, Ireland was at least in theory a kingdom from the perspective of English law. But the Irish were subject to English armed conquest, expropriation of land, and political disenfranchisement, conditions downplayed by current British historiography, according to which the history of Ireland becomes predominantly a part of British state formation. In the wake of the Elizabethan conquest, Ireland became subject to capitalist colonialism through which the agricultural society was 'squeezed . . . to provide labour, or commodities or tribute'.[5] Two of the most palpable forms of this colonization were the Plantation of Ulster, where land expropriated from the indigenous inhabitants was 'operated by settlers, who in some cases employed as labourers the Irish who had previously farmed the land'; and the early seventeenth-century development of an export trade in cattle that produced profits for English owners from Irish land.[6] In a review of recent historiography on early modern Ireland by Jane Ohlmeyer, a dozen pages are on Ireland as kingdom, only two on Ireland as colony.[7] This marks a dramatic shift from the work of D.B. Quinn and Nicholas Canny from the 1960s to the 1980s, in which they compared Elizabethan and Jacobean descriptions of the Irish with descriptions of the Amerindians and construed the colonizing activities of Walter Raleigh, Humphrey Gilbert, and Francis Drake in Ireland as a rehearsal for their activities in the Americas.[8]

In an essay in the *Irish Review* of 1991, Hiram Morgan asserted that Canny and Quinn founded their analysis on faulty premises. Explaining that the intentions and responses of both colonizers and colonized in Ireland differed from those in the Americas, Morgan argued that the 'Tudors set out to reform Ireland not to conquer it', and that 'native aristocrats' unlike 'Amerindian chiefs . . . sought out alliances with other European powers'.[9] Reform itself, however, was a strategy of conquest. Many of the policies thought of as 'reform' by the early modern English in effect destroyed indigenous cultural, economic and political institutions. Such policies as surrender and regrant, which abolished Gaelic titles and entailed the surrender of ownership and use of land to the English sovereign; composition, which imposed only one tax to the English crown but in so doing abolished the customary support of local Gaelic lords; the new colonies of Munster and Ulster, which sought to make more profitable use of land and in the process displaced native inhabitants; and martial law itself, which imposed capital punishment without trial – all were thought of as 'reform' by the early modern English in Ireland. And if the Catholic Irish had greater access to European powers, as witnessed by their negotiations with and aid from Spain, Amerindian chiefs did at times form alliances with European powers.[10] Morgan also noted that the 'constitutional status of Irishmen . . . treated as full subjects, religious disabilities notwith-standing' makes the colonial approach 'untenable'. Under this constitutional status, however, members of early seventeenth-century Irish juries were reg-ularly fined and imprisoned and even physically punished for failing to indict recusants. The example of a jury whose members each had an ear cut off for not returning a verdict favourable to the Crown suffices to question whether inclusion of the Irish under common law was a legal right or a form of colo-nial subjugation.[11] Morgan further argued that the position papers and polit-ical tracts that Canny and Quinn studied were divorced from such events as 'litigation, bribery of officials, billeting of troops, holding of parliament' about which there was 'nothing colonial'. Morgan maintained that the English would have had to have known that they were lying when they represented the Irish as nomads and pagans.

In 1992, Andrew Hadfield responded to Morgan by pointing out that intentions and events are mediated through language and rhetorical strategies – through representations.[12] I would add that textual representations are events, or as Walter Mignolo would say, enactments.[13] Colonialist representa-tions – including historical chronicles, political tracts, epic poems, and maps

– enact the colonizers' appropriation of the memory, language, and space of the colonized, at once recording and destroying what they describe. These representations translate what they describe in the sense of the Italian saying '*tradutorre, traditorre*' ('translator, traitor'), which draws on the Latin verb *tradere,* meaning to entrust and to betray, to pass down and to give up. Interpretation of these representations is a matter of who is speaking to whom and in the context of what activities, what Mignolo calls the 'locus of enunciation'. And this applies to the texts that we are interpreting as well as to our own writing about them. From an epistemological perspective, writing does not mirror the world but creates a relationship to it. From a political perspective, writing is an activity implicated in other actions in the world.

So, for example, Sir John Davies's promotion of the common law in Ireland in his *Discovery of the True Causes why Ireland was Never Entirely Subdued* (London, 1612) needs to be related to his own execution of the law as Attorney General of Ireland from 1603 to 1619. How does his praise for the successful extension of the common law in Ireland – 'that the streams of public justice are derived into every part of the kingdom' – relate to his orders for the threatening, starving, and mutilation of juries whose members did not return verdicts favourable to the English Crown?[14] In this instance, 'public justice' was determined by allegiance to the state and to the interests of the king rather than the extension of common law in Ireland. Beyond this, Davies's basic belief in the superiority of common law over Brehon law was rooted in his view of the cultural and moral superiority of colonists on the Ulster plantation over the native inhabitants, as this passage from his official state correspondence indicates: 'if the civil persons who are to be planted do not exceed the number of natives, [they] will quickly overgrow them as weeds overgrow the good corn'.[15] The colonists on the Ulster plantation are defined as 'civil' whereas native inhabitants are denied such status. The limitations of Davies's legal theory, and the disparity between English legal theory and practice in Ireland generally, did not go unnoticed by early modern Irish historians. Geoffrey Keating found that Davies's attacks on native Irish Brehon law showed his ignorance of the way Gaelic laws functioned in cultural practice, and Philip O'Sullivan Beare criticized the inconsistency and even what he referred to as the 'fiction' of the English law in Ireland.[16] The interpretation of the relation between text and context is clearly a matter of whose political interests are at stake, and not just for seventeenth-century readers but for readers today attempting to interpret early modern English and Irish political thought and history. When John McCavitt pointed out these disparities of theory and practice in Davies's text and context to a late twentieth-century English-speaking academic audience attending a Folger seminar on early modern Ireland, controversy ensued. Those interested in maintaining that the extension of the common law was progress, regardless of how violently it was enforced, wanted to separate writing from events. This is a distinction that keeps us from seeing the darker side of the Renaissance in Ireland, as well as the darker side of progress heralded as the New World Order today. What Enrique Dussel in writing about the Spanish colonization of the Americas has called 'the myth of modernity', the 'justification for genocidal violence' which accompanies the '"rational" concept of "emancipation"', could well be applied to an analysis of the early modern English 'reform' of Ireland.[17]

The connection between sixteenth-century Ireland and contemporary colonial contexts in the Americas is implicitly denied by John Gillingham, who has asserted that 'an imperialist English culture emerged in the twelfth century'.[18] He assumes an unchanging continuity between the view of the Celts as barbarians in the twelfth-century writing of William of Malmesbury and Gerald of Wales and the view of the Irish in sixteenth-century New English tracts. To focus on this perpetuation of an exclusively textual tradition is to overlook the influence of new practices of economic and governmental control and new discourses upon early modern writing about Ireland. In other words, the sixteenth-century accounts of Irish barbarism are related to the English justification of and Irish reaction to the enactment of new policies for the establishment of English rule in Ireland. Furthermore, the work of D. B. Quinn has shown that English colonists in Ireland self-consciously modelled their plans for conquest and plantation upon the Spanish example in the Americas.[19] The identity of medieval and early modern writing that Gillingham asserts also overlooks the colonization of the Americas and the Reformation as events that generated new discourses inflecting the inherited discourse of barbarism.

In what follows, I want to examine some evidence that would further challenge and complicate these arguments – that early modern writing on Ireland is nothing more than the repetition of a medieval discourse on Celtic barbarism, and that early modern writing on Ireland cannot be connected with other colonial texts and contexts because Ireland was a kingdom and not a colony. First, I want to compare the discourse of barbarism in Gerald of Wales's *Topographia* with later adaptations of it to see how these are bound up with new discourses and practices. I will then compare early modern writing on barbarism versus civility in the Irish context with such writing on the Amerindians by the Spanish Catholic Bartolomé de las Casas and the French Protestant Jean de Léry. In the course of this comparison, the question emerges: why do English writers on many occasions represent the Irish as even more alien than these two Continental European writers represent the Amerindians? Finally, I will also look briefly at the response of Irish writers to the English discourse on barbarism, to see not so much how they contradict it, as Joep Leerssen has already shown in his magisterial *Mere Irish and Fíor Ghael*, but also how they criticize it through strategies adapted from Continental European political theory.[20]

Gerald of Wales's *Topographia Hibernica*, or *Topography of Ireland*, is what Foucault would call a foundational text of the discourse that constructs the Irish as barbarians.[21] Imitated and responded to from the twelfth to the seventeenth centuries, the *Topography* initiates a discourse that extends and criticizes the portrayal of the Irish as barbarians. Supporting the papal bull *Laudabiliter* (1155) that granted the English king the right to invade Ireland in order to pursue its moral, cultural, and ecclesiastical reform, Gerald's three-part speech, which he delivered on three successive days at Oxford in 1188, justifies the conquest of Ireland that began with Henry II's military intervention there in 1171–2.[22] In his opening address, Gerald dedicates the text to Henry II, and describes Irish history as appropriated to the king's memory: 'I have, therefore, collected everything . . . thought worthy of being remembered . . . for your attention which scarcely any part of history escapes.'[23] Having discoursed upon the position, wonders, and inhabitants of Ireland, Gerald closes his text with the promise to narrate, as he does in the *Expugnatio Hibernica*, Henry's victories in Ireland: 'I shall attempt to describe the manner in which the Irish world has been added to your titles and triumphs; with what great and laudable valour you have penetrated the secrets of the ocean and the hidden things of nature.'[24] There is a running analogy between Henry's penetration of space and Gerald's penetration of knowledge. Gerald incorporates the history of ancient Ireland from the *Leabhar Gabhála*, or *Book of Invasions*, into chapters 85–90 of the Third Book of his text, but then supplants this Irish narrative of origins with one from the 'British history' of Geoffrey of Monmouth, who claimed that Ireland was uninhabited before the British king Gurguntius gave it to the Basclenses to settle. Gerald's description is a conquest over memory and space. The very title of the text, *Topographia*, writing about place, indicates the spatialization of time, a feature of ethnography, which portrays other cultures in archaic and timeless space, rather than present and changing time, a strategy that the anthropologist Johannes Fabian has termed 'the denial of coevalness'.[25]

In comparing Ireland in the West to the 'countries of the East', Gerald places both cultures not only outside European culture but also in an exotic place of the bizarre and unknown, in what could be seen as an early example of English orientalist discourse.[26] These places are unnatural and fantastic, 'remote parts where [nature] indulges herself in these secret and distant freaks'.[27] Both cultures only come into history at the point where they are conquered. At the end of the text Gerald indicates that the East is the site of the Christian European conquest and colonization of the Moslem world, and thus invites comparison between that crusade and the conquest of Ireland, which he has represented as another crusade, with the twin imperatives of proselytization and economic exploitation. Citing *Laudabiliter*, the Papal Bull which sought to legitimize the English conquest of Ireland as necessitated by the need for ecclesiastical reform, Gerald bemoans the ignorance of the people in matters of faith, and the negligence of the prelates who do not reprimand the people. Both Ireland and the East are also seen as places from which wealth can be extracted. For Gerald, Ireland is an uncultivated place of plenty, which like the East, needs colonization, in its root sense in the Latin verb *colere* – 'to be put to use, to be made of value'.

The Irish are both unfamiliar and familiar, pagan and Christian, treacherous and yet capable of fealty to Henry, uncultivated and yet cultivated. On the one hand they are said to be 'so barbarous as they cannot be said to have any culture', and on the other they are called 'the fountain of the art of music'.[28] Although the clergy are praised for their 'reading and praying', and 'abstinence and asceticism', they are taken to task for their 'negligence in the correction of the people'.[29] Gerald's fascination with 'enormities' such as a bearded hermaphrodite woman with a mane down her back, a man that was half an ox, a man who had intercourse with a cow, and a goat who had intercourse with a woman, all construct the Irish as 'freaks' of nature.[30] And yet they are not evil by nature but by custom. Their customs are so barbarous that it is 'as if they were in another world altogether and cut off from law-abiding people, they know only the barbarous habits in which they were born and brought up, and which they embrace as another nature'.[31] Like Homer's Cyclopes, the Irish before the Norman Conquest inhabit a world that is naturally wondrous and plentiful and yet 'outside the law'. Gerald's allegory of Henry II's subjection of the Irish lords as Jupiter's striking the earth with his thunderbolt repeats Ovid's mythographic history. Just as in the golden age before Jupiter, so in Ireland before the conquest of Henry II, there was no law. Gerald concludes with great optimism for reform; Henry's victory begins a new era of peace and law through the 'protestation of fealty and spontaneous surrender of the Irish chiefs'.[32]

John Derricke in his 1581 *Image of Ireland* imitates the mythographic discourse of Gerald's *Topography* and its narrative of conquest to praise the victories over Irish rebels by the army of Sir Henry Sidney, Lord Deputy of Ireland. Like Gerald, Derricke and his Elizabethan contemporaries represent the Irish as barbarous. Instead of showing a transformation from culturally primitive barbarism to law through the submission of the Irish as Gerald's narrative does, however, Derricke's allegory figures a descent into culturally degenerate barbarism brought about by 'rebellious woodkern' of whom the land must be rid. Unlike Gerald's primitive Irish, who are capable of being reformed by the law and religious reform, Derricke's 'rebellious woodkern' cannot be reformed by religion, civility, the laws, or even God's grace. Rather than merely repeating the view of the Irish as culturally barbaric in Gerald's *Topography*, Derricke's depiction of the Irish woodkerns as 'this graceless cursed race' is formed by new ideologies implicated in new practices.[33]

The Elizabethan conquest was enacted through the new discourse of civility, carried out through enforcement of laws, colonial settlement, and warfare. Although the Statutes of Kilkenny of 1366 attempted to forestall the Gaelicization of the twelfth-century Norman invaders by forbidding them to adopt Irish language and dress, and to marry with the Irish, such laws went largely ignored outside the Pale. Anglo-Normans, or Old English, intermarried with the Irish and adopted their customs and language. A new hybrid culture arose in which Norman feudalism coexisted with and was sometimes merged with

Gaelic political and economic structures.[34] In the mid-sixteenth century, during the Lord Deputyships of Sussex and Sidney, the English attempted a much more thoroughgoing and systematic policy of anglicization: to enforce English law and use of the land through colonial settlement in Laois and Offaly, to the North in Ards and Clandeboye, and to the South in Cork. In these early failed colonial ventures, the Elizabethan governors set out to reorganize the land as shire ground, to enforce inheritance of land through primogeniture, to abolish Gaelic law and language, and to transplant the Irish inhabitants. Such chieftains as Rory Óg O'More (the central rebel protagonist of Derricke's *Image of Ireland*) went into armed rebellion in response to the loss of their lands and the destruction of Gaelic culture that English colonization entailed. The recent archival work of David Edwards shows that for most of the Elizabethan period, the official policy to deal with resistance to English rule was martial law; execution without trial was more the rule than the exception in Elizabethan Ireland.[35] The English failure to make these plantations work also resulted in massacres. Officially state-sanctioned atrocities against civilians included Essex's slaughter of 600 men, women, and children on Rathlin Island in 1574; Sir William Fitzwilliam's order first to offer protection to and then put to the sword hundreds of the Clandeboye O'Neills in Belfast in 1574–5; and Francis Cosby's summoning of the people of Offaly and Laois to Mullaghmast, where English soldiers surrounded them and shot them to death in 1578.[36]

Such violence against both Irish warriors and civilians presided over by Sir Henry Sidney during his term as Lord Deputy (1566–71; 1575–8) is celebrated in the woodcuts and doggerel verse of John Derricke's *Image of Ireland*. In the final part of the text, the defeated rebel Rory Óg O'More praises the execution of his wife and friends as liberation from slavery by Lord Deputy Sidney:

> In fine, 'twas he which made of bondmen free,
> And put to sword for my unstable truth
> My spoused wife, the garland of my youth.
> With many more my dear and special friends,
> Whose breathless corpses were given to flames of fire.

In a marginal note, Derricke explains: 'Rory's friends to the number of sixteen, are slain in a cabin, . . . and afterwards the cabin being set on fire, all their bodies are burned also.' The necessity for this violence is explained in the first two parts of the text where the woodkern are described as evil both by nature and by religious practice. Ireland is no longer a place of miracles, as it was for Gerald, but 'the devil's arse, a peak where rebels most embrace'.[37] The Irish are no longer in need of religious reform but incapable of it. Commenting on the failure of St Patrick to reform the Irish, Derricke represents them as a people cursed by God: 'No strength may prevail whom God does withstand, no physic can cure whom God in his ire striketh, showing that God hath given up Woodkern to a reprobate sense, infecting them with an incurable botch.' The Irish are no longer outside the law, as they were for Gerald before the Norman conquest, but rebels to the law. Derricke comments: 'instead of civility, Woodkerne use villainy'. That villainy is rebellion, which is a sign of irrecoverable damnation, 'O ingratitude most intolerable, and blindness irrecuperable!' Called 'Satan's imps', 'sons of the devil', and 'pernicious members of Satan', the Irish are below the state of 'brute beasts'. Calvinist divine election and the concomitant damnation of the Catholic Irish justify Sidney's conquest. Whereas for Gerald the Irish were capable of artistic cultivation and ecclesiastical reform, for Derricke their clergy and their bards have made these institutions damned and diseased. Derricke blames the rebellion on the instigation of both Irish prelates ('The friar persuades the rebels that it is an high work of charity to kill loyal subjects . . . Behold the plaguey counsel of a poxy friar, the very fruit of papistry') and poets ('The policy of the bard is to incense the rebels to do mischief, by repeating of their forefathers' acts').[38]

The new sixteenth-century Calvinist discourse of predestined damnation is mingled with what could be called a proto-racialist discourse. By proto-racialist discourse I mean the intersection of the early modern notion of race as family lineage or genealogy and as an inherited disposition imposed on a whole group of people. Comparing the Irish to 'graceless grafts / sprung from a wicked tree', Derricke represents Irish evil as inherited through the blood: 'knave father, knave son to the twentieth generation'.[39] All levels of Irish society from chieftain to horse boy are typed as an innately inferior people: 'a pestiferous generation', 'an untoward generation', 'a graceless cursed race'. Likened to 'grasshoppers and caterpillars', 'hogs' and 'dogs', the Irish are sub-human – a 'pestilent brood' for whom even 'hanging and drawing . . . were too good'.[40] The Irish not only have no status in their native land but are enemies from which the land must be rid: 'so bare of heavenly grace, / more foes to country's soil'.[41] This notion of the Irish as inherently and innately evil and so fit for extermination marks a real departure from the medieval discourse of barbarism, in which the Irish are evil not by nature but by custom, and so capable of improvement.

This distinctly early modern discourse of civility as Protestant election and conformity to English law versus barbarism as damnation and rebellion has had, as Seamus Deane has shown in 'Civilians and Barbarians', an afterlife in the representation of politics in late twentieth-century Ireland.[42] Late sixteenth-century responses to this discourse foreshadow recent historiographical debates. Even more widely disseminated than Derricke's popular *Image of Ireland*, the Old English Richard Stanihurst's *Description of Ireland* locates Ireland within the historiography of the three kingdoms, as signalled by its publication in Holinshed's *Chronicles of England, Scotland and Ireland* (1577). Richard Stanihurst describes the Old English of the Pale in relation to English customs, institutions, and history, but relegates the Gaelic Irish to an ethnographic description of an alien people. Born in Dublin, educated at

Oxford, and employed as tutor to the Earl of Kildare, Stanihurst accepts the New English view of the Gaelic Irish as characterized by 'savageness' and 'rebellion'. Like many other early modern writers on Ireland, Stanihurst lifts whole passages directly out of the *Topography* to portray Irish barbarism. The development of Old English culture in the four centuries since the Norman conquest serves in a new way to further marginalize the Gaelic Irish. The author is at pains to distinguish the Old English from the wild Irish and so warns the reader:

> not to impute anie barbarous custome that shall be here laied down, to the cit-
> izens, townsmen, and inhabitants of the English pale, in that they differ little
> or nothing from the ancient customs and dispositions of their progenitors, the
> English and Welsh men, therefore being as mortally behated of the Irish as
> those that are born in England.[43]

Over half the text treats the civility of the Old English as civil founders of cities and schools, scholars, responsible holders of ecclesiastical and public offices, and loyal subjects.[44] Stanihurst defines the civility of the Old English in their speaking English rather than Irish: 'The inhabitants of the English pale have been in old time so much addicted to their civilitie, and so far sequestered from barbarous savageness, as their onlie mother toong was Eng-lish.'[45] This focus on the English language, absent from Gerald's Latin text, unites the discourse on civility versus barbarity with the Renaissance human-ist discourse on the vernacular, one of the most important unifying principles in the emerging concept of nation. Stanihurst's use of 'savageness' as the oppo-site of 'civility' indicates the pressure that New World exploration and colo-nization has brought to bear upon the discourse of barbarousness. As with Shakespeare's 'rude and savage man of Inde' (*Love's Labour's Lost*) and Ralegh's 'Heathen savage' (*History of the World*) in the late sixteenth century, 'savage' tends to be applied more and more to peoples outside Europe, whereas, in a later repetition of this discourse from the *O.E.D.*, barbarous 'tends to be applied to peoples somewhat less remote from civilization'.[46] Stanihurst treats the Gaelic Irish not only as culturally alien but also as politically alien; he fre-quently refers to 'the Irish enemie' (4, 48). And this is not simply textual prac-tice – the repetition of a common term in colonial discourse. Stanihurst also treated the Gaelic Irish as political enemies in his 1593 argument before the Escorial to dissuade the Spanish from aiding O'Neill's revolt against the Eng-lish in the Nine Years' War.

Written in the midst of the Nine Years' War by a New English settler on the Munster plantation, Spenser's *View of the Present State of Ireland* extends Stanihurst's ethnography of Gaelic savagery to include the Old English, and draws on the Calvinist and proto-racialist discourses of Derricke.[47] For Spenser, both Old English and Gaelic Irish 'are all Papists by their profession, but in the same so 'blindly and brutishly informed for the most part that you would rather think them atheists or infidels'.[48] In a rewriting of Irish history reminiscent of Derricke's, Spenser claims that St Patrick's conversion of the Irish had little or no effect because 'religion was generally corrupted with their Popish trumpery'. In Spenser's standard reformation rhetoric, the entire Christian past of Ireland is transformed into a history of corruption in its very origins and further disease in its subsequent effects: 'what other could they learn than such trash as was taught them, and drink of that cup of fornication, with which the purple harlot had then made all nations drunken . . . the dregs thereof have brought great contagion in their souls'. There is no room here for Stanihurst's defence of the civility of the Old English ecclesiastical and scholarly cultural tradition.

Spenser also refutes Stanihurst's separation of Old English from Gaelic culture with the notion that the Old English are even 'more lawless and licentious than the very wild Irish'.[49] For Spenser, the source of Irish barbarism is in Old English degeneracy, their adoption of Irish customs and intermarriage and fosterage with Irish people, 'the two most dangerous infections'. Spenser describes language and ethos as inextricably bound and physically communicated by the child sucking at the mother's breast: 'They moreover draw into themselves together with their suck, even the nature and disposition of their nurses, for the mind follows much the temperature of the body.' Beyond this, Spenser warns against 'marrying with the Irish'; miscegenation is called 'dangerous . . . so perilous as it is not to be adventured'. The result of intermarriage is naturally inherited corruption: 'how can such matching but bring forth an evil race'. As with Derricke, race, in the sense of a genetically inherited disposition, is mapped onto ethnos, or nation, in the early modern sense of a people sharing common customs and language.

Whereas Stanihurst makes Irish culture more familiar to his English readers by separating the Old English from the Gaelic Irish, Spenser defamiliarizes Irish culture by describing Old English and Gaelic Irish as part of an ethnography derived from both ancient European and non-European barbarousness. Spenser distances the Irish from the English both in cultural time and in moral geography. When Spenser discusses ethnography in terms of genealogy, he argues against the Irish claim of Spanish descent in the *Leabhar Gabhála* by characterizing Irish keening for the dead as non-Christian and non-European: 'not proper Spanish but altogether heathenish brought in either by the Scythians or by the Moors, which were Africans . . . for it is the manner of all pagans and infidels to be intemperate in their wailings of their dead'.[50]

As two of Spenser's classical sources, Strabo and Diodorus Siculus, both note, the Scythians were 'man-eating'.[51] Spenser identifies Irish barbarousness with what since Columbus's *Diario* had been the ultimate mark of the inhuman in European representations of the Indians: cannibalism. Spenser's veteran of Irish service, Irenaeus, testifies that the Irish exceed even the savagery of 'the Gauls [who] used to drink their enemies' blood': '. . . so I have seen the Irish do but not [drink] their enemies' but friends' blood'.[52] Later, in the final section of the dialogue where the proposal of destruction by warfare followed by famine is put forward, cannibalism emerges as the desired result of these policies for colonial reformation: 'The end I assure me will be very short and much sooner than can be . . . hoped for . . . being kept from manurance, and their cattle from running abroad by this hard restraint, they would quickly consume themselves and devour one another.'[53] Cannibalism had been the result of the 'late wars in Munster': 'the very carcasses they spared not to scrape out of their graves'.[54] In Book 6 of *The Faerie Queene*, the Irish are mythopoetically represented as the 'savage nation', marauding nomads who 'eat the flesh of men'.[55] This allegorical representation echoes such passages from political tracts in which, for example, Henry Sidney refers to Shane O'Neill as 'that canyball', and John Davies describes the Irish as 'little better than the Cannibals who do hunt one another'.[56]

Most but not all early modern European views of cannibalism and of Amerindians equated them unequivocally with barbarism; Montaigne's sceptical 'De cannibales' is probably the most famous example of this dissent from the dominant discourse. Two sixteenth-century authors who did not attempt to justify European violence against the Amerindians but even criticized it were Bartolomé de Las Casas and Jean de Léry. Their radical departure from previous views of cannibalism needs to be gauged against a genealogy of the word cannibal that can be traced to its first use in Columbus's *Diario*.[57] In this text, native Caribbean informants' accounts of the tribe of 'Caribs who eat men' merge with the medieval European myth of men 'with snouts of dogs, who ate men' and a fantasy of the Oriental, 'Caniba [which] is nothing but the people of the Grand Khan'.[58] Pietro Martire, an Italian humanist who celebrated Spanish exploration and colonization in his *De Orbe Novo Decades* (1530), translated into English in 1555, compared the diet of the cannibals to that of Europeans: 'they eat their own children as we do chickens and pigs'. In André Thevet's 1577 *Cosmographie Universelle*, cannibal becomes a term applied globally to non-Europeans as savages – not only to Amerindians but also to Africans and Asians.[59]

In comparing Bartolomé de Las Casas's and Jean de Léry's defence of Amerindian cannibalism and civility to English accounts of Irish barbarism, I have asked the following questions: what enabled Las Casas and de Léry to represent Amerindian cultural others, however alien in their customs, as civil and moral while English writers represented Irish cultural others as uncivil and immoral? What allowed for this critique of the subjugation of the other in these Spanish and French texts, but prohibited it in English texts? Are there any representations of otherness in Las Casas and de Léry at all comparable to the English representations of the Irish?

In the 1550 debate at Valladolid, Las Casas refuted his opponent Sepulveda's view that the innate savagery of cannibalism justified war against and enslavement of the Indians. In his *Argumentum apologiae, or Defense of the Indians* (1552–3), which records and adds to his argument in the debate, Las

Casas distinguished between the sense of barbarians as people without written language, as opposed to people outside the *polis*, described in Aristotle's
Politics as fiercely warlike and irrational, without their own settled social life
and functioning legal institutions.[60] As Walter Mignolo has observed, the
European humanist denial of Aztec pictographic records and oral tradition as
history because of their not conforming to the Renaissance codification of
knowledge in the form of alphabetic literacy is one of the most powerful acts
of the Spanish conquest of the Americas – the colonization of memory.[61] If
Christian conversion, like the spread of alphabetic literacy, was a strategy of
colonization, for Las Casas his belief that the Indians had souls to convert was
accompanied by his political view of them as a civil people who should not
be subject to conquest. In his *Argumentum*, he represents the Indians through
what he sees as universal human categories of social and political life: 'They
are not ignorant, inhuman, or bestial. Rather, long before they had heard the
word Spaniard they had properly organized states, wisely ordered by excellent laws, religion and custom.'[62] Arguing again from Aristotle, Las Casas considers human sacrifice and the eating of human flesh as 'probable' rather than
actual error. Human sacrifice to the gods is 'fully agreed upon by the known
Indian nations' and 'established by the decrees of their laws'.[63] Las Casas also
considers cannibalism as a universal part of culture by noting that the 'ancient
history of pagans and Catholics alike testifies that almost all peoples used to
do the same thing'.[64] The representation of the Amerindian present as equivalent to the European past could be considered yet another example of the
denial of coevalness. But Las Casas brings his comparison of Indians and
Europeans into the same time-frame. He cites contemporary accounts of
Spanish cannibalism. He also brings the Indians and Spaniards into the same
context in time, by stressing their common and equal ignorance of each other.
The Indians 'are as ignorant of our language as we are of their language and
their religion'.[65] Most importantly, Las Casas finds the morality of the Indians,
'strengthened by the example of so many of their prudent men', to be superior to that of 'Christian soldiers, who exceed the barbarous peoples in their
wicked deeds'.[66]

Whereas Las Casas defends the geographically distant Indian other as civil
and moral, he castigates the more proximate other in Spain, the Moors, as 'the
truly barbaric scum of the nations'.[67] His acceptance of the difference of
Amerindian religious traditions contrasts with his attitude towards Jews and
Mohammedans, which hinges upon a distinction between religious and civil
jurisdiction. Although he asserts that 'Jews, Mohammedans, or idol-
aters . . . are in no way subject to the Church . . . when they celebrate and
observe their rites',[68] he never defends their right of defence against Spanish
conquest. In arguing that 'every nation no matter how barbaric has the right
to defend itself against a more civilized one that wants to conquer it and take
away its freedom', Las Casas identifies the Indians' right of defence with that
of the Spanish:

If war against the Indians were lawful, one nation might rise up against another . . . On this basis the Turks, the Moors – the truly barbaric scum of the nations – with complete right and in accord with the law of nature could carry on war . . . If we admit this, will not everything high and low, divine and human, be thrown into confusion?[69]

The uses of Las Casas's text are fraught with contradictions. As a defence of a nation's right to self-jurisdiction, His argument against the Spanish conquest of the Indians could be extended not just to argue against aggressive warfare by the Moors but also to argue for their expulsion from Spain. Las Casas's shorter and more popular Spanish text *Brevísima relación*, which he wrote to protest and to try to stop the Spanish torture, enslavement, and mass slaughter of the Indians, influenced the English Black Legend of Spain. This same text, and his argument generally for the right of indigenous peoples to resist conquest, later influenced the indigenous political Latin American movements of liberation from colonial rule. The Latin American philosopher Enrique Dussel, who has analysed the Eurocentric myth of modernity as a rationalization for the violence of early modern colonization, discusses Las Casas's critique as a precursor to his own: 'Las Casas attained the maximal critical consciousness by siding with the oppressed Other and by examining critically the premises of modern civilizing violence.'[70]

Las Casas's own writing, as we have seen, however, participates in the discourse of the Islamic 'Other' as barbaric. If we compare his representation of Indians as familiar and Moors as alien with English representations of the Irish, it would appear that the Irish assume a cultural space closer to the Moors than the Indians, but ultimately inferior to both. Whereas Las Casas could view the cultural difference of the Indians as capable of either assimilation or conversion through Christianity, he viewed the cultural difference of the Moors as totally alien and barbaric. Similarly, the English rejected Irish cultural difference as an impediment to English civilization. Whereas Las Casas viewed the Indians as having an indigenous right to political jurisdiction, he saw the Moors as an aggressive threat to Spanish civil jurisdiction, much as the New English viewed the Gaelic Irish assertion of political autonomy as a rebellion against English civil jurisdiction over the land which they claimed by right of the Norman conquest. Whereas Las Casas rejected Sepulveda's view of the Indians as barbarians, incapable of rationality, peace and justice and so, like Aristotle's natural slaves, subject to conquest and slavery, the New English produced a view of the Irish close to this type of barbarian as natural slave. Derricke's woodkern and Spenser's pastoral nomads resemble the barbarian as 'slave by nature', described in Las Casas's interpretation of Aristotle as 'liv[ing] spread out and scattered, dwelling in the forest and in the mountains'.[71] Irish armed resistance to English rule was constituted as an innate character of the Irish, who like the natural slave were 'eager for war, and inclined to every kind of savagery'.[72] David Lloyd's analysis of dominant history's representation of the subaltern applies to both the Moors under Spanish rule and the Irish under English rule: 'the history of the state requires a substrate which is counter to its laws of civility and which it represents as outrageous and violent, in order that the history of domination and criminalization appear as a legitimate process of civilization and the triumph of law'.[73]

Another significant critique of the European subjugation of colonized people comes from the French Calvinist Jean de Léry, whose *Histoire d'un voyage faict en la terre du Brésil* (1578) is a sympathetic and thickly contextual portrayal of Tupinamba culture. As Las Casas had done, de Léry represented Amerindian cannibalism as a socially sanctioned ritual, less barbarous than many contemporary European practices. De Léry protested that European 'big usurers . . . sucking blood and marrow, and eating everyone alive . . . are even more cruel than the savages I speak of'.[74] For de Léry, the modern European practice of capitalism causes 'misery'. In the 1585 and 1611 editions of the text, de Léry added even more examples of European cruelty, including passages from Las Casas's accounts of the Spaniards' torture of the Indians.[75] Thus, the slavery that was part of European colonial conquest is also a mark of early modern European brutality. The particularly brutal religio-political warfare of sixteenth-century Europe is yet another form of bloodthirst that de Léry finds worse than Amerindian cannibalism. In de Léry's account of the St Bartholomew's Day massacre, Catholics butchered Protestants 'in ways more barbarous than those of the savages . . . The livers, hearts, and other parts of these bodies – were they not eaten by the furious murderers, of whom Hell itself stands in horror?'[76] French Catholic savagery is 'even worse and more detestable' than that of the anthropophagous because while the man-eating Indians 'attack only enemy nations . . . the ones over here have plunged into the blood of the kinsmen, neighbours, and compatriots'.[77]

Cannibalism for de Léry also figures as the Catholic savage desire 'not only to eat the flesh of Jesus Christ grossly rather than spiritually, but what was worse, like the savages named Ouetaca . . . they wanted to chew and swallow it raw'.[78] The Ouetaca, because they ate their victims raw and did not speak the language of their enemies, represented the extremity of savagery for de Léry. He saw the Catholics, like the Oueteca, as more savage than the Tupinamba. An ethnography of the Amerindians becomes a way of characterizing the culturally alien as familiar and the culturally familiar enemy as more alien.

To summarize the comparison thus far: if for Las Casas the Indians, though culturally alien, could be viewed as familiar because of civil polity, the Moors, though culturally closer, had to be viewed as more alien than the Indians because of their proximate resistance to Spanish political hegemony. Similarly, if for de Léry the Tupinamba, though culturally alien, could be viewed as familiar because they were a society with coherent rituals, French Catholics, indeed because culturally, politically and physically closer, had to be viewed as more alien than the cannibals because of their proximate violence and the scandal of their religious rituals. When we compare English views of the Irish to these triangulated representations in Las Casas and de Léry, we find that the Irish occupy the space of the culturally alien Indians and the space of the politically resistant Moors and the religiously scandalous French Catholics – and so have to be made even more alien than the Indians. To the English the Irish were political enemies for their rebellion against colonization, religious enemies for their non-conformity to Protestantism. Even though the Irish may be in theory the subjects of a kingdom, they are constructed as enemies in their native land.

When Irish writers criticize English conquest and colonization they employ strategies that resemble these European critiques of colonialism. One of the first Irish texts to narrate the Elizabethan conquest and the aftermath of the Nine Years' War in the reign of James I from the Irish Catholic point of view, Philip O'Sullivan Beare's *Historiae Catholicae Hiberniae Compendium* protests colonial persecution in terms at times reminiscent of Las Casas.[79] For example, O'Sullivan Beare's argument against the English conquest of Ireland repeats the legal basis of Las Casas's defence of the Indians against Spanish conquest. By interpreting the twelfth-century papal bull *Laudabiliter* as granting the English ecclesiastical but not temporal power in Ireland, O'Sullivan Beare follows Las Casas's argument that Alexander VI's Bull to the Kings of Castille exhorted them only to convert the Indians, and not to wage war against and impose political jurisdiction upon them.[80] Furthermore, according to O'Sullivan Beare, since the English had rejected Catholicism under Henry VIII and Elizabeth, the Bull and all English jurisdiction over Ireland had been made completely invalid.[81] Another example of the trace of Las Casas surfaces in O'Sullivan Beare's accounts of English attacks on the civilian population. O'Sullivan Beare represents the Elizabethan conquest of Ireland on the model of Las Casas's harrowing narrative of the Spanish persecution of the Indians. As Las Casas had shown the Spaniards sadistically 'roaring with laughter' as they drowned and stabbed to death both mothers and their infants, O'Sullivan Beare portrays the English Governor who led the massacre at Mullaghmast 'tak[ing] an incredible pleasure in at the same time hanging by the mother's long hair their infant children'.[82] As Las Casas maintained that the Indians had a natural right to defend themselves, so O'Sullivan Beare argues that the Irish have the right to defend themselves not only from such brutal conquest but also from their debarment from citizenship, persecution of their religion, and confiscation of their land. Such accounts of English injustice and brutality were addressed to a Spanish audience, as indicated by the text's publication in Lisbon, its dedication to Philip IV, and its connection with Irish diplomatic strategies to gain Spanish aid for military intervention in Ireland. Striving to forge an alliance for the exiled Irish with the Spanish empire, O'Sullivan Beare is enmeshed in the ideological contradiction of protesting the injustices of English colonization in Ireland, while praising the Spanish sovereign who ruled over an empire perpetrating similar and even worse injustices.

Another Irish writer who criticizes the early modern conquest of Ireland but who, unlike O'Sullivan Beare, accepts the view of Ireland as one of the three kingdoms, is Seathrún Céitinn, or Geoffrey Keating, author of *Foras Feasa ar Éirinn*, literally the 'Foundation of knowledge about Ireland'. Céitinn's insistence upon Ireland as a kingdom was based on the notion of *translatio imperii* from the ancient Irish kingship to fealty to the English monarch at the time of the Norman conquest, a view of history that unites him with many of his Old English compatriots. Unlike that other Old English apologist Stanihurst, however, Céitinn wrote in the Irish language, in fact was the first author to create modern Irish prose as a literary language. The archaeology of Céitinn's text emphasizes the importance of the language in defining the nation and its history. Céitinn criticizes Stanihurst on historiographic grounds that might well be applied to some historians of Ireland today. He criticizes Stanihurst for his ignorance of the ancient Irish sources (he was 'blindly ignorant in the language of the country in which were the ancient records and transactions of the territory, and of every people who inhabited it') and for his opportunism (he 'had expectation of gaining advantage from those by whom he was incited to write evil concerning Ireland').[83] In so far as Stanihurst promotes an English language version of Irish history and directs his text towards the colonizer, he collaborates in what Mignolo would call the 'colonization of memory'. For Céitinn, language is the most important part of culture; so, what distinguishes the Norman conquest as Christian from the Elizabethan conquest as pagan is that the Normans did not suppress the language of the people and expel them from their land, as the early modern colonists did.[84] This distinction can be compared to Las Casas's distinction between the actual forced and violent coercion of the Indians to submit to Spanish rule and religion, and his utopian proposal for religious teaching and freely chosen conversion in a framework that would recognize the civility of the Amerindians' culture and their indigenous right to jurisdiction of their land.

By the seventeenth century, one can find even more explicit and sometimes more pointed comparisons of the effects of colonization in Ireland to those in other parts of the world from the point of view of historical memory, economic resources, and political rights. A royalist and sympathizer with Ormond, the Irish historian Peter Walsh sees a parallel between the authority of Irish sources for ancient Irish history and the validity of ancient sources from the Middle East and Asia for their histories as opposed to the 'ignorance' of Greek sources.[85] Rather than Gerald of Wales and his early modern imitators, Céitinn, whose work Walsh had read in Irish, was his source for Irish history before the English conquest.[86] Like Walsh, John Lynch in his *Cambrensis Eversus* (1662) refutes Gerald of Wales's depiction of Irish barbarism. But historiography is not the only issue here. Although Lynch defends the Irish as loyal subjects to the King of England, he points out that unlike the subjects of other kings, they are not rewarded with offices in the government, from which they are debarred by their religion. The administrative offices, the wealth, and the land are all 'monopolized by the same foreigners'.[87] Lynch quotes Donchadh O'Brian, earl of Thomond, who compares the colonial economic exploitation of Ireland to that of the West Indies: 'Ireland is another India for the English, a more profitable India for them than ever the Indies were to the Spaniards.' The limits of cross-colony identification here are indicated in Lynch's confusion of 'India' with the 'Indies' and his emphasis on the disenfranchisement of the Irish élite rather than the majority of the colonized in either Ireland or the Caribbean: 'Ireland supplied the English not only with immense treasures of ready money, but also with extensive estates and high titles.' Roger Boyle, in explaining the cause of the 1641 rebellion, and in particular the Catholic massacre of Protestants, also compares Ireland to the colonies in the Caribbean. Like Las Casas, he defends violent resistance to the oppression of conquest: 'this implacable enmity of the Irish to the English springs from the same root with that of all other subjected people to their Conquerors . . . That consequently the late unparalleled Massacres . . . had no newer cause or occasion . . . than . . . the frequent ones of European colonies in the Indies'.[88] Whereas Céitinn had referred to Ireland as a kingdom and to the English within it as colonists, in the aftermath of the Cromwellian conquest the division between the Irish nation and the English colony became even wider. In a tract written by one of the Plunketts of Fingall, colonization is described as a form of slavery. The Irish 'are treated by the ruling powers, not as subjects but in the quality of slaves . . . That an antient noble nation is thus enslaved for to support a mean colony, therin planted by the regicide sword of Cromwell . . . 'Tis a burning shame to an antient, illustrious nation to see themselves like worms trod upon by a mean and regicide colony'.[89] Paradoxically, it was because Ireland was by English law not a colony but a kingdom subject to the monarch of England that the rebels of 1641 could maintain that they fought *pro deo, pro rege, pro patria unanimis*. By the same token the English belief in their cultural superiority, divine election, and political jurisdiction over these rebellious Irish subjects legitimized their colonial subjugation under both republic and monarchy.

1997

THE CONSTRUCTION OF GENDER AND THE CULTURAL AND POLITICAL OTHER IN *THE FAERIE QUEENE V* AND *A VIEW OF THE PRESENT STATE OF IRELAND*

The Critics, the Context, and the Case of Radigund

In Ireland, Spenser acquired the land and the living that established the conditions in which he wrote *The Faerie Queene*. He was a scholarship boy, a civil servant who achieved the status of 'gentleman' through obtaining land in Ireland, and ultimately an unsuccessful colonist. Having returned from Ireland to London, he died if not 'for want of bread', as Ben Jonson claimed, then with the loss of his Irish property as a result of the Munster rebellion during which his house was burned and his land overrun.[1] As a colonial bureaucrat working under Lord Grey of Wilton, Deputy of Ireland, Spenser was alienated not only from the rebellious Anglo-Norman and Irish society, which threatened his newly acquired economic and social status as a propertied gentleman in Ireland, but also from the restraining rule of Queen Elizabeth, who recalled his superior, Lord Grey, from Ireland and thus thwarted the policies that Spenser argued in *A View of the Present State of Ireland* would accomplish the total defeat of the Irish necessary for profitable colonization.[2]

I propose to examine how these complex antagonisms in Spenser's social, political, and economic context in Ireland bear upon the construction of the ideological *topoi* of gender and the cultural and political other in *A View of the Present State of Ireland* and *The Faerie Queene V*. Written in 1596 and entered in the Stationers' Register in 1598, *A View* represents the Irish as a feminized, culturally barbaric, and economically intractable society that must be subjected to complete cultural and economic destruction and reorganization by the English colonists.[3] After examining Spenser's representation of the Irish in *A View*, I will explain how the antagonisms in his context are subjected to various conflicted displacements in the allegory of Radigund in *The Faerie Queene V*. The story of Radigund has a central location in 'The Legend of Artegall or of Justice', the book of *The Faerie Queene* that has generally been regarded as having the most direct reference to Ireland. The allegorical political meanings

28

of the story of Radigund, an account of the defeat of an Amazonian queen, have been interpreted in conflicting ways throughout the tradition of Spenser criticism. A review of some interpretations of the Radigund story and of *A View* will help me inquire how certain critical practices on occasion either evade or reveal the social context. The analysis of the work of a few representative and still important critics, Edwin Greenlaw and C.S. Lewis from the earlier part of this century, and more recently Angus Fletcher and Stephen Greenblatt,[4] in turn raises larger questions about how criticism tends to reproduce Spenser's ideology.[5] The reiteration of his ideology is perhaps to some extent the unavoidable consequence of remaining 'faithful to the text'. However, the interpretations that I have selected do not simply repeat Spenser's politics but rather produce complex variations upon them that emphasize disparate meanings, which are in turn registered in different ways, depending on the particular critical theories and practices deployed. In order to pave the way for an analysis of what I see as the fragmented and displaced political allegory of the Radigund story, and of how it recapitulates the politics of *A View*, I will first examine some other explanations of the Radigund story, and of the relevance, or lack of relevance, of *A View* for interpretation of *The Faerie Queene V.*

1

Attention to the political import of Spenser's historical allegory in *The Faerie Queene* has not always been lacking. Both the Variorum edition of *The Works of Edmund Spenser,* edited by Edwin Greenlaw, and Greenlaw's criticism show painstaking archival research into the historical allegory of Spenser's epic and its relation to Spenser's political role in and views on Ireland.[6] Crucial questions arise. What were the critical and ideological interests that motivated Greenlaw's elaboration and reproduction of the ideology of *A View of the Present State of Ireland* in relation to *The Faerie Queene*? What, on the other hand, were the critical and ideological contexts of some later critics that led to the suppression of Spenser's politics in favour of his poetics?

The extensive footnotes of Greenlaw's Variorum edition are the product of late nineteenth-century philology, which pursued what its practitioners saw as the scientific accumulation of relevant literary and historical data. Greenlaw had immense erudition, afforded him by a study of Spenser's complete works, as well as state papers, histories of both England and Ireland, the critical tradition, and the literary sources. Greenlaw also had the confidence of historical positivism, motivating that quest for erudition – that words directly refer to things in the world and that texts refer to facts outside them. However, Greenlaw connects Spenser's poetry and politics in ways that suggest a more explicitly ideological impulse than the latently ideological one of philology. See, for example, his interpretation of the political allegory of the Radigund story: 'It will be remembered that Artegall, disarmed by the beauty of

Radigund, is made to assume the dress of a woman and to perform the tasks of a woman (v. 23–25, vii. 37–41) . . . Here we have an arraignment of womanish methods applied to the solution of the Irish problem; Artegall clad in woman's garments and with distaff in his hands is a fit representative, says Spenser of the course advised by some.'[7] The reference here to 'the Irish problem' makes it clear that Greenlaw interprets the Radigund story with reference to *A View of the Present State of Ireland*. It is tempting to construe Greenlaw's comment as an extension of Spenser's argument in *A View* against the adoption of feminized Irish customs by the Old English (Spenser's name for the descendants of the twelfth-century Anglo-Norman settlers). The connection between *The Faerie Queene* and *A View* was indeed a critical given for Greenlaw's generation. As De Selincourt says in the 1912 Oxford edition of Spenser's poetry: 'the several adventures which befall Sir Artegall are vivid illustrations of the present state of Ireland'.[8] Both Greenlaw and De Selincourt were writing criticism during the first decades of the institution of the study of English literature in the university. This institution was influenced by what Chris Baldick has called 'the social mission of English criticism'.[9] In describing the literary-critical ramifications of World War I, Baldick notes: 'The resurgence of national pride, and the indignant brandishing of the cultural heritage that went with it, acted as a powerful impetus to the establishment of English Literature as a "central" discipline.' That the criticism on Spenser produced in this cultural climate reflects this 'national pride' and 'brandishing of the cultural heritage' should come as no surprise.[10]

The major critical premise of Greenlaw's version of *The Faerie Queene* is that Spenser was 'not merely . . . a poet's poet, but a farsighted student of government who saw clearly the destiny of his nation'.[11] In the 1912 essay 'Spenser and British Imperialism', Greenlaw praises Book 5 as 'the poet's art at its zenith', and he commends the policies, if not the literary merit, of the tract on Ireland. Through Greenlaw's interpretation of these two works, Spenser emerges as 'the laureate of the new England, defending the national policy, which, however cruel and narrow in some of its application, was to enable her to thwart the foes that threatened her destruction'.[12]

Rather than defend Spenser's poem from his politics, Greenlaw defends American and English imperialism as the historical fulfilment of Spenser's policies on Ireland in both Book 5 and *A View*. Greenlaw draws analogies between Spenser's colonial policies and the imperialist practices of late nineteenth-century Britain and America: '. . . if it be granted that the vacillating policy that had been the rule of procedure for many years was preventing real development of the country and was more cruel to the natives than to have the question settled once for all, it is difficult to see wherein Spenser could be censured for the cruelty and barbarousness of his views. The cruelty which he advised was the cruelty of . . . English colonial policy in India and of the American subjugation of the Philippines, cruelty indeed, but a cruelty that was the truest kindness if one be disposed to grant the necessity of the subjugation'.[13] Here Greenlaw writes what today many would characterize as a militant and topical mode of criticism. However, this passage shows a political frankness that at least allows contestation, a feature absent from some subsequent Spenser criticism. Greenlaw acknowledges the American subjugation of the Philippines as evidence of his own political context's implication in the ideology of Spenser. In effect, Greenlaw extends Spenser's view of the English-Irish conflict to apply to the colonization of India. As Greenlaw's analogy of Ireland to India and the Philippines indicates, for Spenser the Irish were not European, were indeed an alien race. Greenlaw reproduces the ideology of *The Faerie Queene* in the image of the imperialist ideology of 1912, and he represents the ideology of 1912, the height of the British empire, as the historical fulfilment of Spenser's poetic prophecy.

Along with this celebration of empire, which later critics assert they depart from, Greenlaw makes a kind of progressive apology. For him the long tradition of class oppression is so pervasive and enduring that it should not enter into our evaluation of Spenser: 'To Spenser and his contemporaries Ireland is the fair realm to be made fit for habitation as part of the English domain; the wild Irish do not enter into the calculation . . . But in England itself would the lower classes have received a whit more consideration in Spenser's time? And what of Fielding's and Goldsmith's account of the miseries which they found in the courts and prisons of the eighteenth century? And Dickens? Why pour vials of wrath on Spenser's head for not being two or three centuries in advance of his time in respect to the doctrine of the equality of men?'[14] This formulation conceals Spenser's characterization of all economic levels in Irish society – from Anglo-Norman aristocratic landed feudal lords to Irish tenants, pastoral farmers, and the 'outlaws and loose people' harboured by them – as one inferior social group.[15] In *A View*, as I will demonstrate, by social level, religion, and what for Spenser is a non-European ethnic identity (alternately Scythian, African, or Moorish), the Irish are constituted as one inferior category, which Spenser further associates with the feminine. Moreover, Spenser's own sense of class identity was sufficiently insecure with respect to the English aristocracy and the Irish feudal lords that his constitution of the Irish as an inferior group can be explained as a defensive strategic position – to ally himself with his superiors and shield himself from any feeling of inferiority to those with whom he lived in greater proximity. Spenser himself was subject to the consequences of the Elizabethan social order. My aim is not to 'pour vials of wrath on Spenser's head', but to explain how Greenlaw's argument persuades against its ostensible end. Instead of neutralizing Spenser's indictment of the Irish, Greenlaw's defence of Spenser's politics emphasizes the repetition of class oppression throughout history.

The frequent absence of Greenlaw as a source in subsequent books and articles on Spenser suggests what an embarrassment his erudition and outspoken judgments may have been for later critics. In 1936, the year the

Variorum edition of Book 5 of *The Faerie Queene* was published, C. S. Lewis distanced himself from the unpleasant burden of historical erudition. For Lewis, the topicality of Spenser's poem 'has become a stumbling-block to poetic readers'.[16] When Lewis argues that 'contemporary allusions in *The Faerie Queene* are now of interest to the critic insofar as they explain how some bad passages came to be bad', we can hear the Arnold of 'Sweetness and Light' whispering over his shoulder, 'where bitter envying and strife are there is every evil work'.[17] For Lewis, what makes Spenser a poet of Arnoldian 'high[er] seriousness' than Ariosto is the 'subjective and immaterial' that lies beneath the surface of the English epic as opposed to the 'actual' of the Italian.[18] Lewis acutely characterizes the difference between the symbolic action of the *Furioso* and the allegory of *The Faerie Queene* in a way that unintentionally explains the mystification of the historical context in Spenser's allegory. Whereas in Ariosto we read both the names and accounts of actual battles he had witnessed, 'in Spenser we shall. . . never find a context in the objective world for the shapes he is going to show us'.[19] Despite Lewis's denial, even criticism as conservative as Greenlaw's had located a good part of the material context for Spenser's allegory in Ireland. If the material context seems inaccessible in Spenser's work, it is because Spenser veils his political commentary with a mystified allegory. Spenser's mode of representation displaces the worldly context through circuitous appropriations of the Irish culture that threatened him, through exclusion of the subjectivity of the Irish, and through definition of them as 'other'.

The disjunction between what Spenser is representing and his mode of representation in *The Faerie Queene* enables Lewis to extend that mystification and abstraction. The rift between the moral dichotomies of the allegory and the historical and social conflicts that these dichotomies attempt to conceal brings to mind Walter Benjamin's analysis of baroque allegory. For Benjamin, what distinguishes the allegory of the sixteenth century from that of the middle ages is the difference between the emblematic and the symbolic: the difference between the sixteenth-century disjunction between things in the world and meanings – where 'any person, any object, any relationship can mean anything else' – and the earlier conjunction between things and meanings.[20] This shift in the mode of representation impinges upon the way the object of history is represented in baroque allegory: 'Once the object has . . . become allegorical, once life has flowed out of it, the object remains behind, dead . . . it lies before the allegorist given over to him utterly, for good or ill. In other words the object is incapable of projecting any meaning of its own . . . In his hands the thing in question becomes something else, speaks of something else, becomes the key to some realm of hidden knowledge, as whose emblem he honours it.'[21] The emblematic, in turn, manifests itself in a peculiar style where 'the written word tends towards the visual', towards the 'sacred character' of 'hieroglyphics', which is in conflict with 'profane comprehensibility'.[22] In formal linguistic terms, Ben Jonson approached this insight about baroque allegory with respect to Spenser's ideolect when he wrote that Spenser, 'in affecting the Ancients, writ no language'.[23]

Even Lewis, who is ostensibly opposed to contaminating the poem's pure hidden knowledge with the taint of the historical object, offers political analogies that reproduce the ideological categories of gender, and the political and cultural other. Witness, for example, his interpretation of the Radigund story: 'the allegory is an attack on uxoriousness . . . which is for Spenser a form of injustice . . . his picture of Radigund is a good commentary on the fact that Amoret has learned "soft silence and submisse obedience" in the Temple of Venus. The doctrine is not very congenial to modern sentiment; but perhaps Spenser's delineation of the cruelty of Radigund . . . if seasoned with our recollections of . . . the Simla memsahibs in Kipling's early work, will go down palatably and profitably enough'.[24] Lewis refers to the doctrine which established the concept of female chastity in the Renaissance: that wives should be 'chaste, silent, and obedient'.[25] By likening the 'Simla memsahibs in Kipling's early work' to Radigund, Lewis reverses the terms of Greenlaw's political exegesis. Whereas for Greenlaw Radigund is Ireland unsuccessfully subdued by the 'womanish methods' of Artegall, as English colonist, for Lewis Radigund becomes the colonialist woman ('memsahib') ruling Artegall, as colonized subject.[26] Lewis's analogy may be construed as reflecting another political meaning of Spenser's allegory: the way in which the female ruler Radigund over Artegall, as I will argue, represents Elizabeth's antagonism to Lord Grey. The apparently contradictory interpretations of Greenlaw and Lewis illuminate the conflicts in the ideology of Spenser's allegory. Spenser represents how the male hero Artegall both subjects and is subjected to the female ruler Radigund. Lewis's analogy shows how Spenser's text provokes a political response – even when politics are ostensibly something to be avoided.

Lewis's division between the political and poetic Spenser is followed by a number of critics of the last generation. As recently as the late 1960s, several books on *The Faerie Queene V* do not discuss *A View*.[27] The interpretation of the poem's allegory in private moral terms suppresses the disturbing implications of the connections between the epic and its context. The resistance to topical readings of Spenser's allegory is a symptom of a larger denial. Just as the historical meaning of Spenser's allegory is denied, so the historical and political function of criticism is implicitly denied. The emphasis on the subject's internal conflicts to the exclusion of historical and social conflicts effects what I would describe as a metaphorization of events. This metaphorization of events, or displacement of action into a state of mind, surfaces in the interpretation of the Radigund story. So Artegall's subjection to Radigund leads him to 'hope based on humility', which qualifies him to 'pursue the ends of justice', to 'free' Irene.[28] Thus Britomart and Radigund, the female warriors of opposing sides, are aspects of Artegall's mind, of 'internal justice', whereas 'Artegall's other actions and decisions represent external justice in the attitudes of a man towards other men'.[29]

A still influential and enormously complex work of Spenser criticism, Angus Fletcher's *The Prophetic Moment*, continued the division between the political and poetic Spenser, even though Fletcher attempted to attend to historical and sociological categories. Fletcher claimed that the critical outlook of *A View* was of little significance for the mythographic outlook of the epic. However, the historical gaps that resulted from this privileging of the mythographic over the critical surface in the discussion of Artegall as what Hobsbawm calls 'the social bandit': a type of Robin Hood 'who brings justice to a world where laws either do not exist or have failed somehow to work, usually through a governor's malfeasance'.[30] Fletcher's analysis of the hero of Book 5, Artegall, in terms of the social bandit tends not to emphasize that Artegall figures as the official representative of Gloriana's justice, just as Lord Grey, upon whom Artegall is modelled, functioned as official representative of Elizabeth's justice in Ireland. Nor did Fletcher's socio-mythographic interpretation take into account that the rebels who surrounded Spenser in Munster called themselves 'Robin Hoods', which is how Spenser refers to them in *A View*.[31] Fletcher noted: 'There is some irony in the fact that Spenser's Kilcolman house was burned down by bandits who considered themselves social, while his last official appointment in the service of Queen Elizabeth . . . was the office of sheriff.'[32] There is another irony here. Fletcher's comment overlooks the irony of Spenser, always on the side of the sheriff, in appropriating his enemies' role as social bandit to his official hero Artegall. Again, the ideological content and the historical reference of Spenser's allegory are even more conflicted and complex, I think, than Fletcher's analysis of Artegall as social bandit allowed.

Politics come to the fore, as they have for earlier critics, in Fletcher's interpretation of the Radigund story. According to his reading, the enemy Radigund 'gives a bad name to the chivalric ideal', and this is significant because chivalry is the 'poetic system of historical ideals which subtend the actual political life of the period'.[33] However, the gap between chivalry as an ideal and as a practice, implicit in this formulation, receives little attention. In practice the English in sixteenth-century Ireland were using guns, as were the Anglo-Norman lords and Gaelic Irish kerns. With regard to chivalric status, Anglo-Norman lords, however hibernicized their social customs, still had the titles, the coats of arms, the generations-old feudal claim to their land that made them more traditionally chivalric than the newly landed colonists, of whom Spenser was one. By portraying Artegall's enemy Radigund as a debased version of chivalry, Spenser may be displacing his own anxiety about the more chivalric identity of his Hiberno-Norman adversaries.[34] When it comes to giving a bad name to chivalry in practice, there is the example of Lord Grey at Smerwick, where he ordered the massacre of 600 Italian and Spanish prisoners who had surrendered on the condition that their lives be spared.[35]

Fletcher's comment on Radigund's defeat of Artegall also raises questions about the ideology of gender. For Fletcher, the allegory functions in terms primarily sexual, as the following passage demonstrates: 'the crime is rape, the victim a man instead of a woman. Another woman [Britomart] must punish Radigund'.[36] The interpretation of Radigund's defeat of Artegall as a rape reveals the displacement of narrative action, as well as the displacement of social-historical roles. It is Artegall who is attracted to Radigund when he sees her face covered with blood, her body prostrate on the ground from his blow. As the analysis of Artegall as social bandit implicitly endorsed Spenser's appropriation of the role of social bandit to the officer of the law, this account of the Radigund story projected the role of sexual victim upon the aggressor.

Even more provocative questions about the ideology of gender, particularly as it intersects with social status, are raised by those recent critics who set out to analyse the poem in relation to A View, but still metaphorize the historical context. Of these critics, the most impressive is Stephen Greenblatt, whose chapter on Spenser in Renaissance Self-Fashioning redirected attention to the historical grounding of The Faerie Queene.[37] Greenblatt's discussion of Spenser's 'self-fashioning' as a gentleman through his acquisition of land in Ireland significantly contributes to our understanding of the precariousness of that identity, how it was dependent on acts of military aggression, which were in turn subject to Elizabeth's willingness to fund them. Greenblatt contended that the destruction of the erotic Bower of Blisse, in The Faerie Queene 2.12, illustrates Freud's observation in Civilization and Its Discontents that 'Civilization behaves towards sexuality as a people or stratum of its population does which has subjected another one to its exploitation'.[38] According to Greenblatt, 'The Bower of Blisse must be destroyed because it threatens civility, which for Spenser is achieved only through renunciation and the constant exercise of power'.[39]

Greenblatt explained the text in relation to the social context by linking the burning of houses and the felling of groves in the destruction of the Bower of Bliss with the colonial policy of Lord Grey, which Spenser defended in A View. However, his explanation did not connect this violence with sexual exploitation. Marguerite Waller has criticized Greenblatt's text because, as she writes, 'it exercises the very cognitive imperialism it deplores'.[40] Rather than pursue what seems like an ad hominem argument (Waller does call Greenblatt 'unselfconsciously sexist'),[41] I am more concerned to explain how the methodology which Greenblatt deployed privileges the subjectivity of men of a certain social stratum. Greenblatt's eclectic methodology combined theoretical approaches from different disciplines – among which both anthropology (especially as practised by Clifford Geertz) and psychoanalysis are important. What Waller calls 'cognitive imperialism' is an effect of the focus of Greenblatt's critical practice. The limitations of these methods allowed Greenblatt to see the effects of oppression only in relation to the subjectivity of the oppressors. According to Freud, the ruling class represses its own sexuality, but this is to say nothing of the way the ruling class sexually exploits the underclass and the colonized. The subjectivity of the cultural other is also blurred at times by Geertz's methodology, which, as Vincent Crapanzano has argued in his analysis of 'Deep Play', presents 'no understanding of the native from the native's point of view'.[42]

The occlusion of the cultural other produced by these methods is revealed in Greenblatt's interpretation of an allusion to the New World in the proem to *The Faerie Queene II.* The passage reads:

> Who euer heard of th'Indian *Peru?*
> Or who in venturous vessell measured
> The *Amazons* huge river now found trew?
> Of fruitfullest *Virginia* who did ever vew?
>
> Yet all these were, when no man did them know;
> (*Faerie Queene* 2 Proem 2.6–9–3.1)[43]

Greenblatt comments: 'For a moment the work hovers on the brink of asserting its status as a newfound land, but Spenser immediately shatters such an assertion by invoking the gaze of royal power.

> And thou, O fairest Princesse vnder sky
> In this faire mirrhour maist behost thy face,
> And thine owne realmes in lond of Faery,
> And in this antique Image thy great auncestry.
> (2 Proem 4)

In an instant the "other world" has been transformed into a mirror.'[44] Here Greenblatt showed how the language of this proem obliterates the status of the poem as an alternate world. But we also need to see that Spenser has obliterated the consciousness of the native inhabitants in those 'newfound' lands. '[A]ll these were, when no man did them know' indicates that only the consciousness of 'who in venturous vessell measured' can know and represent the New World. The consciousness of the colonist displaces that of the colonized.

When we consider that Radigund is an Amazonian queen, that the 'huge river' in Spenser's proem was named by the Spaniards for the female warriors they saw there, and that Radigund is an alien female onto whom Spenser displaces the role of Artegall/Lord Grey as aggressor, the bearing of Greenblatt's explanation of *The Faerie Queene II* upon an understanding of the Radigund story emerges. The displacement of the consciousness of the other is effected in Book 2, as well as in the story of Radigund. Spenser's evasion of the cultural other, which Greenblatt's discussion discloses with respect to the Bower of Bliss but seems to occlude in the analysis of the proem to Book 2, is extended in part through a particular deployment of Freudian method. This method may permit an evasion of events and of the sexual effects of violence upon the subjected through the metaphor of the oppressor's self-imposed sexual repression. In the proem to Book 2, the metaphor of the newfound land conceals the colonists' appropriation of the Indians' land. New Historicism's treatment of history needs to acknowledge this in order to avoid reproducing the ideological assumptions underlying colonialism's creation of the concept 'New World'.

Although such critics as Andrew Hadfield and Willy Maley, among oth-ers,[45] have done a great deal to substantiate Greenblatt's important insight that 'Ireland is not only in book 5 of *The Faerie Queene*; it pervades the poem',[46] prior to their carefully contextualized readings, much criticism still attempted to evade the bearing of the Irish context upon Spenser's work. A case in point is Kenneth Gross's rhetorical analysis of *A View*, which stops short of recog-nizing the tract's political aim: to convince the crown of the need to extermi-nate a majority of the Irish, to relocate those remaining, and to transform all Ireland into the rented property of English settlers.[47] Gross writes of *A View* that 'it tends to present the English themselves as amongst the most effective agents of evil in Ireland, on account of the very rigidity with which they have instituted the machinery of cultural reform, making an idol of policy and refusing to accommodate their laws and statutes to the flux of time and human desire, or the more chaotic laws of the Irish genius loci'.[48] The assertion that Spenser thinks the English should accommodate native Irish custom is con-tradicted by key parts of *A View*: 'since we cannot now apply laws fit to the people . . . we will apply people and fit them to the laws'.[49] And as for what Gross calls the 'more chaotic laws of the Irish genius loci', witness the in-terchange between Irenius, 'the authorial voice', and Eudoxus, 'the good humanist who should be truly convinced by the man of action':[50]

> Irenius: And therefore where you think that good and sound laws might amend and reform things amiss there you think surely amiss, for it is vain to prescribe laws where no man careth for them . . . but all the realm is first to be reformed.
> Eudoxus: How then do you think the reformation thereof to be begun, if not by laws and ordinances?
> Irenius: Even by the sword, for all those evils must first be cut away with a strong hand before any good can be planted, like as the corrupt branches and the unwholesome boughs are first to be pruned, and the foul moss cleansed and scraped away, before the tree can bring forth any good fruit.[51]

This passage, which introduces the third and final section of *A View*, shows that there is no 'genius loci' for Spenser, only corrupt Irish branches that must be cut away by the sword of a strong English hand.[52] He lays waste to what will later become Wordsworth's violated woodsprites. Most questionable of all is Gross's epigraph to his chapter on *A View*, taken from Wallace Stevens's 'Notes Toward a Supreme Fiction':

> From this the poem springs: that we live in a place
> That is not our own and, much more not ourselves
> And hard it is in spite of blazoned days.[53]

To equate the alienation evoked in Stevens's poem – including the alienation of language from the world it describes – with Spenser's alienation from Ire-land is to suggest that the colonist's alienation is not social, not political, not cultural, but rather ontological or existential alienation. Gross's analysis, I think, implicitly denies the continued effectiveness of the terms of Spenser's discourse, the discourse of barbarity versus civility that Seamus Deane and other cultural critics of present-day Ireland have argued still informs political practice.[54] Gross's rhetorical analysis of A View in Spenserian Poetics valiantly attempts to translate Spenser's alienation in terms with which a contemporary American academic audience can sympathize. Unfortunately, the cultural and political conflicts of Spenser's context are lost in translation. There is the further risk in such rhetorical analysis that our own political conflicts are circumscribed from discussion, as they were not in Greenlaw's old historicist criticism. If Spenser criticism since Greenblatt has at times glossed over rather than analysed Spenser's ideology, as Greenlaw had done, it is because we live in a time when conquest and expropriation, though still practised, are no longer fashionable.

2

The importance of A View needs to be understood in its relation both to Irish history and to Spenser's poetic mediation of Irish history in The Faerie Queene. Spenser not only witnessed and participated in the administration of martial law under Lord Grey but also actively defended Grey's policies in A View. Greenblatt summarizes these policies as 'the burning of mean hovels and crops with the deliberate intention of starving the inhabitants, forced relocations of peoples, the manipulation of treason charges so as to facilitate the seizure of lands, the needless repetition of acts of military "justice" calculated to intimidate and break the spirit'.[55] I propose to extend the work of Greenblatt, to indicate how Spenser's texts are informed by his context: how both A View and The Faerie Queene V displace that context through false genealogies and through a taxonomy of virtue versus vice. In the case of the tract, I want to suggest the continued effectivity of its policies in seventeenth-century Irish history. In the case of Book 5, I am concerned to show how the object of history may be in part disinterred from the allegory, that form which Benjamin describes as leaving the object 'dead . . . and incapable of projecting any meaning of its own'.[56]

In his essay on Spenser, Yeats attributes the burning of Spenser's house by the local Munster people in 1599 to their having heard some rumours of A View.[57] Cromwell suggests no less than Yeats. In a letter regarding the forfeit and reinstatement of Spenser's grandson's land, Cromwell grants William Spenser's land back to him: first, because he has now renounced the 'Popish religion', and, secondly, because 'his grandfather was that Edmund Spenser who, by his writings touching on the reduction of the Irish to civility, brought on the odium of that nation, and for these works and other good services Queen Elizabeth conferred on him the said estate which the said William Spenser now claims'.[58] Cromwell's words here echo those of A View, as his own 'to hell or Connaught' policy was modelled on that of A View. Nicholas

Canny has pointed to how Spenser's *View* became a discourse of a periodical character. From the 1615 publication of *A Survey of the Present State of Ireland*, signed 'E.S.', to *The Interests of the English in the Irish Transplantation* of 1655, and *The Present State of Ireland* of 1673, among others, Spenser's *View* is alluded to, quoted, and imitated again and again.[59] These texts formed the basic policies for the seventeenth-century conquest of Ireland.

A View, which takes the form of a dialogue between Irenius, a veteran of the English colony in Ireland, and Eudoxus, his humanist interlocutor, is divided into three parts – all of which are informed by Spenser's experience in Ireland and the transformation of that experience into the allegory of *The Faerie Queene*. In the first section, Spenser criticizes the previous English reform strategy. The second section describes how 'barbarous' Irish customs have corrupted the Old English, called by modern historians Anglo-Normans, who had been in Ireland since the twelfth century. In the third and final section, Spenser argues for the policies of extermination and relocation.[60]

The previous reform policy, codified in the Statutes of Kilkenny (1366), had attempted to maintain English identity and political hegemony by keeping the English racially, culturally, and economically separate from the Irish. Everything from the adoption of Irish language and dress to intermarriage and tanistry (the Gaelic system of political succession), and Irish gavelkind, or communal 'ownership' of land as opposed to private property, was forbidden to the Old English.[61] In *A View* Spenser observes that 'the old English in Ireland . . . through licentious conversing with the Irish, or marrying or fostering with them . . . have degendered from their ancient dignities and are now grown as Irish as O'Hanlan's breech'.[62] Spenser recognizes that the laws had not effectively prevented the mingling of the two cultures.

Particularly troubling to Spenser is the privilege granted to these fully hibernicized Norman lords, that they held land and were recognized by the queen while they were, in fact, largely integrated into the alien culture of the Irish. In order to confront their authority, he has to create a claim to earlier origin and greater authenticity for the Elizabethan English colonists. So, he omits the fact that it was ironically Pope Adrian IV who granted Ireland to the English during the twelfth century.[63] Instead Spenser asserts the prior claim of Arthur. By tracing the genealogy of power to Arthur, Spenser appeals to the Tudor myth of their Welsh descent from Arthur, a myth also employed in *The Faerie Queene* 3.3, where it is prophesied to Britomart that she will marry Artegall, the hero of Book 5. The mention of the priority of the English claim to Ireland through Arthur in *A View* indicates that Spenser's genealogy in *The Faerie Queene* is invested with a historical and political validity as well as a mythopoetic force. It is Artegall who takes the place of Arthur in the genealogy of the Tudors in *The Faerie Queene* III, and also Artegall who, in Book 5, undertakes the quest to free Irene, or Ireland. At least since the eighteenth century, Artegall has been recognized as referring to Arthur Lord Grey of Wilton, the Lord Deputy of Ireland under whom Spenser served.[64]

Spenser's comments on language in *A View* also express his concern with creating prior English origins in Ireland. For example, he reverts to a false etymology to explain the cry of the Irish as they retreat from battle; 'cummericke' becomes 'Briton, help'.[65] There is a pun on the Welsh word 'cummeraig' meaning 'Welsh,' which in Spenser's mythology signifies Tudor.[66] This quasiparanomastic trope is translated into narrative action as the Briton knight Artegall saves Irene, or Ireland, to the enthusiastic shouts of the native people, glad to be free of the tyrant Grantorto, whose description is modelled on that of an Irish kern, or warrior. The Irish origins of Ireland are called illegitimate in *A View* and appropriated into a false British origin in both *A View* and *The Faerie Queene*.

Spenser also argues the moral superiority of the English to the Irish and Hiberno-Normans in both tract and epic. The moral qualities attributed to the Irish constitute a taxonomy of vice as opposed to the array of virtues embodied in the hero knights and the titles of each book of *The Faerie Queene*. As opposed to the 'holiness' of Redcrosse Knight, the defender of Una, the one true Protestant faith, the Irish are 'all Papists . . . but . . . so blindly and brutishly informed . . . that you would rather call them atheists or infidels'.[67] In contrast to Guyon the Knight of Temperance, the Irish are repeatedly called 'wild', 'licentious', 'intemperate'. Unlike Britomart's valued chastity is the lewdness of the Irish women. In describing the mantle worn by Irish men and women alike, Spenser particularly protests its wearing by the *Monashut,* or vagrant women: 'it is her cloak and safeguard, and also a coverlet for her lewd exercise . . . and when her bastard is born it serves instead of all swaddling clothes'. The Old English through 'licentious conversing' with the Irish have 'degendered from their ancient dignities'. Unlike the justice of Artegall in Book 5, 'lawlessness' characterizes the Irish; their assemblies are 'full of the scum of loose people'. Juxtaposed against the civil Calidore of the Book of Courtesy are the 'barbarous' and 'uncivil' (the most frequently used adjectives in *A View*) Irish. Their custom of wailing for their dead is 'heathenish, brought thither by the Scythians, or the Moors, which were Africans'. The Irish for Spenser are indeed descended from Africans; in support of this he cites their manner of farming and riding horses.[68]

It has been noted that Spenser's depiction of the Irish in the first section of *A View* owes a great deal to Giraldus Cambrensis.[69] However, the use of Cambrensis within Spenser's radical proposals for colonization makes the old ethnographic descriptions serve an emerging discourse of race. Nineteenth-century racial discourse, economically motivated by the full-blown European imperialist exploitation of Africans, Asians, Arabs and other colonized peoples, certainly takes forms different from that of Spenser's ethnographic description of the Irish. Nevertheless, his use of this ethnography to further his argument for colonization, cultural reorganization, and even extermination becomes a way to constitute the disparate groups within Irish society as a type of unified racial other. While Spenser's construction of disparate economic groups within Ireland as one social category does not correspond to real conditions,[70] he attempts to overcome this with a definition of the Irish as an antagonistic racial other, with the power to corrupt and subsume the Old English through social contact and intermarriage. He describes the Irish as not only primitive and barbaric, but also as African and Asian, and pagan. But, as we will see, his attempt to recapitulate this ethnography in an economic-sociography reveals the gap between these two accounts of the Irish. His own social and economic anxieties about those higher up in the social order seem, at least in part, to motivate his ethnographic description.

In *A View* the moral degeneracy of the Irish is not just a catalogue of ethnographic vices but the product of material practices which thwarted the efficient and profitable English exploitation of Irish people and land. Spenser's descriptions of the Irish laid the way for his proposals for action: the thoroughgoing destruction and reorganization of every aspect of Irish life – economic, political, and cultural.[71] He outlines how this destruction and reorganization will be accomplished in a highly detailed five-part proposal. The order and purpose of the plan reveals that Spenser's complaints against Irish customs are the description of symptoms that have a much more threatening cause in political and economic practice. The order of the plan is as follows: 1) military defeat of the entire country – including the starvation of the civilian population; 2) the institution of military control of the entire country to be accompanied by the introduction of English settlers into the largely depopulated land; 3) required sworn allegiance to the crown and subjection to a mandatory census for the tithe; 4) the abolition of transhumance, the Irish system of pastoral farming (all who kept cattle would have to plough the land; any stragglers would be imprisoned and executed); 5) the missionary endeavour, which was to be preceded by instruction in English grammar. Religion and language are relatively insignificant factors in this plan; of primary importance are land and money. In the calculation of how to get the best return on the investment of troops and money in the conquest of Ireland, the first order of the day is to get rid of those intractable people, who through raids and rebellions resist appropriation of their land.

The moral complaints of the second part of *A View* become economic complaints in the third section. Whereas earlier Spenser claims that encroachment upon the land of the Old English is due to their moral degeneration in intermarrying with the Irish, later he emphasizes the economic consequences of the loss of land to the Irish. At first besieged by obsessions with sex, Spenser's ultimate concern is with money. In the third section of *A View*, he explains how money is being lost because of gavelkind (here confused with tanistry), whereby the Irish transformed private property into the communal property of the clan: 'how those Irish captains of countries have encroached upon the Queen's freeholders and tenants, how they have translated the tenure of them from English holdings into Irish tanistry and defeated Her

Majesty at all her rights and duties, which are to accrue to her thereout, as wardships, liveries, marriages, and fines and alienations, with many other commodities which now are kept from Her Majesty to the value of £60,000 yearly, I dare undertake, in all Ireland by that which I know in one county'.[72] Spenser's use of the verb 'undertake' in this reckoning of revenue lost through 'tanistry' suggests an association with his own economic position in Ireland. For as an 'undertaker', an English settler to whom the crown granted property in Ireland, Spenser held and rented out land confiscated from the Anglo-Norman Sir John of Desmond.[73]

Both the defeat of tanistry and the specific defeat of Desmond may be construed in the stories of Pollente and the Gyant in Book 5.2. The feudal lord and social bandit Desmond, who forfeited his estates because he was charged with treason, may be part of the political reference of Pollente, described as 'expert in battell and in deedes of armes', and one who 'him selfe vppon the rich doth tyrannize' (5.2.5, 6). Artegall cuts off Pollente's head, which then: 'He pitcht vpon a pole on high ordayned / Where many years it afterwards remayned' (5.2.19.4–5). In 1582, the head of John of Desmond, cut off by Colonel Zouche, was sent to Lord Grey at Dublin Castle. It was placed on a pike outside for all to see – including Spenser, who lived at Dublin Castle, where he was serving under Lord Grey.[74] Over 3,000 acres of Munster land and Desmond's Kilcolman Castle were granted as reward to Spenser for his service in Ireland.[75] And it was at Kilcolman Castle that he wrote the concluding books of *The Faerie Queene*.

The defeat of gavelkind may be construed in another figure in Book 5.2, the Gyant, around whom 'the vulgar . . . flock' because of his promise that he 'all things would reduce unto equality' (5.2.32, 33). Critics of the early part of this century saw the defeat of the Gyant as an argument against the Anabaptists, or against pre-capitalist socialism, and even, by historical extension, as the defeat of the principles of the French Revolution.[76] While these extensions of the political meaning of the allegory across history might seem anachronistic, such interpretations remind us of the continuing political relevance of *The Faerie Queene*. Spenser's defence of 'private property' is an important part of his allegory of justice.

In proposing a specifically Irish reference for the Gyant, I want to consider the relevance of Spenser's own economic context – the fact that he was engaged in the appropriation and renting of land formerly held by feudal title, as Desmond's land was until he rebelled and his title was revoked. These two stories that follow one another in Book 5.2 indicate Spenser's dual protest, his opposition to both the rebellious feudalism of the Hiberno-Normans and the intractable custom of Irish gavelkind. The appropriation and redistribution of land, outlined in *A View* and informing the stories of Pollente and the Gyant, also inform the story of the defeat of Radigund.

3

The story of Radigund in Book 5, cantos 5 and 7, of *The Faerie Queene* can be analysed in terms of the disjunction between historical content and allegorical form, which Benjamin asserts is characteristic of the baroque. Through the strategies of appropriation and expropriation both of cultural identity and of land, Spenser's representation of the subjection of Artegall to Radigund figures a description of social decay, recapitulated in *A View of the Present State of Ireland*. Along with the oppositions of English versus Irish, civilian versus barbarian, which define the colonist versus the native in Spenser's tract, is the opposition of masculine versus feminine. Now I want to explore how these oppositions figure in the story of Radigund in Book 5. Britomart's and Talus's conquering Radigund and her Amazonian women allegorically represents the policy of military force, outlined in *A View*. And just as cultural/racial identities are rearranged in Spenser's allegory, so too the political/gender roles of female queen and male subject are both mirrored and inverted. As Lauren Silberman observes in her discussion of androgynous discourse in Book 3: 'Certainly (the highly problematic) Book 5 provides a very different view of female rule in regard to all women who are not Elizabeth.'[77]

The characterization and narrative fate of Artegall in Books 5.5 and 7 can be deciphered as the appropriation of an alien cultural identity to the Elizabethan colonist, since 'gall' in Irish means foreign, making Artegall as Lord Grey a foreign Arthur. Artegall's first appearance in the poem (3.4.39.2) where he is called a 'stranger knight' further suggests this meaning. As the text of *A View* illustrates, Spenser was well aware of this Irish word; for there he notes 'it is at this day amongst all the Irish a common use to call any strange inhabitants there amongst them Gald'.[78] He does not make explicit, however, that 'gall' was the name the Irish gave to the Anglo-Normans, or Old English. The Irish called the Elizabethan settlers 'Saxain', or 'sasanach'.[79] Whereas in *A View* Spenser creates a genealogical origin for the English colonist through the Tudor myth of their descent from the Briton settlement of Arthur's time, here in *The Faerie Queene* Artegall is a 'foreign' Arthur.

Artegall's fate is like that of the Hiberno-Normans who are described in *A View* as 'degendered', 'through licentious conversing with the Irish'.[80] Artegall is defeated by Radigund through his attraction to her 'beautie' and 'feature excellent' (5.5.12.7; 13.6). As soon as he is overcome by the sight of her, she flies up to attack him. In the simile describing her assault on Artegall, he is a 'gentle falcon', and she 'like as a Puttocke' or bird of prey (5.15.1). Only two other times in the poem does Spenser use this word. First, 'puttocke' describes those storming the house of Alma (2.11.11), who closely resemble Irish fighters.[81] Another time the word is used in the phrase 'like puttocks claws' (5.12.30.3) to describe the long nails of Envy, who attacks Artegall when he is recalled to Gloriana's court after rescuing Irene. The word 'puttock' occurs again in *A View* to describe the Irish, from whom the Old English are now indistinguishable: 'Growen to be as very puttockes as the wild Irish'.[82] Radigund is associated with the influence of the Irish upon the Old English, as Artegall is associated with the 'degendering' of the Old English. Since he assents to Radigund's terms in battle, he is responsible for his own defeat: he 'to her yeelded of his owne accord' (5.5.17.2).

Artegall is degenerated according to his gender role as well as his political role. Made to do women's work and wear women's clothes by Radigund, he is like the Old English in their adoption of Irish customs. Spenser's particular emphasis on dress in his depiction of the Old English becoming Irish in *A View* makes it tempting to view the effeminization of Artegall as a narrative translation of the 'degendering' of the Old English. In *A View*, directly after a passage in which Irenius laments the 'evil race' brought forth through marrying with the Irish, Irenius speaks of the law against the wearing of Irish apparel, which is not observed by the Old English. Eudoxus, in response, likens the corruption of the Old English to that of the Lydians: 'Cyrus changed their apparel . . . and instead of their short warlike coats, clothed them in long garments like wives . . . they became most tender and effeminate whereby it appeareth that there is not a little of the garment to the fashioning of the mind and condition.'[83] More evidence for this construction of the sociopolitical meaning of this sartorial allegory comes from the Irish etymology of Radigund's name: 'rad' in Irish means to 'grant' or 'bestow', while 'guna' means 'women's clothes'.[84]

The depiction of Radigund as a rebellious female, who inverts the subjection of woman to man decreed by natural law, makes her analogous to the Irish, whose 'barbarity' demands they be 'reduced to civility' by the English. The characterization of the 'licentious Irish' in *A View* is prefigured in the narrator's moralizing comment on Radigund's subjection of Artegall:

> Such is the crueltie of womenkynd,
> When they haue shaken off the shamefast band,
> With which wise Nature did them strongly bynd,
> T'obay the heasts of mans well ruling hand,
> That then all rule and reason they withstand,
> To purchase a licentious libertie.
> But vertuous women wisely vnderstand,
> That they were borne to base humilitie,
> Vnless the heavens them lift to lawfull soueraintie.
> (5.5.25.1–9)

In *A View* the Irish are often described as 'licentious' or as 'living licentiously'.[85] Their effect upon the Hiberno-Normans is described as follows: 'they have become flat libertines and fall to flat licentiousness, more boldly daring to disobey the law than any Irish dare'.[86] Also, according to Spenser's ethnology, Irish women, like Radigund and like their ancestors the 'Old Spaniards' or 'Africans', usurp a ruling hand, for they have, as Spenser writes, 'the trust and care of all things both at home and in the fields'.[87]

Perhaps the most perverse aspect of Radigund's inversion of natural law is that it can be read as a rehearsal for the policy Spenser recommends the English follow in subduing the Irish. He describes what should be done with the Irish once they are defeated: 'I would have them first unarmed utterly, and stripped of all their warlike weapons, and then these conditions set down and made known to them, that they shall be brought and removed . . . into Leinster, where they shall . . . become good subjects to labour thenceforth for their living.'[88] Similarly, Radigund both disarms her captives and sets them to work:

> First she doth them of warlike arms despoile,
> And cloth in womens weedes: And then with threat
> Doth them compell to worke, to earn their meat.
> (5.4.31.3–5)

Like Spenser's plan to reduce the Irish through starvation – even more forcefully stated in *A Briefe Note* than in *A View* ('force must be the instrument but famine must be the meane'[89]) – Radigund prevents rebellion through strict control of food:

> Ne doth she giue them other thing to eat,
> But bread and water, or like feeble thing,
> Them to disable from reuenge aduenturing.
> (5.4.31.7–9)

And when Radigund asserts 'like a rebel stout I will him use' (5.51.3), it is as though Artegall is to Radigund as an Irish rebel is to Grey.

When Britomart, Artegall's betrothed, defeats Radigund and frees Artegall from 'women's thralldom' (5.5.21.9), critics from Lewis to Fletcher tell us that the order of law is restored. But the language in which this restoration is achieved reveals the contradictions in Spenser's claims about the universality of the law in *The Faerie Queene* and *A View*. Britomart as a figure of Elizabeth is unlike other women. The chastity of Elizabeth and Britomart is distinguished from Radigund's 'licentious libertie'. Elizabeth and Britomart are capable of lawful rule because 'the heavens them lift to lawful soueraintie' (5.5.25.9). The lines describing Britomart's establishment of justice, after she frees Artegall and re-arms him, express this alienation of Britomart from other women. She finally enforces the subjection of women to men:

> And changing all that forme of common weale,
> The liberty of women did repeale,
> Which they had long vsurpt; and them restoring
> To mens subiection, did true Iustice deale.
> (5.7.42.4–7)

The use of 'common weale' here suggests that this restoration of gender roles also connotes a change of economy and of government, for 'weale' means both wealth and community. Britomart's overturning of 'common weale' is prophetic of the overturning of both common law and Irish Brehon law in *A View*.

In fact, the actions which attend this change of 'common weale' correspond point for point with Spenser's reorganization of Irish society in the third part of *A View*. First, the women of Radegone are reduced by military force, as the Irish were to be. Spenser uses the same language of husbandry that he uses in *A View* to describe this part of the 'reform'.[90] Britomart's and Talus's martial victory is narrated as follows:

> She with one stroke both head and helmet cleft.
> Which dreadfull sight, when all her warlike traine
> There present saw, each one of sense bereft,
> Fled fast into the towne, and her sole victor left.
>
> But yet so fast they could not home retrate,
> But that swift *Talus* did the foremost win;
> And pressing through the preace vnto the gate,
> Pelmell with them attonce did enter in.
> There then a piteous slaughter did begin:
> For all that euer came within his reach,
> He with his yron flaile did thresh so thin,
> That he no worke at all left for the leach:
> Like to an hideous storme, which nothing may empeach.
>
> (5.7.34.6–9; 35, 1–9)

This slaughter is metaphorized as a threshing, then a blood letting, and then as a natural disaster.

Following the first step of military defeat in Spenser's policy comes the appropriation of land and of all political power by the English. The description of Britomart freeing the knights from captivity conforms to the order of economic and political appropriation of Ireland in *A View*:

> For all those Knights, which long in captiue shade
> Had shrowded bene, she did from thraldome free;
> And magistrates of all that city made,
> And gaue to them great liuing and large fee.
>
> (5.7.43.1–4)

'Those Knights' are like Spenser's threatened colonists who would become magistrates and acquire land to rent, 'great living and large fee', if Spenser's proposals were carried out.

The third step of reform in *A View*, the swearing of allegiance to the Queen, in the poem is replaced by the swearing of allegiance to Artegall, which is instituted by Britomart:

> And that they should for ever faithful bee,
> Made them sweare fealty to *Artegall*.
>
> (5.7.43.5–6)

This final appropriation to Artegall of the role of Britomart, or of the Queen, reveals a further displacement of the historical context by the text of the allegory. At this point in the poem, Artegall is triumphant, restored to manhood and power, unlike Lord Grey, who was recalled from Ireland in disgrace – not because of his cruelty but because of the enormous expense and inefficiency of his methods. The roles of Elizabeth and Grey are reversed in this story. At the end of 5.7, Britomart appears for the last time in the poem. She pines for Artegall, whereas he rides off to rescue Irene, who figures allegorically as Ireland. At the centre of Canto 5, what had been, in fact, Grey's defeat becomes a triumph of his methods of slaughter and appropriation, which Spenser defends and systematizes in A View.

What I have argued here is how a return to the footnotes can help us to understand the bearing of Spenser's material context in Ireland upon the political allegory of The Faerie Queene. His protest in A View against the Hiberno-Norman's alliance with the Irish and Elizabeth's withdrawal of support from Grey's iron fist policies informs the allegorical displacement of identities in Faerie Queene V. In the construction of the identity of the hero knight Artegall, the alien identities of Hiberno-Norman lord and powerful sovereign queen are both appropriated and inverted. Similarly, the reproduction of the political allegory through the critical tradition continues the process of appropriation and inversion. The institution of Spenser criticism at times extends the strategies of his 'fashioning of a gentleman'. Spenser criticism has as much to do with the creation of the middle-class subject as Spenser's allegory itself. The process is a complex and convoluted one, motivated by political oppositions within Spenser's context as well as those within the contexts of his critics.

1990

REPRESENTATIONS OF WOMEN IN SOME EARLY MODERN ENGLISH TRACTS ON THE COLONIZATION OF IRELAND

Since D. B. Quinn's *The Elizabethans and the Irish*, the history of early modern Ireland has been the subject of a wide range of studies, but only recently has women's role in that history received attention.[1] Similarly, Nicholas Canny's article on 'Edmund Spenser and the Development of an Anglo-Irish Identity' initiated a debate about whether sixteenth-century tracts on Ireland express a unified colonialist ideology, but only recently has the construction of sexuality in these texts come under scrutiny.[2] It is not surprising that those studying the history of women in early modern Ireland do not often turn to the English tracts for evidence, except with great caution and reservation. So much related in these documents is indebted to the stereotypes of a colonialist discourse, initiated by Giraldus Cambrensis in the twelfth century, rather than to observation or encounter.[3] Recent work on the history of women in early modern Ireland presents us with a sense of what is not being represented in the English settlers' descriptions. Such aspects of women's lives in Gaelic Ireland as their right to hold and acquire their own land and to keep their own names while married are not referred to in these tracts, which do not yield transparent information about actual Irish women of the period, although there are fascinating references to their activities. Spenser writes that Irish women had 'the trust and care of all things both at home and in the fields'.[4] And at least one woman, the foster mother of Murrogh O'Brien, is said to have drunk the blood of her child's head as she grieved when he had been drawn and quartered by the English.[5] The character of these texts as colonialist discourse makes the representation of women as a symbolic category or 'gender' the more useful focus, rather than some unmediated sense of 'women'.

In their construction of gender, the tracts have more to tell about the subjectivity of the colonizers than that of the colonized. New historicists have analysed the subjectivity of the colonizer in Spenser's ethnography of the Irish in *A View of the Present State of Ireland* in relation to his 'fashioning of a gentleman' in *The Faerie Queene*.[6] While this criticism makes readers of Spenser more aware of his historical context, its focus on the canonical Spenser to the exclusion of other authors of tracts on Ireland tends to grant *A View* an influence it did not have in 1596, when it circulated in manuscript but was not published. Treating Spenser's text as representative also overlooks important ideological differences among the tracts. *A View* is but one of many tracts on Ireland from the reigns of Elizabeth and James. A far more widely known text was Richard Stanihurst's 'Description of Ireland', first published in 1577 in Holinshed's *Chronicles*.[7] References to Stanihurst's text in later tracts, which both imitate and refute it, attest to its influence. The Irish-born Stanihurst's 'Description' contrasts with the majority of these tracts, which were written by Englishmen in the royal army or government of the Lord Deputy for Ireland.[8] Even within this category, a close examination of gender in the tracts reveals no one unified subjectivity.

What can be learned from these tracts is how representations of gender signify social, political, and religious conflicts in the colonial context. My analysis of the representation of women in English descriptions of Ireland, like Louis Montrose's analysis of Ralegh's *Discoverie of Guiana*, deploys Joan Scott's concept of gender as a 'primary way of signifying relationships of power'.[9] Scott divides 'gender as a constitutive element of social relationships' into four parts: (1) 'culturally available symbols that evoke multiple (and often contradictory) representations'; (2) 'normative concepts that set forth interpretations of the meanings of the symbols, that attempt to limit and contain their metaphoric possibilities'; (3) 'a notion of politics and reference to social institutions'; (4) 'subjective identity'.[10] My discussion of early modern tracts on Ireland addresses all four categories: how symbols and normative concepts conflict with one another; how the social groups and institutions with which the authors were affiliated influence representations of groups and institutions; how the identities of these authors are formed in their texts.

A comparison of the tracts with one another shows that certain topics – namely language, religion, nakedness, and even Irish people as a group – are typed as feminine. The construction of these topics as feminine reveals both the author's attitude towards the Irish and his chief ideological concerns. The shifts from text to text disrupt a sense of binary fixity – both in terms of discourse on Englishness versus Irishness and in terms of discourse on masculinity versus femininity. Neither of these binary oppositions is statically set, even within the forty-year period 1577–1617 from which the tracts examined here are taken. Every ideological category described – ethnicity, religion, status, and gender – is inflected by the particular ideological affiliations of the author. Attention to each author's context tells a great deal about how and why he uses the representation of gender to symbolize other ideological categories. The diverse ways in which particular authors characterize particular topics as feminine complicates an understanding of the debate on the colonization of Ireland. In some cases, the descriptions of women in other colonial contexts, as well as prescriptions for English women's conduct, shed light on these gendered representations in the tracts. Finally, the portrayal of Elizabeth – as woman and director of the colonial enterprise – figures prominently in several tracts and relates in complex ways to representations of the colonized. One such tract is Richard Beacon's *Solon His Follie* which, along with Herbert's

Croftus Sive de Hibernia Liber, has often been compared to Spenser's *View*.[11] Beacon, like Spenser, served on the Munster provincial council and was an undertaker, an English colonist who was granted land confiscated from the Irish and who undertook to meet the requirements for plantation. For both Beacon and Spenser, service in Ireland was a means to get land, wealth, and power. Written in the form of an allegorical humanist dialogue, *Solon* contains allegorical figures both of the Irish and of Elizabeth that need to be decoded in relation to symbols in other tracts and literary texts.

In order to understand early modern tracts on Ireland, it is important to understand the social context of their authors in Ireland. The three social groups represented in these texts are New English, Old English, and Irish. Almost all the authors discussed here were New English Protestants, late six-teenth-century and early seventeenth-century colonists. This group includes Spenser, Beacon, Davies, Moryson, and Riche. The descendants of those Anglo-Normans who had invaded Ireland in the twelfth century were referred to by these New English authors as Old English. Stanihurst, whose family had been part of the English administration of Ireland since the fourteenth cen-tury, identifies himself as Old English. Many of the Old English, unlike the New English, were fairly well assimilated into Gaelic society through inter-marriage with the Irish, a common Catholic religion, and the Irish language. As Spenser puts it:

> great houses there be of the old English in Ireland which through licentious conversing with the Irish or marrying and fostering with them . . . have degen-dered from their ancient dignities and are grown as Irish as O'Hanlan's breech.[12]

According to Spenser, intermarrying with the Irish and allowing their chil-dren to be raised by foster parents in the Irish custom had caused the Old English to go native. Even in 1610, after the defeat of the Irish lords in the Nine Years' War, Barnabe Riche expresses what had become a commonplace of the tract on Ireland: 'It is holden for a Maxime in Ireland, that ten English will sooner become Irish, then one Irish will be found to turne English.'[13]

By far the largest group in Ireland was 'the wild and mere' Irish. From reading Spenser's *View*, one might get the impression that Gaelic society was made up of nothing but unruly fighting men, nomads, and generally 'loose people'. Recent research by social historians, however, has shown that early modern Irish society was not comprised only of greater and lesser overlords and Scottish mercenaries. There were also fishermen, traders, prosperous farmers, craftsmen, smaller tenants and peasants, who, though subject to overlords, at least had the advantage of being able to move and 'to choose the most favourable working conditions'.[14]

This analysis of gender in the tracts on Ireland begins with Richard Stani-hurst's 'Description of Ireland' not only because of its wide circulation and influence, but also because it represents an Old English perspective that serves by contrast to better define that of the New English. In Stanihurst's text, the representation of women is related to the attitude towards Old English and Irish. He is at pains to distinguish himself and the Old English as civilized inhabitants of the English pale, the counties of Louth, Meath, Dublin, and Kildare, controlled since the twelfth century by the royal administration. Stanihurst was not only a Dubliner but a recusant Catholic.[15] Religion – either Catholic or Protestant – does not concern him in his description of either Old English or mere Irish. He aims to distinguish the Old English from the Irish according to other customs. Interestingly enough, his first description of people concerns their knowledge of English. He insists not only that the 'inhabitants of the English pale' had English 'as their only moother toong' but that English had spread to Ulster, Munster, and especially Wexford. He tells a story about how an Englishman thought he heard the natives speaking Irish when they were actually speaking 'old ancient Chaucer English'.[16] 'Inhabitants of the meaner sort' are singled out for speaking 'neither good English nor Irish'. In this context Stanihurst criticizes the pronunciation of Irish women:

> And whereas commonllie in all countries the women speake most neatlie and pertlie, which Tullie in his third booke of *De oratore* . . . seemed to have observed . . . yet . . . in Ireland it falleth out contrary. For the women have in their pronunciation a harsh and brode kind of pronunciation, with uttering their words so peevishlie and faintlie, as though they were half sicke, and ready to call for a posset. And most commonlie in words of two syllables they give the last accent . . . And if they could be weened from that courrupt custome, there is none that could dislike of their English.[17]

Irish women's speech is less feminine than Cicero claims is women's speech in general. Like the 'meaner sort', women are less secure in their English, and beyond that perhaps even less willing to speak English since they sound 'half sicke' when they do so. These women could be made more civilized if, like Eliza Doolittle, they could only learn how to speak more correctly. Women here are used to stand for what is more conservative, less civilized, and yet clearly capable of reform in Irish culture. Stanihurst sees nothing inherently evil about the Irish language, which, as he points out, has even lent some words to English.

Spenser's comments on Irish women's role as bearers of culture through nurture and language show that he, too, views language as an indicator of civilization. Unlike Stanihurst, however, he sees no hope of reform for the Irish. For Spenser, the Irish language is tied up with intermarriage and fostering with the Irish, all three of which are positively evil. Whereas Stanihurst can sympathetically report: 'They love tenderly their foster children, and bequeath to them a childes portion, whereby they nourish sure friendship', Spenser's account of an Irish wet nurse's effect upon a child suggests that physical contact with the Irish – particularly with Irish women – is itself contaminating:

> the chief cause of bringing in the Irish language amongst them was specially
> their fostering and marrying with the Irish, which are the two most dangerous
> infections, for first the child that sucketh the milk of the nurse must of necessity learn his first speech of her, the which being the first that is enured to his
> tongue is ever after most pleasing unto him, insomuch as though he afterwards
> be taught English, yet the smack of the first will always abide with him, and
> not only of the speech, but of the manners and conditions. . . They . . . draw
> into themselves together with their suck, even the nature and disposition of
> their nurses, for the mind followeth much the temperature of the body; and
> also the words are the image of the mind, so as they proceeding from the mind,
> the mind must be needs effected with the words; so that the speech being Irish,
> the heart must needs be Irish . . . how can such matching but bring forth an
> evil race, seeing that commonly the child taketh most of his nature of the
> mother, besides speech, manners, inclination, which are for the most part
> agreeable to the inclinations of their mothers, for by them they are first framed
> and fashioned.[18]

This passage is remarkable for what it says about Spenser's view of language, intermarriage between English and Irish, and the ideology of motherhood. The analogy between the child's learning language and sucking milk through the breast suggests the most physical and erotic sense of language, as well a linguistically conditioned way of perceiving the world. Cultural identity is deep for Spenser, not something easily susceptible to adaptation or reform. Intermarriage clearly means intermarriage with Irish women, not men, and it is evil since these women are responsible for raising and thus forming the cultural identity of the children. The cultural influence of the mother is so strong that others can never eradicate it; her children are 'framed or fashioned' by her nursing, speech, and very 'inclinations'.

Riche's comments on language are marked by religion rather than gender. For Spenser the missionary endeavour would come only after complete military defeat accompanied by mass starvation and forced relocation. Religion, however, is of utmost importance for the radical Protestant Riche. He commends the king's order for a translation of the New Testament into Irish.[19] Just following this exhortation to spread the true faith in Irish, Riche in one breath says: 'For the Irish to inure themselves to speake English, I thinke it were happy'; in another, he reserves this happiness for Protestants: 'If never a Papist throughout that whole country could either speak or so much as understand a word of English.'[20] Riche does not so much resent the mere Irish as he does the more powerful Catholic Old English. Old English recusants who threatened New English control of the Irish parliament in the early seventeenth century are the object of Riche's recurring complaint, 'poperie is the onely plague-sore that hath so poysoned Ireland'.[21]

Riche represents Catholicism through anecdotes and symbols that associate it with sex and women. While Spenser's babies are sucking in language, Riche's are 'nuzeled from their cradles in the very puddle of Popery'.[22] Riche had inherited the language of the reformation, which also characterizes this passage in *A View*: 'What other could they learn than such trash as was taught them, and drink of that cup of fornication with which the purple harlot had then made all nations drunken?'[23] Riche draws out the image of the Catholic church as the whore of Babylon in at least two directions – both by producing variations on the symbol in his context and by attaching it to particular women in this context. To dramatize the disloyalty of recusants, Riche tells the story of how a married woman rationalizes her adultery:

> That at my marriage day, this mouth of mine made inviolable promise to my husbande of continencie; and therefore with the other parts of my bodie, for my lips are onely vowed to my husband, and for him I will reserve them. . . . this Woman was as firme in the promise she made to her husband, as a number of Papists in their oaths they do make to the king.[24]

The recusant's allegiance to the king is likened to a woman's vow of sexual fidelity to her husband; her pretended faithfulness involves a clever equivocation of meaning. The recusant gives lip service to the king and the rest of his body to the church. At other times Riche refers to the actual prostitution of wives on their husbands' behalf: 'Some women there hath been that have prostituted themselves, thereby to advance her husband's credit, sometimes to save her husband's life.'[25] The placement of this discussion of cuckoldry in the context of Riche's sardonic mock praise of the Irish – 'iealousie is no generall sickness in Ireland' – suggests that prostitution for political advancement thrives there. Catholic women of all classes – both ladies and alehouse keepers, both English and Irish – receive Riche's censure. In *The Irish Hubbub, or The English Hue and Crie* (1617), Riche rails against English 'runnagates, that for their misled lives in England do come running over into Ireland', and particularly singles out 'Recusants' as 'more hurtful than all the rest'.[26] He goes on to complain about the sort of English women among these recusants who have come to Ireland:

> there have bin as ungracious and wicked women, that when by their misled lives, they have . . . made themselves so notorious, that they were become odious to all honest company in England, have then transported themselves into Ireland, where they have so insinuated themselves amongst our Ladies and Gentlewomen, . . . by whom they were so entertained, graced and countenanced, that those women that had lived before in good name and fame, and finding themselves to be but slightly regarded, thought it more wisdom to forget their former modestie, and for companies sake to follow the fashion.[27]

Among the working women of Dublin, Riche castigates the 'Tavernekeepers'. Despite his protests against 'idelnesse whoredome and many other vile abhominations', his main complaint is not moral but clearly economic. The problem with these women is that they are making too much of a profit:

> They have a number of young ydle Huswives, that are both verie lothsome, filthie and abhominable. . . and these they call Taverne-keepers, the most of them known harlots; these do take in both Ale and Beere by the Barrell from those that do brue, and they sell it forth againe by the potte, after twoe pence for a Wine quart. And this. . . is a principall cause for the tolleration of many enormities; for the gaine that is gotten by it must needes be great, when they buy mault in Dublyn, at haulfe the price that it is sold for at London, and they sell their drinke in Dublyn, at double the rate they doe in London.[28]

Riche defends this description against the objections of a woman reader in his *True and Kinde Excuse, written in Defence of that Booke, intituled A New Description of Irelande* (1612):

> At an honest Alderman's house in Dublyne, . . . a woman (if I may tearme her to bee a woman that hath forgotten to blush) but such a creature there was that amongst the wholl assembly, beeganne to picke quarrelles both at me and my booke, belying and slaundering both it and me, with such false and untrue reportes, that a number of those that had never read the booke itselfe, beleeved all to be true that shee reported: And thus being carried from hand to hand I was brought into a generall obloquie throughout the whole citie of Dublyne, but especially amongst the citizens wives.[29]

This passage presents evidence of early modern Irish women's literacy and also highlights the portrayal of Irish women as a significant aspect of Riche's work for both author and reader.

Riche was also the author of a conduct book entitled *My Ladies Looking Glasse*, which distinguishes 'a good woman from a bad' in terms that connect the intractable colonized subject in Ireland with the unruly woman in England.[30] Just as he personifies 'Sinne' as 'she. . . that began on the sudden to play the Rebell' in *My Ladies Looking Glasse*, so too, in *The Description of Ireland*, he rails against 'Popery that hath set afoot so many rebellions in Ireland. . . that it hath ruined the whole realm and made it subject to the oppression of. . . Rebels'.[31] *My Ladies Looking Glasse* also contains not only such anti-Catholic tirades but even complaints about the rebellious Irish who can 'tell you news from the Pope, how he meanes to give assistance to the Earl of Tyrone, of men, money, munition and shipping, and of all other necessaries, and to send him into Ireland'.[32] Even the title of one of his Irish tracts, *A Looking Glasse for Ireland* (1599), suggests that Riche's text conceives of the regulation of women's conduct as analogous to the regulation of the colonized.

While Riche complains of prostitution in alehouses, the corrupting effects of English recusant women, of Catholicism itself as a kind of symbolic adultery, Spenser rails against the wandering women in the context of a diatribe against the wearing of Irish dress. Men, too, are criticized for the wearing of mantles; but while these Irish men are outlaws, rebels, and thieves, women who wear them are 'wandering' and 'lewd':

> In summer ye shall find her arrayed commonly in her smock and mantle to be more ready for her light services; in winter and in her travel it is her cloak and safeguard and also a coverlet for her lewd exercise, and when she hath filled her vessel, under it she can hide both her burden and her blame.[33]

While Spenser does not always represent the Irish as women nor Irish customs as feminine, when it comes to describing the sexual looseness of the Irish, he does. Irish women in tracts by Davies, Moryson, and Riche appear naked more often than dressed. These images of female nudity express fascination and repulsion. Two passages from Fynes Moryson's *Itinerary* display these different responses to a woman's nakedness:

> He coming to the house of Ocane, a great lord among them, was met at the door with sixteen women, all naked, excepting their loose mantles; whereof eight or ten were very fair and two seemed very Nymphs. With which strange sight his eyes being dazzled, they led him into the house, and there sitting down by the fire, with crossed legs like tailors, and so low as could not but offend chaste eyes, desired him to sit down with them. Soon after, Ocane . . . came in all naked except a loose mantel and shoes, which he put off as soon as he came in, and . . . desired him to put off his apparel, which he thought to be a burden to him, and to sit naked by the fire with this naked company. But the Baron, when he came to himself after some astonishment at this strange sight, professed that he was so inflamed therewith as for shame he durst not put off his apparel . . . At Cork I have seen with these eyes young maides stark naked grinding of corn with certain stones to make cakes thereof, and striking off into the tub of meal such reliques thereof as stick upon their belly, thighs, and more unseemly parts.[34]

On the one hand, the sight of fair Irish women sitting naked around the fire evokes sexual arousal and shame; on the other, the lack of separation between a woman's naked body and the grain she works provokes disgust. Similarly, Barnabe Riche writes:

> if I should tel, how my selfe have seene a woman sitting with a Mustarde Quearne betweene her bare thighes, grinding of Oatmeale, I thinke a man would have little life to eate of the bread.[35]

In the description of the woman working, the body becomes the site of contamination – of the filth of the lower bodily stratum. Woman's nakedness also stands for Ireland's savagery, in Moryson's account of an Italian friar's exclamation upon seeing Armagh: 'Vain Armagh city, I did thee pity, / Thy meat's rawness and women's nakedness.'[36] The selection of raw meat (and all the associations of this with cannibalism) and naked women as markers of identity are similar to those found in sixteenth-century descriptions of Native Americans. Michel de Certeau comments on Jean de Léry's account of naked Tupi women mourning and then preparing a dead man's body for a cannibal feast: 'The nakedness of these women is a very ambivalent vision. Their savagery fascinates and threatens. . . the native world, like the diabolical cosmos, becomes Woman. It is declined in the feminine gender.'[37]

If Davies's and Spenser's representations of Irish women betray ambivalence, their depictions of their sovereign queen are also mixed with attraction and fear. Elizabeth is both masculine ruler and feminine subject. She has a masculine identity as ruler of her subjects and a feminine identity as the object of male desire, and as the passive medium of divine intervention in history. In his dedication to the queen in *Solon His Follie*, Beacon refers to how she had achieved 'the greatest magnificence of a Prince'.[38] But Beacon portrays Elizabeth's power as feminine when he addresses her as 'Circe. . . who has graunted vnto dumb creatures liberty of speech'. He also expresses his relation to Elizabeth as that of a courtier imitating a suffering Petrarchan lover before the queen as object of desire: 'And with the fonde lover in Petrarke, must thou of force make me a sorrowful minister thereof? And with the silly birds fast tied and bound, must I represent the face of thy loving thoughts?'[39] For Davies, Elizabeth is an effective ruler, outdoing her masculine predecessors in her efforts to conquer and colonize Ireland, and she is the passive means through which God establishes his higher power. On the one hand, Davies praises Elizabeth for 'spend[ing] more treasure to save and reduce the land of Ireland than all her progenitors'.[40] On the other hand, he treats her as the passive instrument of God: 'Who can tell whether the Divine Wisdom . . . did not reserve this work to be done by a Queen, that it might rather appear to be His own immediate work?'[41] For Spenser, Elizabeth's power by metonymy is 'the sword' that Irenius interprets as 'the royal power of the prince, which ought to stretch itself forth in her chief strength', and which Eudoxus translates into practice: 'an infinite charge to her majesty to send over such an army as should tread down all that standeth before them on foot and lay on the ground all the stiff necked people of that land'.[42] These images of Elizabeth as prince and lady follow a convention that she herself exploited in her public self-representation. In her speech before the troops at Tilbury, she played on this theme: 'I know I have the body of a weak and feeble woman, but I have the heart and Stomach of a King.'[43]

Beyond the convention of the queen's dual-gendered identity, Beacon's and Spenser's tracts further complicate the construction of the queen's identity, since she had authority over their colonial endeavours. Elizabeth not only had the power to 'spend treasure' on the army and the legal administrative system in Ireland but also to recall her English servants in Ireland and to prohibit their criticism of her colonial policies. By writing critically about the administration of Irish affairs in the 1590s, Beacon and Spenser risked the queen's displeasure. *A View* explicitly vindicates Spenser's former superior in Ireland, Lord Grey. Elizabeth had recalled Grey from his post as Lord Deputy of Ireland in part because of the embarrassment to the crown caused by the massacre at Smerwick, where 600 Italians and Spaniards, who had surrendered on the promise that their lives would be spared, were executed. In *A View*, Irenius, a veteran of the English conquest of Ireland, graphically pictures the famine, cannibalism, and mass extermination of people brought about by Grey's policies:

> Out of every corner of the woods and glens they came creeping forth upon their hands, for their legs could not bear them. They looked anatomies of death, they spake like ghosts crying out of their graves, they did eat of the dead carrions. . . Yet sure in all that war there perished not many by the sword, but all by the extremity of famine, which they themselves had wrought.[44]

The Irish are blamed for having brought famine upon themselves. It is no wonder that Eudoxus 'greatly pit[ies]' not the effects of this violence upon its immediate victims but the effects of its retelling upon the queen: 'being by nature full of mercy and clemency, who is most inclinable to such pitiful complaints and will not endure to hear such tragedies made of her people'.[45] Spenser fears that Elizabeth will not countenance such violence. His criticism of the queen is that while 'by nature' her 'compassion' will not allow her to approve of such violence, by policy she would want Ireland 'made ready for reformation'. For Spenser, this reformation can only be achieved by the scorched earth policies of Grey:

> So I remember that in the late government of that good Lord Grey, when after long travail and many perilous assays. . . he had brought things almost to this pass ye speak of, that it was even made ready for reformation.[46]

Beacon's tract expresses a similarly vexed relation to Elizabeth's power. While slavishly praising the queen for her reformation of Ireland in the dedication to *Solon His Follie*, Beacon, too, turns out to be a supporter of Grey, and implicitly a critic of Elizabeth. Furthermore, Beacon has his own axe to grind, since he had been recalled from Ireland by Elizabeth's Privy Council. In his case the offence was his practice of imposing excessive fines upon the people of Munster, where he served as Attorney General from 1587 to 1591. The aspiring civil servant Beacon mediates his antagonism towards Elizabeth by representing her in an allegorical figure that is gendered and within the tradition of tracts on Ireland conventionally used to depict the Irish. He calls Elizabeth 'Circe' who 'hath once again graunted unto dumbe creatures liberty of speech'.[47] Here Beacon allegorizes Elizabeth's lifting a prohibition against public debate of her Irish policy as Circe's disenchantment of the men she had once turned into swine. This reverses the conventional figure of Circe as the corrupting influence of the Irish upon the Old English or Anglo-Normans.

After recounting the customs of the wilde Irish in his 'Description of Ireland', Stanihurst produces this simile:

> Againe, the verie English of birth, conversant with the savage sort of people become degenerat, and as though they had tasted of Circes poisoned cup, are quite altered.[48]

Later in 1612, Davies repeats the same image, in which the power of Irish customs to transform the English into beasts is likened to Circe's cup:

> These were the Irish customs which the English colonies did embrace and use after they had rejected the civil and honourable laws and customs of England... like those who had drunk of Circe's cup, and were turned into very beasts, and yet took such pleasure in their beastly manner of life as they would not return to their shape of men again.[49]

That Circe is a woman, a seductress, and an alien whose drink turns men into beasts makes her an apt image for what these New English colonists saw as the corrupting influence of the Irish. That Beacon likens Elizabeth's allowing him to publish *Solon His Follie* to Circe's restoring beasts to men implicitly means that her earlier silencing of him or of other critics was like Circe's turning men into beasts. Like the wild Irish who deprived the Old English colonists of their identity as English, Elizabeth had limited, or in some cases, deprived her colonial servants of their autonomy and power in Ireland. If the wild Irish posed the threat of Gaelic power for the New English colonist, Elizabeth posed a threat to these men from the centre of English power. Both Irish and Elizabeth are constructed as woman, seductress, and alien.

While Beacon describes Elizabeth through an exotic feminine figure usually associated with the wild Irish, he allegorizes the Irish in terms traditionally associated with the queen. At the opening of Beacon's allegorical dialogue, Solon, while in the garden of the Temple of Venus, recounts a dream vision:

> This night I seemed to beholde faire Diana with a beautiful Dove glistering like golde, placed upon her shoulder, slyding and wavering everywhere, in such sorte, as it seemed to me to be in great ieopardy of falling, but forthwith mooved with compassion I stretched my right hande, to better and reforme the place of her standing: wherewith I might beholde Diana with a sharpe and sowre countenaunce to threaten the losse of my hand.[50]

The great Diana figure of late sixteenth-century England was Elizabeth herself. In the 'Letter to Raleigh', Spenser explained his portrayal of Elizabeth as Belphoebe and Cynthia: 'Phoebe and Cynthia both being names of Diana'.[51] Raleigh formed a private cult that later became public in which Elizabeth was adored as the moon. Elizabeth herself exploited this literary conceit in her public self-presentation; she posed for portraits wearing the crescent moon of

Diana in her hair. It makes perfect allegorical sense that this vision of Diana should appear to Solon while sleeping in the garden of Venus, since Diana and Venus were linked iconographically in the cult of Elizabeth. Such works as John Davies's 'Of Cynthia' and *Hymns to Astraea* portray Elizabeth as the virginal Diana and Venus, Queen of Beauty.[52] As John King has pointed out, the figure of Diana also symbolized Elizabeth's 'universal imperium' and Protestant and national independence, as in the Dutch engraving of the bare-breasted Diana defeating the Pope.[53] Given this public cult of Elizabeth as Diana, Epimenides' explanation of the dream reverses a culturally dominant image: 'The people of Salamina is the threatening Diana, hating all reformation.'[54] Diana is not the Virgin Queen nor is she the symbol of Protestant national independence; she is the Catholic people of Ireland.

If we recall the myth of Actaeon, frequently alluded to in Petrarchan love lyrics, the image of threatening Diana as the Irish people explains the complexity of the colonist's relation to the colonized and to the queen. The story, in Ovid's *Metamorphoses* 3.173–252, tells how Actaeon, spying the naked Diana bathing, is turned by her into a stag and then hunted down and devoured by his own hounds. Beacon's allegory, like the myth, contains the elements of eroticism and dismemberment. He describes the threatening Diana first as 'the faire Diana'. And just as the Diana of the myth is angered by Actaeon's intrusion, so, too, is Beacon's Diana. The two details that significantly distinguish Beacon's dream vision from the myth of Actaeon are the substitution of the golden dove for Diana's nakedness and the loss of Solon's hand for Actaeon's metamorphosis and the stag's mangled flesh. Epimenides decodes the meaning of the dove as 'the pleasaunt countrie of Salamina'. The golden dove has associations not only with the doves of Venus' chariot but also with the *Golden Hind*, the ship Drake sailed when he plundered Spanish treasure, and with the mythic land of gold, 'El Dorado', which Walter Raleigh searched for in his voyage to Guiana. The object of desire is the golden dove, suggesting both the commodity of gold and the merchant vessel to transport that commodity. That the dove is 'slyding and wavering everywhere . . . in great jeopardy of falling' means that Diana cannot control her. Diana's sharp and sour countenance threatens the loss of Solon's hand, which is explained as 'the difficulties and dangers which shall oppose you in this action of reformation'. If Ovid's Diana silences Actaeon by turning him into a stag, Beacon's Diana, too, threatens to silence Solon by depriving him of the hand that wields both sword and pen. It is interesting to note how the violence of the Irish opposed to the 'reform' of colonization is allegorically assigned to a feminine figure. At the same time, if we think back to the image of Elizabeth as Circe, who 'graunted speech unto dumb creatures', and to the convention of Elizabeth as Diana, it is possible to read a double allegory of conflicted meanings here. Perhaps the text also suggests, against Beacon's explicit attempts to fix its meaning, that Elizabeth is not in control of the Irish people; that her attempts to silence or restrain her colonial servants are as much a threat to the reformation of Ireland, and to the New English reformer, as the opposition of the Irish itself.

While this analysis is by no means exhaustive – either in terms of texts or topics – what still emerges from it is a sense that, though all these texts portray some aspects of Irish culture as feminine, it is not always the same aspect that is marked by gender, nor is that aspect always represented in the same way. The reasons for these differences lie in the specific circumstances and beliefs of each author. Stanihurst's description of the mispronunciation of English words by Irish women portrays the assimilation, however imperfect, of the Irish to English culture. This optimistic view is characteristic of his 'Description' as a whole, which gives the impression of the legitimacy and relative success of Old English power in Ireland. Spenser's castigation of the Irish language as it is tied to 'dangerous' Irish manners and morals portrays a colonial society in which assimilation means the degeneration of his Old English rivals into Irishness. From the vantage point of 1596, in the middle of the Nine Years' War, in which the Irish led by Hugh O'Neill rebelled against English rule, colonization by peaceful means has failed. Writing after the defeat of O'Neill and the Gaelic chiefs in 1603, Riche occupies a New English position much more secure with respect to Irish culture but still in competition with the Old English recusant élite. Riche's approval of an Irish language bible to promote the spread of Protestantism shows that Gaelic culture is not as threatening as is Old English Catholicism. A third antagonism, not against the Irish or their Catholicism but against the queen in her power to direct colonial policy, is shared by Beacon and Spenser, but significantly not by Riche and Davies, both of whom wrote in the reign of James I. Despite all these differences, the conflation of Elizabeth with Circe and of the Irish with Diana shows how thoroughly the representation of gender is the representation of power relationships. Filtered through the desires and fears of the subject, the power relations of waking life are inverted in a dream, when the colonized are represented as a woman in power.

1993

SPENSER'S RELATION TO THE IRISH LANGUAGE
The Sons of Milesio in *A View, Faerie Queene V,* and the *Leabhar Gabhála*

At the centre of *A View of the Present State of Ireland*, Spenser describes how perception and emotion are linguistically conditioned: 'the words are the image of the mind, so as they proceeding from the mind, the mind must be needs effected with the words; so that the speech being Irish, the heart must needs be Irish'.[1] The context of this passage is a tirade against the Old English customs of marrying and fostering with the Irish, 'from which the evil custom of language chiefly proceedeth'. While Irenius finds the Old English love of Irish 'unnatural', Eudoxus finds their linguistically going native contrary to the practice of Roman colonial conquest: 'for it hath been ever the use of the conqueror to despise the language of the conquered, and to force him by all means to learn his'. Irenius's rationale for proposing instruction in English letters and grammar as part of a general reform of Irish society would seem not only to confirm Eudoxus's point of view but to enforce the conqueror's disdain upon the conquered:

> whereby they will in short time grow up to that civil conversation, that both the children will loathe their former rudeness in which they were bred, and also their parents will... perceive the foulness of their own brutish behaviour.[2]

Spenser's relation to the Irish language was much more ambivalent and complex than these two alternatives of love and disdain. Neither fluent in Irish, as the Anglo-Norman Old English who had begun the process of going Gaelic in the twelfth century were, nor merely monoglot in English, as few, if any, sixteenth-century New English bureaucrats in Ireland could have been, Spenser was a poet with a keen attention to language and a full understanding of its power. Despite some evidence of his knowledge of Irish (however imperfect) and his interest in Irish chronicles and bardic poetry, since the 1950s there has been almost no critical attention to Spenser's relation to Irish language and literature and how this affected his writing.[3] It will be the purpose of this article to reconstruct, at least in part, Spenser's linguistic context in Ireland, to examine his comments about Irish writing in *A View*, and to compare the story of the sons of Milesio in *Faerie Queene* 5.4 with the version in the *Leabhar Gabhála* (which he also refers to in *A View*) in order to investigate how the poet mediated his relation to Irish lore through his poetry.

Before Spenser went to Ireland, he may very well have read some Irish words in Richard Stanihurst's 'Description of Ireland', published in Holinshed's *Chronicles* (1577).[4] Like Spenser's *Shepheardes Calender* (1579), Stanihurst's work was dedicated to a member of the Sidney family (Stanihurst's text to Henry, Spenser's to Philip); and Spenser used his Sidney connections to help gain an appointment in Ireland.[5] Although the Dublin-born Old English Stanihurst defends the Englishness of the Pale and displays no great knowledge or love of Irish, he does mention Irish words that also occur in the *Shepheardes Calender*. Spenser uses the Irish 'glenne' in the Aprill Eclogue (l. 26) and 'kernes' (an English plural of the Irish noun) in the Julye Eclogue (l. 199).[6] If the glosses on these words – 'country Hamlet' for 'glenne' [valley] and 'churle' [peasant] for 'kerne' [Irish *ceithearnach*: horseboy] – betray a less than exact knowledge of Irish, part of Spenser's confusion may lie in his reading of Stanihurst's text. Two passages from Stanihurst might very well have inspired the Spenserian link between kerne and churle. In the first, Stanihurst describes the pride of place that the Gaelic Irish felt they deserved in respect to both Old and New English:

> For the Irish man standeth so much upon his gentilitie, that he termeth anie one of the English sept, and planted in Ireland, Bobdeagh Galteagh, that is English churle: but if he be an Englishman borne, then he nameth him, Bobdeagh Saxonnegh, that is, a Saxon churle.[7]

Just following this translation of an Irish taunt into English, Stanihurst describes the 'kern' as an 'ordinarie souldier', but he suggests the etymology of kern derives from the wild behaviour of these soldiers:

> Kerne signifieth (as noble men of deepe iudgement informed me) a shower of hell, because they are taken for no better than for rakehels, or the divels blacke gard, by reason of the stinking sturre they keepe, wheresoever they be.[8]

Both kerne and churle are lowly creatures in Stanihurst's account as they are in Spenser's text. The word 'kern' also figures prominently in another near-contemporary text, also associated with the Sidney faction, John Derricke's *Image of Ireland with A Discoverie of Woodkarne* (1581), which eulogizes Sir Henry's campaign in Ireland. Derricke, like Spenser, associates 'kern' with 'churl', or as D. B. Quinn says in the glossary to his edition 'the disreputable Irish peasantry'.[9]

If Spenser had encountered a few Irish words in his reading before he left for Ireland, during his eighteen years there he must have learned a great deal more. In the sixteenth century most of the Irish outside the Pale – and many of those within it – were primarily Irish speakers; it was only in the seventeenth century, with the disruption of the Gaelic order that followed the defeat of O'Neill at Kinsale and the further colonization of the entire island, that the Irish language began to decline.[10] Even the descendants of Cromwellian settlers were Irish speakers by 1700. The Ireland of 1750, in which the majority of Catholics in the North were native speakers while the majority of gentry throughout the country had English as a first language, could best be described as bilingual.[11] In sixteenth-century Ireland, Irish was the dominant language, which meant that the English needed to use Irish both in speaking to their subjects and in describing their activities. As Stanihurst comments in 'The Description': 'the English pale is more willing to learn Irish than the Irishman is willing to learn English: we must imbrace their language, and they detest ours'.[12] Stanihurst's 'Description' mentions the influence of Gaelic upon English: 'As for the word bater, that in English purporteth a lane, bearing to an high waie, I take it for a meere Irish word that crept unwares into the English, through the dailie intercourse of the English and Irish inhabitants.'[13]

More than a few 'meere Irish' or truly Gaelic words crept all too consciously into the correspondence of the Lord Deputy for Ireland, which Spenser, who served as Lord Grey's Secretary (1580–82), had to draft and copy.[14] Spenser's duties as secretary included not only letter-writing in Dublin but also accompanying the Lord Deputy on military campaigns all over the country, which would have necessitated their contact with Irish speakers. One such campaign found Grey and Spenser in the western part of the Dingle peninsula (still part of the Kerry Gaeltacht) at Smerwick, from which a letter in Spenser's hand survives.[15]

Spenser's use of Irish in documents written in his hand from the State Papers Ireland and later in *A View of the Present State of Ireland* displays an instrumental approach to the language – a sort of intelligence-gathering.[16] The list of Irish words common to both the State Papers and *A View* amassed by Roland Smith in 1958 includes nine words that pertain to geography, warfare, politics, and law. Among these are 'glenne' and 'kerne', now used correctly. Such words as 'bawne' [Ir. *badhbhdhún, bábhún, bódhún*: a fortified enclosure] and 'rath' [Ir. *ráth*: earthen rampart, or round trench] relate to the surveillance of land. Such words as 'galloglas' [Ir. *gall-óglách*: literally, foreign young warrior; a Scots mercenary), 'tanist' [*tánaiste*: elected leader of the sept]; and 'tanistry' [*tánaishtecht*: the custom of choosing the leader of the sept] relate to intelligence gathering about the Gaelic military and political order. Such words as 'creat' [Mid. Irish *cáeraighecht*: a herd of cattle driven from place to place for pasture] and 'garron' [Ir. *gearrán*: gelding, small horse] designate property, in an account of gallowglasses encountered in battle and in a bill against Roche, Spenser's neighbour in Kilcolman with whom he was involved in legal disputes.[17] Another Irish word that occurs in the State Papers in Spenser's hand, but not in *A View*, is 'vriaghs', the *árach* or 'binding, or covenant' of the ancient laws. That the 1563 treaty between the queen and Shane O'Neill also contains this word shows that the mastery of Irish vocabulary was necessary not only to the secretary and planter in Ireland but also to the queen and her Privy Council in England.[18] Indeed, there was even an Irish primer composed for Elizabeth so that she could learn the language.[19]

Spenser's interest in Irish went beyond the necessity that he had to know at least some rudiments of the language in order to work as secretary to the lord deputy and to live as a colonist in Munster. In *A View*, when Eudoxus assumes the lack of a written culture in Ireland, Irenius sharply rebukes him: 'ye are therein much deceived, for it is certain that Ireland hath the use of letters very anciently, and long before England'.[20] In the same breath that Irenius admits his dependence upon Irish sources, he undercuts their reliability:

> I do herein rely upon those bards or Irish chronicles, though the Irish them-selves, through their ignorance in matters of learning, and deep judgement, do most constantly believe and avouch them, but unto them besides I add my own reading.

The scrutiny to which Irenius subjects his Irish sources, 'likeness of manners and customs, affinity of words and names, properties of natures and uses', amounts to a search for what will make sense to his interlocutor Eudoxus, or by extension Spenser's English reader: 'a probability of things which I leave unto your judgement to believe or refuse'. Spenser both respects the antiquity of Irish literature and undermines the authority of its writers – referring to their 'ignorance of art and pure learning' – in order to appropriate the role of judge and disseminator of these 'relics of true antiquity, though disguised, which a well-eyed man may haply discover and find out'. His dual roles as antiquarian and political policy analyst involve him in simultaneously pre-serving Irish antiquities and controlling them as the production of what he argues is an inferior culture.

Irenius claims that in addition to his own research on the antiquities of Ireland he has sought out the help of an Irish translator to understand Bardic poetry:

> Yea, truly, I have caused diverse of them to be translated unto me, that I might understand them, and surely they savoured of sweet wit and good invention, but skilled not in the goodly ornaments of poetry.[21]

On the one hand, Spenser excludes Irish bardic compositions from consider-ation as poetic art and limits them to the realm of natural beauty in com-mending the 'pretty flowers of their own natural device'. On the other hand, he clearly finds interest in their 'good invention', their choice of topics, or subject matter, called *invenio* in rhetoric. Such contact with a learned Irish poet or chronicler could help to explain not only Spenser's appreciation for the antiquity of the language but also his knowledge of its topics and stories.

One example of the antiquarian and poet's familiarity with Irish language sources is in his treatment of the myths about the invasions of Ireland. In rail-ing against Irish 'forged histories of their own antiquity, which they deliver to fools and make them believe them for true',[22] Irenius rehearses four different invasion stories in the following order:

> first of all one Gathelus, the son of Cecropes, or Argos, who having married the King of Egypt's daughter, thence sailed with her into Spain, and there inhabited, then that of Nemed and his four sons who coming out of Scythia peopled Ireland and inhabited with his sons two hundred and fifty years, till he was overcome of the Giants dwelling then in Ireland, and at last quite banished and rooted out; after whom two hundred years the sons of one Dela, being Scythians, arrived there again and possessed the whole land, of which the youngest called Slaynius in the end made himself monarch; lastly of the four sons of Milesius, King of Spain, which conquered the land from the Scythians, and inhabiting it with Spaniards, called it of the youngest, Hibernia.[23]

In comparing Spenser's account with the versions of the invasions of Ireland recounted in the *Leabhar Gabhála* and the works of Nennius, Giraldus Cambrensis, Campion, and Holinshed, Roland Smith pointed out that only in the *Leabhar Gabhála* and in *A View* does the story of Gaedel (Spenser's Gathelus) occur first, and only Spenser follows the Irish spelling of Nemed from the *Leabhar Gabhála*.[24] Finally, while Spenser may have drawn the story of the 'sons of Milesius, King of Spain' from Giraldus, he may just as well have taken it from the *Leabhar Gabhála*. In any case Spenser was not dependent on Campion, Holinshed or Nennius for this story since they all refer to 'foure brethren Spaniards', rather than to the 'four sons of Milesius', the '*Maic Milead*' of the *Leabhar Gabhála*.

Spenser had been acquainted with the story of the sons of Milesius even before writing *A View* (1596), as can be seen in the story of the sons of Milesio in *Faerie Queene* 5.4–20. Roland Smith went to great lengths to show how many different Irish intertexts could have influenced Spenser's version of the story, including not only the *Leabhar Gabhála*, but also the *Benshenchas*, the *Book of Lecan*, and the *Senchas Már*, or *Ancient Laws of Ireland*.[25] In order to prove that these texts could have been sources for Spenser, Smith emphasized their similarities to the story in Book 5. The *Leabhar Gabhála* provided the story of a dispute between two brothers over land; exchange of wives; a genealogical tract from the *Book of Lecan* contained the detail of contested dowry; and the *Benshenchas* included the plot element of the *Ancient Laws of Ireland* which yielded the judgement that if one travels over sea to retrieve flotsam, it belongs to him and not the original owner of land. All these texts create a much fuller sense of the Irish textual and cultural context.

Such source study, however, does not ask how and why Spenser altered this traditional material. If we examine the significant changes that he makes in his telling of the story of the Milesian invasion we might have a sharper sense of why it occurs in the legend of Justice of Book 5, and what Spenser's version of the story has to say about his relation to Irish traditional lore, and his use of that lore to express the relation between English and Irish culture.

Spenser's story of the sons of Milesius can be summarized into the following plot elements. The story opens when Artegall happens upon a dispute between two brothers, from which their wives attempt to dissuade them. Next, Artegall interrupts 'their greedy bickerment' and questions 'the cause of their dissent' (5.4.6.8, 9).[26] Brasidas, the elder brother, proceeds to tell that they are the sons of Milesio, who leaves each of them an equal inheritance. They each inherit one of 'Two Ilands' (7.5). Trouble starts when the 'devouring Sea' washes Brasidas's land away 'unto [his] brothers share' (8.2–3). Things get even worse for Brasidas when his betrothed Philtera, '[w]ith whom a goodly doure [he] should have got' (8.8), leaves him for his younger brother Amidas. Lucy, Amidas's betrothed, throws herself into the sea in an attempt to end her grief in death. On the verge of drowning, she finds a treasure chest which she clings to and which brings her to Brasidas's shore. Brasidas saves her life, and in recompense she gives him herself and her treasure 'in dowry free' (12.8). Meanwhile Philtera claims the treasure is actually hers, and Amidas maintains the truth of her story to Artegall. At this point Artegall steps in to judge the case. He commands the brothers 'let each lay down his sword' (16.7). Artegall asks Amidas by what right he holds onto the land which the sea washed from his brother's island onto his own. Then with analogous reasoning, Artegall asks Brasidas by what right he keeps the dowry that landed on his shore. The answer in each case is the same: 'what the sea unto you sent, your own should seeme' (17.9, 18.9). Justice turns out to be the will of the sea:

> For equall right in equall things doth stand,
> For what the mighty Sea hath once possest
> And plucked quite from all possessors hand,
> Whether by rage of waues, that neuer rest,
> Or else by wracke, that wretches hath distrest,
> He may dispose by his imperiall might,
> As thing at randon left, to whom he list.
> So *Amidas*, the land was yours first hight,
> And so the threasure yours is *Bracidas* by right.
>
> (5.4.19)

Though Artegall claims that the judgement maintains 'equall right', Amidas and Philtra are 'displeased', presumably because of their loss of the treasure, but Brasidas and Lucy are 'right glad' (20.2, 3).

Spenser changed the story from the *Leabhar Gabhála* about the Milesian invasion and conquest of Ireland into a story about inheritance and law. In the *Leabhar Gabhála*, the story begins with the judgement of Amorgen (one of the sons of Míl) who tells his brothers that they must sail 'over nine waves' before they return to Ireland to attempt to conquer it.[27] While in the *Leabhar Gabhála* druidic winds that put 'gravel upon the surface of the sea'[28] drive the sons of Míl back to Ireland, they have clearly sought this invasion and are willing to fight for the possession of land:

Fir torachta tuinide!
Dar nói tonna mara mun-glassa,
Ni ragaid mani déib cumachtachaib –
Clandtar crib! Airlicther cath!
[Men seeking a possession!
Over nine great green-shouldered waves,
Ye shall not go, unless with powerful gods!
Be it settled swiftly! Be battle permitted!][29]

In *The Faerie Queene*, the arbitrary decree of the sea that carries land, treasure, and a woman and leaves them wherever it wills replaces the desire of the sons of Míl to invade, engage in battle, and conquer all of Ireland. What was a battle for 'fixed ownership' [*tuinide*] in the Irish myth becomes the chance windfall of flotsam and jetsam in Spenser's narrative. Spenser treats the land the same as moveable property, not inherently linked either to the people who live there or to those who insist upon their right through battle.

That Spenser made his story about 'Two Ilands' rather than one suggests a conscious attempt to enlarge a myth about the island of Ireland to a myth about the relation between Ireland and its neighbouring island. The sense that Brasidas's island has become 'impaired' while Amidas's has 'increased' suggests an allegorical rendering of the English appropriation of Irish land.

It is significant that Artegall instructs the two brothers to lay down their weapons as a condition upon which he will grant them a judgement and solution to their disagreement. In the story of the sons of Míl, Amorgen divides the land of Ireland between his two brothers, Eremón and Eber, with Eremón inheriting the North and Eber the South.[30] On the one hand, in the Irish account, the sons of Míl overturn Amorgen's judgement in favour of a battle which results in Erimón's sovereignty over the entire island of Ireland. (He is said to rule all of Ireland for seventeen years.)[31] On the other hand, in Spenser's narrative, the sons of Milesio lay down their swords and submit to Artegall's judgement, even though they are not equally happy with the resulting division of property. Unlike *A View*, which recommends the English military conquest of Ireland, and Irish versions of the Milesian invasion, which tell a story of battle leading to unity under a single kingship, Spenser's story allegorically represents a legal solution to the problem of land ownership which evades warfare.

The principle according to which Artegall reasons for the division of property is the power of the sea, which is referred to as its 'imperiall might'. Spenser's use of the adjective 'imperiall' is significant here. One of the justifications of English power in Ireland, according to *A View*, is the legal right and will of the sovereign, 'the Empresse' to whom *The Faerie Queene* is dedicated and whose rule guaranteed the legal right of the New English to pursue armed conquest, to confiscate land, and to establish plantations. And this whole process of taking over ownership of Ireland was in the sixteenth century, and continued to be in the following three centuries, as much or more by litigation as by warfare. The sovereignty over Ireland established by Eremón is replaced by the 'imperial might' of the sea, the might of English law.

What does this all have to do with Spenser's relation to the Irish language and its literature? In his roles as antiquarian and government servant he was engaged in gaining some knowledge of the Irish language and of Irish antiquities in order to control Irish culture for English purposes. To a certain extent both in *A View* and in *The Faerie Queene*, Spenser performed the antiquarian role as preserver of culture. By the same token, the poet completely reworked these sources to established new myths to explain a new culture – specifically that of the English living in Ireland. If Spenser undercut the truth value of Irish antiquities in *A View*, in the Proem to *Faerie Queene II* he feared that his audience might subject his own 'famous antique historie' and judge it 'painted forgery' rather than 'matter of just memory' (1.2, 4, 5). The judgement depends on whose memory and whose justice are in question. Ironically evoking the mysterious and imaginative origins of his narrative, Spenser declares that what he does is to 'vouch antiquities, which nobody can know' (Proem II, 1.9). My point is that some of these antiquities can be known in the body of ancient Irish texts. Because of Spenser's admitted interest in and reliance upon Irish lore, the whole question of how the poet used Irish myths to explain an English fiction with a historical allegory deserves further attention. I have tried to show that both in *A View*, where the antiquarian undercuts the truth status of Irish myths, and in *The Faerie Queene*, where the poet transforms them into his own mythopoetic 'matter of just memory', Spenser's use of Irish traditional lore enacts his very ambivalent relation to Irish language and literature – both its preservation and destruction.

1996

AJAX IN ULSTER AND ARIOSTO IN IRELAND
Translating the *Orlando Furioso*

When Sir John Harington returned from a disastrous expedition to Ireland with Essex in the autumn of 1599, the queen greeted his arrival at court with, 'What, did the foole brynge *you* too? Go backe to your businesse'.[1] From Harington's correspondence we can glean that at least part of Elizabeth's anger was due to his meeting with Hugh O'Neill, the Earl of Tyrone, to whom the poet read and to whose sons he presented a copy of his English translation of *Orlando Furioso* (1591). In a letter dated February 20, 1600, Harington writes to Sir Anthony Standen:

> I came to court in the very heat and height of all displeasures: after I had been there but an hour, I was threatened with the Fleet; I answered poetically, 'that coming so late from the land-service, I hoped that I should not be prest to serve in her Majesty's fleet in Fleet street'. After three days every man wondered to see me at liberty; but though, in conscience, there was neither rhyme nor reason to punish me for going to see Tyrone; yet if my rhyme had not been better liked than my reason (I mean when I gave the young Baron of Dungannon an Ariosto), I think I had lain by the heels for it.[2]

Harington believed he was saved from his godmother the queen's anger at his visit to Tyrone because she esteemed his poetic wit more than his political sense. (As the author of the *Metamorphosis of Ajax* [pronounced a-jakes] (1596) on the invention of the w.c., Harington had a reputation for outrageous humour and satire of contemporary figures.) He implies that the queen understood that from his point of view poetry was the main reason for the visit, or at least that was his story. In some sense Harington's rhyme was his reason. For by his own account, written just four months earlier in a letter to Sir Justice Carew, the meeting with O'Neill was concerned more with Harington's poetry than with matters of state.

Why was Harington socializing with and reading poetry to O'Neill? Part of the answer, I think, lies in the imaginative relation between Ireland and his *Orlando Furioso*, as attested to both in Harington's letters from Ireland and in his marginalia and commentary upon his translation. Not only was Ireland the site of one of Harington's transgressions, as the queen's reaction to his return indicates, but it figures in his translation of the *Furioso* and his letters as a radically 'other' sort of place. Throughout his translation he makes recourse to an imaginative image of Ireland in order to explain some of the ancient, exotic, chivalric, and magical elements of the story. And as seen throughout his letters from Ireland, the fictional world of the *Furioso* informs his description of contemporary history.

As early as 1586, Harington lived in Ireland for several months. He was attempting to establish himself as an undertaker on the Munster plantation, but the venture proved a failure.[3] From the perspective of cultural exchange, however, his visit to Ireland was a success. Five years after his stay, references to Irish customs, legend, and magic appear in marginal notes and commentary, and even word choices for his English *Orlando Furioso* (1591). For instance, he uses the word 'oes', which, as he explains in the marginalia, refers to 'the mud that the tyde leaveth behind on the banks';[4] the Irish *ós*, like the Old Norse *hóss* and the Latin *ôs*, is used in poetry for the mouth of a river.

At the very outset of the Bodleian manuscript of Harington's *Furioso*, the translator comments on Ferrau's swearing upon his mother's life (I.30): 'Yt was the manor in spayn and is now in Ireland to swear by ye life of thier parents.'[5] In this note Harington draws an analogy between literary medieval Spain and historical early modern Ireland, an analogy that displays several strategies in common with early modern ethnography. This analogy between the fantastical narrative of the *Furioso* and contemporary social practice shows the permeability between the exotic in fiction and the foreign in ethnographic writing that characterizes the use of myth to describe culturally alien people in such disparate texts as Columbus's *Diario* and Spenser's *View*. In such discourse the foreign is not only fantastical but also primitive. Harington's use of the past tense in reference to Spain ('Yt *was* the manor in spayn') and of the present in reference to Ireland ('and *is* now in Ireland') [emphasis mine] illustrates how colonialist discourse represents the colonized cultures as archaic. The displacement of the subjects of ethnographic description into a time that precedes that of the observer is what Johannes Fabian has called the 'denial of coevality'.[6] This denial of historical contemporaneousness figures as a rhetorical strategy in the legitimization of European sovereignty over the Americas and English sovereignty over Ireland.[7] Harington's connection of Ireland with Spain also follows an Irish myth of Spanish origins that descends from the Gaelic *Leabhar Gabhála*, in which the sons of Míl were said to have come from Spain to conquer Ireland.[8] This Irish text was a source for the same story in the twelfth-century *Topography of Ireland* by Gerald of Wales, and in the late sixteenth-century *A View of the Present State of Ireland* by Edmund Spenser, who denies this genealogy in favour of the myth of descent from the Scythians.[9] Both Gerald and Spenser make Ireland the site of the primitive and culturally barbaric. In contrast, Harington here seems to favour a view of the Irish as primitive and yet noble, like the Spanish medieval paladin Ferrau. The Gaelic Irish myth of their descent from the Spanish sons of Míl was a story frequently repeated by bardic poets and even by Irish historians as late as the seventeenth century to emphasize just such an ancient noble genealogy.[10]

Harington's description of the Irish troops in the Tenth Book – a longer and more detailed description than that in the Italian – is also coloured by the ethnographic tradition:

> Then come the Irish, men of valiant harts
> And active limbs, in personages tall;
> They naked use to go in manie parts,
> But with a mantell yet they cover all;
> Short swords they use to carrie and long darts
> To fight both neare and farre aloofe withall,
> And of these bands the lords and leaders are
> The noble Earls of Ormond and Kildare
>
> (OF 10.73)

In translating Ariosto's Italian, Harington adds such details as the athletic tall bodies of the Irish, which had been described by Gerald of Wales, and their nakedness, which was also depicted by Barnabe Riche, Fynes Morison, and Edmund Spenser.[11] By mentioning the 'mantell', which in Spenser's *View* is both the site of illicit intercourse and a cloak to hide the rebel's identity,[12] Harington's translation alludes to rebellion in Ireland. The Italian version of this stanza refers to 'il conte di Desmonda' rather than to the Earl of Ormond. No doubt Harington changed the stanza to omit any reference to the attainted rebel Gerald Fitzgerald, earl of Desmond, whose defeat leading to the confiscation of his lands paved the way for the Munster plantation.

Alongside the ethnographic representation of the Irish as primitive, if noble, warriors, and even in conflict with that tradition, is the representation of the Irish Oberto as a perfect chivalric hero in the story of Olimpia in *Furioso* 11.[13] Ariosto's Oberto is an exemplar of chivalry; he fights against the Ebudans who feed the women they capture in their raids to a voracious sea monster, and he is the particular protector of Olimpia. Left stranded by her husband Bireno, Olimpia is abducted by pirates to Ebuda where she is chained to a rock as a naked lunch for the sea monster, until Orlando rescues her, and Oberto falls in love with her and promises to protect her:

> And straight he promist that he would attend her
> And set her in her countrey if he may
> And mauger all her enemies defend her
> And take revenge on him did her betray,
> And that he might both men and mony lend her
> He would to pawne his realme of Ireland lay
> Nor till she were restor'd aske no repaiment,
> And straight he sought about to get her rayment.
>
> (OF 11.58)

Oberto is an exemplar of service to the lady. Unlike Ruggiero, who in a similar situation attempts to rape the naked Angelica, Oberto clothes and protects Olimpia. As soon as he falls in love with the naked damsel, Oberto straight away takes revenge upon Bireno, who had abandoned her, and restores her to her rightful throne.

In Harington's version Oberto is even more idealized, and the story is allegorized as a moral fable. Although Harington follows the basic outlines of Ariosto's story, his translation leaves out the frankly sexual desire of Ariosto's Oberto, how he 'kept recalling vividly to mind' Olimpia's 'limbs so splendid' ('sì belle membre, che forza è ad or ad or se ne rimembre' [11.75]). If in the ethnographic tradition the Irish are generally portrayed as loose and licentious, Harington's Irish Oberto is singularly proper. In Harington's 'Allegorie' for this canto, Oberto's clothing of Olimpia becomes a restoration of her 'modesty and sobrietie'. As Harington explains, 'By the Iland is signified pride and looseness of life', while 'pirats' are 'flatterers that go roving about to entise [women] thither, robbing them indeed of all their comely garments of modesty and sobrietie and at last leave them naked upon the shore, to be devoured by the most ugly and mishapen monsters . . . as filthy diseases, deformities'.[14] Contrary to Harington's allegory, Ariosto's story of Olimpia ends not in her ruin but in Oberto's being seduced by her splendid nakedness, which inspires him to do whatever he can for her. Harington's 'allegorie' of Olimpia's rescue by Oberto transforms the story from an erotic adventure into a moral exemplum, or cautionary tale.

Throughout his commentaries Harington often attempts to either reprove or explain away the poem's eroticism – or, as he says in his 'Moral' on the story of Richiardetto's seduction of Fiordispina, 'where any light and lascivious matter falls [his aim is] . . . to salve it'.[15] For the more sentimental and moralized tastes of his English audience, Harington translates the poem into a vehicle for instruction. His allegories on the poem can be seen as imitations of the earlier Italian allegories that were part of the text's literary canonization in the century after Ariosto's death; but the English translator's allegories are also peculiarly anecdotal and personal.[16] Harington's allegories, like his morals and histories, which follow every canto, relate the events of the poem to quotidian events in an attempt to make possible the sort of autobiographical reading encouraged in the lines he adds to the opening of Book 3: 'For some there are may fortune in this booke / As in a glasse their acts and haps to looke' (7.2.7–8). Just such an autobiographical and moralized reading of the poem appears in one of Harington's letters from Ireland, where he describes how a Galway woman identified with the story of Olimpia:

> My Ariosto has been entertained into Gallway before I came. When I got thither, a great lady, a young lady, and a fair lady, read herself asleep, nay dead with a tale of it; the verse I think, so lively figured her fortune: for, as Olimpia was forsaken by the ungrateful Byreno, so had this lady been left by her unkind Sir Calisthenes, whose hard dealing with her cannot be excused, no not by Demosthenes.[17]

The Galway woman interprets the story as a version of her own life and as an allegory of a seduced and abandoned woman, similar to that in Harington's commentary.

Harington portrays Ireland not only as an archaic and idealized literary realm but also as a supernatural one. In the description of St Patrick's Purgatory, Ariosto's 'Ibernia fabulosa' becomes Harington's 'Irish Ile / Where men do tell straunge tales' (10.77–8). In his marginalia, Harington makes reference to the Irish conception of the sí, the spirits or fairies. His comment on the 'great assemble / of sprights' summoned by Melissa in Merlin's cave (3.21.7–8) brings to mind the Irish myth of the *Tuatha Dé Danann*, earlier inhabitants of Ireland, who lived in fairy forts underground: 'Some hold opinion that there be spirits in the aire and likewise in the earth.'[18] At the end of the Twelfth Book, Harington again refers to Irish magical lore, this time to explain Ferraw's enchanted invulnerability:

> [S]ome say it is a great practise in Ireland to charme girdles and the like perswading men that while they weare theme they cannot be hurt with any weapon, and who can tell whether the divell may not sometime protect some of his servants?[19]

As an example of this, Harington then proceeds to tell a story about how when his 'valient cosen, sir Henrie Harington', was taken prisoner 'in a vile and treacherous Parlee', a rescue party of one hundred of Harington's men were unable to lay even a hand on his captor 'Rorie Oge (a notable rebell of Ireland)':

> I say these hundred men well appointed beset the house strongly, being made of nothing but bardels and durt, yet the villen [i.e. Rorie Og], er they could get in gat up in his shirt and gave the knight xiiii wounds verie deadly and after gate thorow them all without hurt where a mouse almost could not have got betweene them, and I have heard it affirmed in Ireland that it was with meere witchcraft.

The legend of Rory Óg O'More's witchcraft stems from the correspondence of Sir Henry Sidney to the court from the English plantation of the midlands, against which Rory Óg led the resistance. As Lord Deputy in the late 1570s, Sidney characterized Rory Óg's escapes from the largest search and destroy mission the midlands had ever seen as 'sorcerie or enchauntement', no doubt in order to save face.[20]

In a letter from Athlone, written while he was on campaign in Ireland in 1599, Harington recites the same story about the magical escape of the enchanted Rory Óg. This time Harington tells the story to illustrate the sort of Irish credulity that he claims has infected the English in Ireland:

> I verily think the idle faith which possesses the Irishry concerning magic and witchcraft seized our men and lost the victory. For when my cozen Sir H.

Harington in a treacherous parlye with Rorie Ogie, a notable rebel, was taken
and conveyed to his habitation a prisoner; his friends not complying with the
terms offerd for his ransom, sent a large band to his rescue, which the rebel seeing to surround his house, rose in his shirt, and gave Sir Henry fourteen griev-
ous wounds, then made his way through the whole band and escaped,
notwithstanding his walls were only mud. Such was their panick, as verily
thinking he effected all by dint of witchery, and had by magic compell'd them
not to touch him. And this belief does much daunt our soldiers when they
come to deal with the Irishry, as I can well perceive from their discourse.[21]

The context for this story is the Irish victory over English troops in the Curlew
mountains, on August 5, 1599. Not only was the President of Connaught,
Conyers Clifford, killed at the engagement but he lost nearly a third of his
1,700 men.[22] Harington resorts to the same explanation for defeat in order to
save face as Sidney had: the Irish were magically possessed. The appearance
of the wondrous escape of Rory Óg in both Harington's commentary on the
Orlando Furioso and in his letters from Ireland shows the convertability of the
fictional and the historical in his writing. That the fictional story of Ferraw
could be interpreted in relation to Sir Henrie Sidney's propaganda about Rory
taken as fact, and that the fact of English defeat on the battlefield could then
be explained away by the same fictional fact, reveals an imagination in which
the ideological and the fictional, the legendary and the historical are all trans-
latable in terms of each other.

Just two months after the defeat in the Curlew mountains, Harington paid
a visit to O'Neill during which he presented a copy of his *Furioso* to the Irish
lord's sons. The events immediately leading up to this visit explain why the
queen viewed it as such a transgression. On September 7, 1599, Essex was
surprised into a parley at Louth and conversed privately with Tyrone.[23] A
truce permitting the Irish to hold all they possessed was the result. This agree-
ment was considered particularly shameful by Elizabeth, who excoriated
Essex for his incompetence.[24] Along with Essex's unexpected departure from
Ireland in late September 1599, the truce was the major reason for the queen's
outrage on his return to court. It was on September 17, during the period of
this cease-fire, that Harington went with Sir William Warren to visit O'Neill.
In the letter recounting the visit, Harington portrays Warren's purpose as the
negotiation of a continued truce with O'Neill, and his own as the leisurely
pursuit of poetic entertainment and conversation with the great lord.

O'Neill's connections with the English establishment in part account for
the warm welcome that Harington received and for his flattering portrayal of
his host. Harington's very first words about O'Neill present him as extrava-
gantly self-deprecating and anxious to remind his New English guests of his
longtime association with them:

when I came, the earl used far greater respect to me than I expected; and began
debasing his own manner of hard life, comparing himself to wolves, that fill

their bellies sometime, and fast as long for it; then excused himself to me that he could no better call to mind myself, and some of my friends that had done him some courtesy in England; and been oft in his company at my Lord of Ormand's; saying, these troubles had made him forget almost all his friends.[25]

Harington also mentions O'Neill's asking after his cousin Sir Henry Harington, who had suffered 'an imputation of want of courage, for the last defeat at Arkloo'.[26] O'Neill's defence of Henry Harington, with all the specifics of 'time, place, and persons', suggests that he knew the poet's cousin very well. In his rise to power, O'Neill's network of connections with the New English, going back to his fosterage in the Pale and his fighting to defend its Northern border, had been extremely important. Among his New English allies were both Henry Harington and Henry Warren, whom O'Neill actually identified as men 'willing to enter into bonds on his behalf' and who did so when he had to go to court to defend himself for the hanging of Hugh Gavelach MacShane in 1590.[27] Harington refers to this previous reliance upon Warren as a factor in convincing O'Neill to prolong the truce, 'which he would never have agreed to, but in confidence of my lord's honourable dealing with him'.

Harington refers to these practical considerations of politics only in passing and prefers to paint an idealized and almost elegiac portrait of O'Neill, as though he were a hero out of the *Orlando Furioso*. At this time, the parts of Ireland outside the Pale were largely organized according to what historians for want of a better term call 'bastard feudalism'. As described by Katharine Simms, 'bastard feudalism' entailed a 'utilitarian attitude of the late medieval Gaelic lord to the vassal relationship' that depended on an exchange of military service for protection, and monetary tribute for hosting.[28] In contrast, Harington's account of O'Neill's court reveals a fascination with the soldiers' bond of personal loyalty to their lord:

> His guard, for the most part, were beardless boys without shirts; who, in the frost, wade as familiarly through rivers as water spaniels. With what charm such a master makes them love him I know not, but if he bid come, they come; if go, they go; if he sayd this, they do it.[29]

Whether this is Harington's romanticization of the scene through his own very literary perspective, or an accurate rendering of the remnant of an older pre-feudal sense of Gaelic vassalage, he marvels at O'Neill's charisma. Harington conveys O'Neill's self-presentation as an aristocrat of great personal honour, protesting that he sought only 'freedom of conscience, without which he would not live, though the queen would give him Ireland'. The elegiac tone in Harington's account also emerges in his reading aloud the lines on fortune's wheel at the beginning of Canto 45 of the *Furioso*:

> Looke how much higher Fortune doth erect
> The Clyming wight on her unstable wheele,

> So much the nigher may a man expect
> To see his head where late he saw his heele.

In his commentary on Canto 45, Harington connected this passage with the dramatic change from Elizabeth's life in prison to her becoming 'of the sodain a crowned Queene'.[30] His reading this passage to O'Neill suggests that Harington saw a parallel between Elizabeth and O'Neill as figures of great power, and thereby subject to great gains and losses.

If Harington's *Furioso* was a vehicle for the translation of Irish culture as a fictional world in his writing, it also became a vehicle for anglicization in Ireland. In presenting his 'Ariosto' as a gift to O'Neill's sons, Harington mentions their 'learning the English tongue', that 'their teachers took [the book] very thankfully', and that 'O'Neill solemnly swore his boys should read all the book over to him'.[31] Harington thought that his translation would be part of their education in English. By the same token the reception of Harington's work in Ireland influenced his interpretation of his experiences there. That his translation 'had been entertained into Galway before [his] arrival there' and that the copy he brought to O'Neill was 'got in Dublin', and that during this visit 'the earl . . . called to see it openly, and would needs hear some part of it read' all suggest that Harington found an audience for his work in Ireland.[32] He even blandly asserts in a passage marked by extraordinary naïvety that he thought his warm reception in Ireland might bode well for his future career:

> The Irish lords, gentry, yea and citizens where I come, I have found so apt to offer me kindness, so desirous of my acquaintance, that my friends think it a presage of a fortune I might rise to in this kingdom.[33]

And this from a man who referred to the Irish enemy in battle as 'vermyn'.[34] At least in these passages where he focuses on the Irish as readers of his translation, Harington, unlike so many other English writers of his time, was able to understand the Irish as not so radically other.

Indeed, six years after this meeting with O'Neill, Harington would write about Ireland in sympathetic terms that contrast sharply with the usual New English discourse of the period: 'As for the beggerlynes of yt, no wonder yf war and spoyle make beggers . . . Neyther ys the cowntry without rare examples of fidelyty in servants, of love and chastyte in matrons, howsoever some pens have taxed the one with trechery, the other with incontynency.'[35] If Harington's fascination with Ireland as archaic and magical reveals the typical New English view of the Irish as not fully civilized and not fully human, his acknowledgment here of the conditions of conquest to which the people were subject shows that he was capable of viewing Ireland as more than literary fantasy. Nevertheless, his literary work looms large in his representation of Ireland, and in turn his English *Furioso* would have an effect on Irish literary taste and on the representation of Britain.

An anonymous late seventeenth-century Irish language prose romance entitled *Orlando agus Melora* shows this influence. The text survives in only three manuscripts: two at Trinity College Dublin, the earliest written *circa* 1679, the other dated 1696, and a third at the British Library, written sometime between 1698 and 1715.[36] This text can be called a translation of the *Orlando Furioso* only in the loosest sense. I think it would be wrong, however, to reject the Italian poem as an 'indirect source' and to play down the possibility of English and European influences as Draak, one of the editors of the Irish Orlando manuscripts, does.[37] So far, no one has noticed that the story of *Orlando agus Melora* roughly recalls Ariosto's account of Orlando's rescue from madness by the English knight Astolfo. In the Irish romance, Orlando, son of the king of Thessaly, is put under a spell that leaves him entrapped in the Forest of Wonders and reduced to muteness. Like Astolfo, Melora, who rescues Orlando, is a British knight who quests after the cures that will free Orlando from captivity and restore him to his human state. There is another interesting similarity here. In Ariosto, just before Astolfo cures Orlando, the madman's companions do not recognize him – his face resembles a beast's more than a man's – and he is unable to speak lucidly (*OF* 39.45, 57). Similarly, in the Irish romance, just before Melora rescues Orlando, he is unrecognizable and cannot speak; there is nothing human in his appearance ('gan aithne, gan urlabhra, gan én-ní do dheilbh dhaonda fair'[38]). That the knight who rescues Orlando from the spell that Merlin has cast on him is a woman, Melora, who goes on her quest to free Orlando out of love for him, suggests that she is modelled not simply on Astolfo but also on Ariosto's warrior maiden Bradamante, who rescues her beloved Ruggiero from entrapment by the magician Atlante.

Robin Flower originally suggested the story of Bradamante's rescue of Ruggiero from Atlante in Canto 4 of *Orlando Furioso* as the Ariostean source for this Irish romance in his commentary on it in the *Catalogue of Irish Manuscripts in the British Museum*.[39] The portrayal of Melora is indebted in more ways than one to Ariosto's warrior maiden Bradamante. Melora is repeatedly called 'Ridire an Earraidh Ghurim' ('Knight of the Blue Attire'), just as Bradamante is frequently identified by her white plume and shield. Like Bradamante, Melora often so impresses her audience with her martial prowess that they believe she is a man until she reveals her secret identity as a woman.[40] It seems to me that the Irish author may well have conflated these two stories – the one of Astolfo's rescue of Orlando from madness and the other of Bradamante's rescue of Ruggiero from enchantment – into the story of Melora's rescue of Orlando.

In addition to noting the possible source of the Irish Orlando romance in the story of Bradamante's quest on behalf of her beloved, Flower also pointed out that Sir John Harington's 1591 translation of the *Orlando Furioso* was well known in Ireland. As we have seen, at least according to Harington's own account, it was. It is interesting to note that the manuscript of *Orlando agus*

Melora in the British Library, like the 1696 manuscript at Trinity College
(T.C.D. 1335), was penned by the scribe Uilliam Ó Loinsigh, who was from
the literary district of South Ulster, Northern Leinster, the very area around
Dundalk where Harington met with O'Neill and presented his 'Ariosto' as a
gift. This area of South Armagh–North Louth, called Oriel, is the site of a long
Gaelic literary tradition. The scribe of the earlier manuscript from 1679
(T.C.D. 1399) was also from East Ulster. In an edition of a text also found in
T.C.D. 1399, the 'Pursuit of Gruaidh Ghriansholus', Cecile O'Rahilly argues
that the scribe, and possibly the author, was the East Ulster poet Eoghan Ó
Donnghaile.[41] Scribes often were the authors of the Irish prose romances and
learned how to write these romances in the process of copying them.[42]
Closely following the text of this earlier version, the 1696 manuscript in Ó
Loinsigh's hand includes his lovely pen-and-ink drawings. These illustrations
show that the scribe knew the English *Furioso*, since they closely imitate the
engravings to the 1591 edition of Harington's translation. The Porro engravings that were printed in Harington's 1591 English translation are taken from
the 1584 Franceschi edition of Ariosto's *Orlando Furioso* printed in Venice,
another text that might have been a source for Ó Loinsigh's illustrations,
although a less likely one than Harington's translation.[43] Harington was also
known in Ireland as the first translator of Ovid's *Amores* into a European vernacular, and as such was a model for the adaptation of Ovid by Irish writers
of lyric love poetry.[44] There is ample evidence of the circulation of Harington's
work in early modern Ireland

Ó Loinsigh's drawings in T.C.D. 1335 follow in overall composition and
in minute detail the Porro engravings that Harington used to illustrate his
translation. Both the Porro engraving for *Furioso* 3 (figure 1) and the drawing
on p. 24, fol.16v, of the manuscript (figure 2) represent a sequence of three
simultaneous actions. In the engraving for Canto 3, Bradamante kneels before
the sorceress Melissa, then at the right, visits Merlin's tomb and at the far left
sees a vision of her descendants. In the drawing, Orlando's three visions in the
Forest of Wonders are depicted: first the two hands with swords fighting, then
on the left the harper with one hand, one eye, and one leg, and on the far right
the hag, An Mhilltionach (the destructive one), foretelling his future. In both
engraving and drawing, an arch frames each of the three actions. At the centre of both illustrations a craggy tree-trunk shaped rock juts up, forming the
roof of a rocky cave above and enclosing rows of arches and pillars below. In
the top left portion of both pictures a rotunda of several storeys, each con-
taining arches, sits atop a mountainous cliff, and at the far right on another
cliff stands a dog raising his left front paw. One detail that Ó Loinsigh leaves
out is the skyline of a city in the top centre of the Porro engraving. So many
other details in both pictures, such as the clump of foliage bursting forth from
a rocky crevice on the left, the arched doorway on the lower left centre, and
the posture, gesture, and dress of the figures on the left (Bradamante in the
engraving, and Orlando in the drawing) so exactly resemble each other that

Figure 1: Engraving for Canto 3, from *Ludovico Ariosto's Orlando Furioso Translated into English Heroical Verse by Sir John Harington* (London, 1591), courtesy of the Cambridge University Library.

Figure 2: Trinity College Manuscript 1335, fol. 16v, courtesy of the Manuscripts Department, Trinity College Library

Figure 3: Engraving for Canto 42 from *Ludovico Ariosto's Orlando Furioso Translated into English Heroical Verse by Sir John Harington* (London, 1591), courtesy of the Cambridge University Library.

Ó Loinsigh had to have seen the Porro illustrations. Ó Loinsigh's only other illustration for the story (figure 4) – a picture of Melora thrusting her sword into the King of Africa which appears on p. 49 (fol. 29 r) – copies the lower portion of the Porro engraving for Canto 42, in which Orlando battles Gradasso (figure 3). Again, such details as the angle and shape of Gradasso's upraised scimitar, the crosshatching on the backside of the saddle, Orlando's horse rearing forward, the shape of the plume atop his helmet, his shield held back behind his left arm – all are imitated in Ó Loinsigh's drawing.

While it might seem at first that the stories that correspond to these illustrations have nothing to do with each other, there are actually connections between them. The illustration of Orlando's duel with Gradasso, in the midst of which occurs Orlando's duel with the African king Agramante in *Furioso* 42, is used to illustrate Melora's duel with the king of Africa. Whereas Orlando slays his opponents, however, Melora simply brings hers to the point of submission. Even if these duels differ in their details, the image of knights fighting on horseback certainly is important for both the Italian and the Irish Orlando stories. Indeed, following Alan Bruford's generalization that 'horses hardly figure at all in the Romantic tales', it would seem the *Orlando agus Melora* is nearly unique among the Irish prose romances in its frequent description of travel by and combat on horses.[45]

In the case of the story of Bradamante's visit to the cave of Merlin in *Furioso* 3 and Orlando's journey to the Forest of Wonders in *Orlando agus Melora*, the analogies are more substantial. Both stories involve journeys to enchanted places; in both Merlin casts the enchantment; both stories involve prophecies of the future; and both precede a quest to rescue a prisoner. In *Furioso* 4, Bradamante sets off to find the magic ring to rescue her beloved Ruggiero, and in *Orlando agus Melora*, Melora sets off on the quest to find the spear of Longinus to break into the dungeon where Orlando is imprisoned, the carbuncle of the King of Narsinga's daughter to banish the darkness, and the oil from the pig Tuis to restore Orlando's voice.

The fantastical narrative of *Orlando agus Melora* makes no explicit allusion to any Irish context. The only recognizably Celtic character in the story is the druid Merlin. He conspires with the Spanish knight Mador to have Orlando enchanted, imprisoned, and reduced to bestiality in the Forest of Wonders, so that he cannot marry his beloved Melora. That the villains of this Irish prose romance are the Celtic druid and the Spanish knight, while the heroine is many times referred to as British or from Britain, tempts me to speculate on the text as a political allegory.[46] Orlando's father King Gustabhus (Gustavus) – a particularly bizarre name in an Irish language text – may allude to the Protestant hero King Gustavus Adolphus of Sweden. Irish mercenaries stationed in Bohemia would have recognized Gustavus as the name of the enemy. In an allegorical political reading of this text, the plot against Orlando by the druid Merlin and the Spanish Mador could stand for the late sixteenth-century Irish alliance with Catholic Spain in the final years of the Nine Years'

Figure 4: Trinity College Manuscript 1335, fol. 29r, courtesy of the Manuscripts Department, Trinity College Library

War, and the Irish hopes for Spanish intervention in Ireland that run throughout the State Papers in the 1620s right up to England's treaty with Spain in
1630. The British Melora and her band of knights would then stand for the
English who defeated the Spanish-backed Hugh O'Neill in 1603 and the
papally supported Owen Roe O'Neill in 1649. Her rescue of and marriage
with Orlando, son of the Protestant Gustavus, would in this context represent
the English rescue of and union with a Protestant Ireland.

As plausible as this political allegory of the romance is, it raises questions
about why an audience reading in Irish would want to read about a British
hero. Why was a story alluding to the Italian Orlando adapted into the Irish
language? How can we position this Irish romance in relation to its audience?
For example, what was the audience for prose romance in Ireland in the seventeenth century? How were these romances read? Do we know anything
about who was reading this text and why? And what can all of this tell us
about the cultural effects and uses of translation? In addition to attesting to
the enormous popularity of the *Orlando Furioso* throughout Europe – even the
farthest western reaches of Ireland – the Irish adaptation of elements from the
work also shows the popularity of romances in Ireland. Just seven years
before the earliest of the three manuscripts of *Orlando agus Melora*, the English translator Francis Kirkman commented on how he pitched his translation
of the third part of Jeronimo Fernandez's *Belianis de Grecia*, published as *The
Honour of Chivalrie* (1671–72), to an Irish audience:

> The encouragement I received by writing the Second Part of this History, hath
> induced me to prosecute it with a Third Part; wherein, I will assure you, I have
> out-done the Second, both in language, and contrivance of the story. And I
> have taken more than ordinary pains in describing the ancient Kingdom of Ire-
> land, and many principal Cities and Towns long since ruined. If what I have
> written be but pleasing to you, I may in short time please you further by writ-
> ing another History of this nature.[47]

In this same preface Kirkman wrote of the popularity of another romance in
Ireland, *The Seven Wise Masters*, which he claimed to be held:

> of so great esteem in Ireland, that next to the Horn-Book and Knowledge of
> Letters, Children are in general put to read in this; and I know by this Book
> several have learned to read well, so great is the pleasure that Young and Old
> take in the Reading thereof.[48]

Since Kirkman himself translated a version of *The Seven Wise Masters* in 1674
this might seem simply like self-promotion. However, Kaarina Hollo has
shown that references to *The Seven Wise Masters* abound in early modern Ireland. The text is mentioned along with other romances, described as 'school
books', in advertisements of what was for sale in Dublin bookshops in the late
seventeenth century. *The Seven Wise Masters* is also repeatedly mentioned in

versions of an Irish poem entitled 'Pléaráca na Ruarcach', translated as 'O'Rourke's Feast'.[49] See for example this English translation of 1782:

> Do ye thus treat your pastors?
> Ye, who scarcely were bred
> To the *Seven Wise Masters*;
> That when with the Pope
> I was getting my lore,
> Ye were roasting potatoes
> Not far from Sheemor.[50]

It would appear that schoolchildren in Ireland were reading these English translations of Continental romances in order to learn how to read, and perhaps in some cases even to learn English. The translations were so popular that they may have influenced the writing of Irish adaptations of Continental romance. The use of prose romances as school texts in which students learned how to read the language suggests a similar use of Irish romances for English readers – although undoubtedly on a much smaller scale, since we are talking about an exclusively manuscript culture in Irish and a relatively small number of English speakers who would take the trouble to become literate in the language of the colonized underclass.

The paratexts to *Orlando agus Melora* suggest that the manuscript was produced for English-speaking students of the Irish language. Following the story of *Orlando agus Melora* in T.C.D. 1335 are a Latin-Irish glossary (fol. 41r–60v) as well as a guide to the pronunciation of Irish and a grammar, written in Irish (fol. 63r–71v), and then in English (fol. 72r–79r). The glossary is clearly in Ó Loinsigh's hand, and at the end of this paratext (fol. 61r) his signature appears, along with the date, 'mdcxcvi' (1696) and place, 'do scriobh mbaile atha cliath' (written Dublin), where he produced this copy. The grammar and pronunciation guides contain his characteristic pen-and-ink decorative borders on fols. 61r, 63r, 71v, and 72r. An illustration most connected to the Orlando story appears just above the first chapter of 'don aibéidir go sonnraghach' ('on defining or specifying [the characteristics of] the alphabet'): a border with the Medusa head flanked by two knights on horseback pictured from the rear (fol. 63r, see figure 5). Most of the synonyms provided in the glossary are fairly straightforward – e.g. poeta, filidh; patriarcha, úasal athair [54r]; but a few suggest the possibility of an allegorical reading: Orpheus, uiait'ne (harmony); Apollo, grian (sun); Babilon, Confusio. In this last case, there is no translation into Irish; instead a symbolic meaning in Latin is provided – and one which is usually associated with the Protestant view of the error of Roman Catholicism as the Whore of Babylon. All this suggests the use of the text to learn the Irish language – and most likely by English-speaking Protestants.

The manuscript dated 1696 also identifies the person who commissioned it to be copied as Edward Lhuyd (1660–1709), curator of Antiquities at the

75.

caib. 1.

ɗon aibcioin. go Soinaʒaċ.

Uiʒ liʒne pioċeᴅo ᴅo bi ʁaᴅa ó ʁoin aʒ na ʁen ʒcoᴅlaib ina naibciom ᴅo Sʒniobᴅcoin aʒuʁ ᴅo cuinᴅcoiʁ ʁioʁ an an oʁᴅuʒaʁa aᴅ ᴅiaiʒ (uiʒ) b.l.ʁ. n.h. o. ᴅ. c. q. m. ʒ. nʒ. z. ʁ. ᴅ. ᴅ. 1. o. u. ᴅ. ᴅᴅ. ᴅᴅ. ʁo.

Ni hi ʁuᴅ am an aibciom ċleaċᴅmoio eniṁoṁaiʒ na haimṁiʁeʁi anoiʁ aʁ aibciom aʁ aʁ an ʁeoᴅlaʁa aᴅ ᴅiaiʒ aʒ ᴅʒʁ leiʁ na laiᴅneaċaib, aʒuʁ leiʁ an cciuᴅ eiʁo ᴅon euʁoiʁ on nʒʁeiʒ ᴅ̄ ᴅuaiʒ a leiᴅ a nᴦʁmiʁ; aʒuʁ anoʁouʒ liᴅʁʒᴅa i. a.b.c.ᴅ.e.ʁ. ʒ.h.i.k.l.m.n.o.p. q.ʁ.ʁ. ᴅ. u.x. y. z. ᴅʁi liʒʁʒᴅa pioċeʒo.

Ⱥ ᴅaiᴅ ciuʒ liʒne ᴅon ᴅʁuiṁʁ k.q.x.y.z. aʁ naċ biᴅh maċᴅanaʁ leoᴅʁa a bʁoᴅlaib ʁioʁ ʒcoiᴅeiʒe aʁ mon beiᴅ ʁocal coṁaiʒ̄ an aʒ ᴅeaʁ ó ᴅlṁʒaᴅ eiʁe ċoiʒcniᴅe mʒ aʁ leiʁ an ʁna ʁoclaiᴅʒ̄ aᴅ ᴅiaiʒ maʁ aᴅa k. ʁan bʁoċʁa kaillaṁ Q. ʁan bʁoiċalʁa [quinᴅai] caᴅaiʁ ʁan chṁa) Ⱦ ʁan bʁoċalʁa Ⱦnoʁon aiṁ oᴅ̄ne . y ʁan bʁoċalʁa york . aiṁṁ baile aʁaxaib Ⱦ ʁan bʁoċalʁa zaċaʁiaʁ aiṁṁ oᴅne . Ni ċuiniṁ w. ʁan aibci= oiṁ ʒcoiᴅeiʒe maʁ ᴅo ṁ con u. aṁaiṁ a haiᴅ ᴅʁiṁ.

Ⱡniʁ an ʒcuma ʁoʁ ʁniʁ an oʁᴅʒaʁa ᴅo ᴅaiʁᴅlnaṁaʁ ᴅiᴅ aṁ ʁo q̄ liʒʁib na ʒcoiᴅeiʒe aʒa ainm no ʁloiṁʒᴅ ʁᴅeiʁialᴅa ʁa leiᴅh

Figure 5: Trinity College Manuscript 1335, fol. 63r, courtesy of the Manuscripts Department, Trinity College Library

Ashmolean Museum at Oxford and author of *Archaeologica Britannica: an Account of the Languages, Histories, and Customs of Great Britain, from collections and observations in Travels through Wales, Cornwall, Bas-Bretagne, Ireland, and Scotland. Vol. i. Glossography.*[51] Published in 1707, the very year of the parliamentary union of England with Scotland as Great Britain, Lhuyd's *Archaeologica Britannica* was the first comparative dictionary of the Celtic languages. Lhuyd included the 'British Etymologicon', comparing English, Welsh, and Greek words, the Latin-Irish dictionary of Francis O'Molloy (Rome, 1677), an anonymous Irish grammar (Louvain 1669), as well as his own original compilations, among them 'A Comparative Vocabulary of the Original Languages of Britain and Ireland' (including Welsh, Cornish, and Irish), and an Irish-English dictionary, based on Irish manuscript sources. Through comparing the Welsh and Irish languages etymologically, Lhuyd was able to show that they were both Celtic languages. He based his dictionary upon 'Vocabularium Hibernicum et Latinum', an Irish-Latin dictionary in manuscript written by Richard Plunkett in 1662, with additions from the major canonical works of Irish prose, including Geoffrey Keating's *Foras Feasa ar Éirinn*. Lhuyd wrote a preface to his dictionary in Irish, in which he explains how he learned the language:

> It is but reasonable. . . that I here make an Apology for Undertaking to write and publish a dictionary in a different language from my native tongue; and which I did not learn by Ear from any Person whose native language it was. For though 'tis true, I travelled through Ireland and the North-West of the Highlands of Scotland, partly to make remarks on the natural curiosities, and partly to review the old monuments of those nations; yet frequently meeting and conversing with those who spoke English, I learned very little Irish in that Progress: and therefore it is from Books, for the most part, that I have acquired the little knowledge I have in that language.[52]

Lhuyd makes it clear that he gained his knowledge of Irish from reading texts rather than from conversing with native speakers. The presence of a glossary and pronunciation guide in the copy of the *Orlando agus Melora* that he commissioned suggests that one of the uses of this text was for his philological research.

Why would Lhuyd have been interested in this text – hardly of the same stature as the 'Irish Bible' and Keating's 'Chronological History of Ireland', both of which he acknowledges as sources?[53] Lhuyd's explanation of his motive for studying Irish provides clues to why he may have been interested in the Irish *Orlando* with its British heroine Melora. According to the 1724 translation of his Preface reprinted by William Nicolson, Lhuyd found his knowledge of 'the old British language . . . imperfect and defective'. This led him to the 'conjecture that a little skill in the old Irish words, would be very useful . . . in explaining those antient British words'.[54] By 'British' Lhuyd means Welsh; for in the Irish original of his text the words that he consistently uses are *Breatnach* (the Irish for 'Welsh') and *Seanbhreatnuigh* (the Irish for 'Old Welsh'). In fact, in the translation, Lhuyd's own nationality is referred to as 'not English' but 'old Briton', which in the original Irish is '*nach . . . Sasanach ach Sinbhreatnach*' meaning 'not English but old Welsh'.[55] His account of this genealogy complicates matters even further as he locates his descent through the male line as deriving from 'the province of Reged in Scotland, in the Fourth Century, before the Saxons came to Great Britain'.[56] Briton, or British (Irish: *Breatnach*) encompasses the meaning Welsh and even points to ancient Brythonic as opposed to Gaelic roots in Scotland, whereas the island of Great Britain (*Inis Mhoirbhreatuin*) can refer to England, Scotland, and Wales. Lhuyd's sense of what Britain is clearly relates to the Irish sense of *Breatain*, a term which as it is used in Keating's *Foras Feasa ar Éirinn* can mean: 1) Wales, 2) Roman Britain, or the isle of Britain without Scotland; 3) the entire island of Great Britain. Given the origin of *Breatain* as a name for Wales that was then applied to the whole island of Britain, it is ironic that this term came to be associated in early modern English with an English-dominated culture and political system, initiated at the time of Henry VIII, and represented in the parliamentary union of England and Scotland as Great Britain in 1707. In *Orlando agus Melora*, it would appear that the meaning of Breatain is also an issue. Melora is repeatedly described as '*as criochaibh Breatan*', 'from the territory of Britain'.[57] That Britain here primarily means Wales becomes clear when Melora speaks with Uranus, a servant of the King of Asia, who helps her in the quest to get the oil of the pig Tuis, which will restore Orlando's speech. Uranus also is '*as criochaibh Breatan*' and he speaks to Melora in the British language ('*a tteangaidh na Briotaine*').[58] According to Lhuyd's dictionary, while *Breatain* may have the different meanings of Wales and Britain in the sense of Great Britain, *Briotanis* means 'the Brittish tongue' in the sense that he uses the word British throughout the *Archaeologica,* that is as the Welsh language. Lhuyd's dictionary reveals that Welsh and Irish are both Celtic languages with common etymologies; the romance of *Orlando agus Melora* tells the story of a Welsh knight Melora in the Irish language.

It is difficult to determine to what extent the English term 'British', standing for an English-dominated cultural and political identity throughout the British Isles, is either resisted by or felt as an influence upon the linguistic consciousness of the Welsh antiquarian who commissioned the *Orlando agus Melora* and the Irish scribe who copied the tale for him. The publication of Lhuyd's *Archaeologica Britannica* in the same year as the parliamentary union of England and Scotland into Great Britain would argue that Lhuyd was well aware of the political significance of this term. Perhaps his late seventeenth-century commissioning of the text to be copied is dictated by its topical interest as the story of a British heroine. That it might have been written as an allegory for a Protestant English-speaking audience learning to read Irish makes the topical interest in the text all the more likely. On the other hand, that *Breatnach* means 'Welsh' in Irish, which both Lhuyd and Ó Loinsigh would have been aware of, reveals the invention and manipulation of the 'British' tradition, as evidenced by the Tudor myth of their Arthurian Welsh origins, to the parliamentary use of the term 'Great Britain' to impose the English claim to sovereignty throughout the British Isles.

In addition to this shared sense of the affinity between Irish and Welsh, Lhuyd's dictionary and the Irish *Orlando* also show a concern with representing Celtic culture as European and civilized. Before and even after Lhuyd wrote his treatise on the common etymologies of Irish and Welsh, the mythical theory that Irish was a language of 'Scythian' derivation was used at times to promote the view of the Irish as 'savages' and of Irish culture as barbaric, as in John Pinkerton's *Dissertation on the Origins and Progress of the Scythians or Goths*.[59] This can be seen as a kind of philological extension of the politically motivated Scythian myth of Irish origins promulgated by Edmund Spenser in his *View of the Present State of Ireland* to legitimize the English colonization of Ireland.[60] In contrast to Elizabethan and Jacobean English writers who had described Irish culture and language as barbaric, Lhuyd's research on Gaelic and Welsh sought to prove that both are ancient, European, and hence civilized languages. And so he argues in the preface to his dictionary: 'It is undoubtedly true that they were the first languages of the British Isles . . . but it is as certain that they were the most antient and best preserved of any languages in the West of Europe.'[61] Lhuyd is in fact way ahead of his time in finding evidence of the common linguistic roots of the Celtic languages with the European languages:

> The famous and learned nations of France, Italy, and Spain will not be capable of giving an account of those languages which (a) Menage [*Dictionaire etymologique de la langue française*] and (b) Aldrete [*Del Origen y principio de la lengua Castellana o Romance*], and many other learned Persons endeavoured to do, and indeed made laudable essays that way; if they do not arrive to some Perfection in the Knowledge of your Language and ours.[62]

The Appendix to Lhuyd's 'British Etymologicon' actually includes a glossary that compares Irish not only to Latin, Greek, and Welsh but also to Danish, French, German, Italian, Polish, Spanish, and Turkish.

While Lhuyd demonstrates that Irish and Welsh are European languages, the anonymous author of *Orlando agus Melora* displays the capacity of the Irish language to tell a story inspired by European models – the Spanish and Italian prose romances that were being circulated in Ireland as well as Harington's translation of the *Furioso*. That the hero of this Irish romance is Welsh, and that she gathers around her a band of knights from Babylon, India, and Asia to help her rescue Orlando, creates a kind of cosmopolitan context for the romance, not unlike that of the *Orlando Furioso*, where national identities often seem so interchangeable they are hard to keep track of. On the one hand, this cosmopolitanism may veer towards a view of an emerging empire – an Irish language vision of a British empire. On the other hand, as a literarily cosmopolitan text the *Orlando agus Melora* attempts to incorporate elements from other literary traditions into Irish. Like Harington's translation of the *Orlando Furioso*, itself an intertext for the Irish romance, the *Orlando agus Melora* translates the story into a new cultural context, to meet the tastes of the translator's audience and to expand the capacities of his native language. The use of this loose adaptation of the *Orlando Furioso* into Irish for philological research into the Irish and Welsh languages indicates that the anonymous author contributed towards the understanding of his language in ways that, from his own local point of view, he might never have been able to anticipate. In a sense the anonymous author's writing of the text was part of a larger seventeenth-century Irish cultural movement to hibernicize Continental cultural material, while Lhuyd's reading began an exciting development – not to be furthered until the work of the great German philologists of the nineteenth century – to place the study of Celtic languages within a cosmopolitan European framework.

1999

THE JANUS FACE OF MACHIAVELLI
Adapting *The Prince* and the *Discourses* in Early Modern Ireland

The anonymous author of *Breve relacion de la presente persecucion de Irlanda*, published in Seville in 1619, attacked those writers 'imputing a lack of civility to the Irish' whom he defended for 'holding on so tenaciously to their Catholic, salutary, and ancient customs, and shielding themselves to such a degree against the profane novelties errors, vices and Machiavellian or Calvinistic policy that [such writers] would like to see introduced'.[1] Here, Machiavelli is portrayed as the source of everything dangerously innovative, heretical, and evil in politics. The demonization of Machiavelli was widespread in the early modern period. The view of his influence as immoral ranged from the earliest criticisms of his work by the Jesuits to the image of the villainous Machiavel on the popular Elizabethan stage.[2] In *Breve relacion de la presente persecucion de Irlanda*, the label 'Machiavellian' is meant to stick to the New English in Ireland, and specifically to their religious ideology as it found expression in their politics. This author's equation of Machiavellian and Calvinistic political philosophy sounds like an early modern version of Brendan Bradshaw's interpretation of the intellectual roots of Spenser's severe justice in the English Protestant, indeed Calvinist, support for 'coercion as an instrument of social reform'.[3] The same word – *policia* – is used to describe both the 'civility' that the Irish have been accused of lacking and the 'policy' that the New English have proposed to reform this lack. For the author of *Breve relacion* the policies that he complains of – forcing attendance at Anglican services, packing the parliament with Protestants, and keeping Catholics from holding civil offices – all correspond with Bradshaw's view of English reform as coercion.

If the author of *Breve relacion* views New English reform in Ireland as a kind of Machiavellian social manipulation – the application of radical change, if necessary by force, associated with *The Prince* – more recently both intellectual historians and literary critics have been speculating about the indebtedness of New English political writing to the republicanism of the *Discourses*. Much of this work has focused on Richard Beacon's tract on the colonization of Ireland, *Solon His Follie* (Oxford, 1594), because it is the first printed English text to make use of Machiavelli's *Discourses* and a point of comparison for Edmund Spenser's *View of the Present State of Ireland*. Sidney Anglo was the first to identify Beacon's debt to Machiavelli, the Machiavelli of both *The*

91

Prince and the *Discourses*. Anglo did not characterize this debt in terms of a coherent political philosophy but rather identified passages quoted and precepts adopted from the Florentine master.[4] Arguing that Beacon made a much more systematic use of Machiavellian political theory, Markku Peltonen has analysed *Solon His Follie* as part of an emerging republicanism in England prior to the English revolution. For Peltonen, this text is ultimately not so much about the need to reform Ireland as it is about the 'loftier goal' to reform England; he sees the conquest of Ireland and the reform of the common-weale as 'hardly fully compatible'.[5]

The strain in this illuminating argument has in part to do with the weight given to Machiavelli at the expense of other sources that Beacon deploys. Not only is *Solon His Follie* an allegory, based on the story from Plutarch's *Lives* of how Solon feigned madness to speak about the outlawed topic of the Athenian colonization of Salamis, but the text is also a dense bricolage of passages from Bodin's *De Republica*, and to a lesser extent from Lipsius's *Politics*, Guicciardini's *Historia d'Italia*, as well as from Machiavelli's *Prince* and *Discourses*. In my own essay on the intellectual genealogy of the text, I stressed the tension between the strong monarchical rule that Beacon took from Bodin and the republican notions of mixed constitution, the return to first principles, and the protection of the people from the nobility that Beacon took from Machiavelli.[6] Andrew Hadfield has speculated about a similar tension in Spenser's *View*. For Hadfield, this text oscillates between the seemingly contradictory poles of Bodin's 'law of equity' – 'the founding of a central authority sanctioned by God whose duty is to protect itself' – and the republican politics of Machiavelli, critical of monarchy and defending the rights of citizens.[7] Hadfield's reading of Spenser's Machiavelli as the republican critic of the *Discourses* rather than the observer of *real politik* in *The Prince* sharply contrasts with Edwin Greenlaw's analysis at the turn of the last century.[8] Both Hadfield's and Greenlaw's readings have been questioned by Vincent Carey, who finds Spenser's interpretation, and the New English interpretation of Machiavelli in general, to be based on isolated precepts rather than a systematic understanding of either *The Prince* or the *Discourses*.[9] Carey particularly takes issue with Peltonen's reading of *Solon His Follie* as a text primarily about England rather than Ireland. In a more carefully contextualized reading of the text, Carey stresses the text's allegorical references through figures from Plutarch's *Lives* to Irish law (e.g. Solon's *Seisachtheia* as the composition of taxation in Connacht) and even to its author's own career in Ireland (e.g. the unjustly accused Camillus as Beacon, who saw himself as unfairly recalled from Ireland).

Solon His Follie is not exclusively about Ireland any more than it is primarily about England; rather it is about the relationship between England and Ireland. This relationship between England as an emerging empire and Ireland as a colony motivates both Spenser's and Beacon's use of Machiavelli. The New English appropriation of Machiavelli is characterized not by the incompatibility of republic with empire, or of reform with conquest, but by the relationship between these apparently diametrically opposed concepts. In Beacon's and Spenser's writing, republicanism is the alternate face of imperial expansion. They did not see a conflict between the analysis of how to achieve and maintain power in extreme conflict in *The Prince* and the commentary on how Rome maintained its republican institutions while expanding its power through empire in the *Discourses*.[10]

My title 'The Janus Face of Machiavelli' addresses not only the two sides of the Florentine political theorist – that of his *Prince* and *Discourses*, of empire and republic – but also the various uses to which his political language could be put in Irish as well as New English texts. As Marc Caball has shown, the extreme conflict brought about by the early modern English conquest of Ireland and the Irish resistance to it was subjected to political analysis in bardic poetry.[11] The representation of this dramatic cultural and political change in the bardic poetry of Eochaidh Ó hEódhusa, I would like to argue, shows traces of such Machiavellian concepts as the interplay between the man of power's *virtù* and the female *fortuna*, as well as the analogy between Roman historical example and the present.

Machiavelli's analysis of Rome's strategies for conquest and the rule of conquered peoples was a large part of what Beacon and Spenser adopted from *The Prince* and the *Discourses*. In *The Prince* iii, Machiavelli recommends settlements or colonies for governing a conquered people 'differing in language, customs, and institutions', a proposal endorsed by Beacon and Spenser, as it was by the New English generally.[12] Beacon repeatedly stresses the need to 'deduct colonies', and Spenser makes the plantation of colonists part of his plan for the reorganization of society following the military defeat of all rebels.[13] Although the policy of colonization is a commonplace of New English writing, and so perhaps not directly or only derived from a reading of *The Prince*, certain details in Beacon's and Spenser's analyses show a debt to Machiavelli. The whole first section of *A View* can be read as an in-depth exploration of Machiavelli's differences in 'language, customs, and institutions' of the conquered people. Spenser, however, makes significant changes: he substitutes religion for language and, in dramatic contrast to Machiavelli's functional analysis, morally judges all three features of Irish society to be 'evils'.[14] Spenser also analyses the success of the Norman conquest of England, contrasted with the failure of the conquest of Ireland, as caused by the adherence to Machiavelli's advice that the conquering prince ought to live in the defeated territory in person in the first instance, and the impossibility of this in the second.[15] And although Spenser's and Beacon's support for garrisons contradicts Machiavelli's criticism of them, their insistence upon harsh military retaliation against the nobility echoes the Italian's advice to 'crush the nobles'.[16]

Machiavelli advocates the strategic use of violence in the *Discourses* as well, particularly in Book II, which is devoted to the expansion of Rome. As

Lisa Jardine has shown in her work on Gabriel Harvey's annotations to his copy of Livy's *Decades*, such English initiators of colonies in Ireland as Sir Thomas Smith and his son had been applying Machiavelli's analysis of Roman colonization to their endeavours as early as 1570.[17] Many of Machiavelli's observations – both his specific examples and the principles deduced from them – are explicitly invoked by Beacon. Beacon seconds Machiavelli's insistence upon the need for strongly disciplined troops and the readiness of those troops to fight in order to avoid the servitude of paying tribute.[18] Like Machiavelli, Beacon also argues against 'the meane course' in conquest.[19] Beacon's quotation from Camillus's speech to the Roman senate on extending citizenship to the conquered Latins holds out the possibility of conquest by extreme 'bountie and liberalitie' as well as by sharp punishment.[20] To the extent that Beacon entertains the possibility – at least hypothetically – of persuasion as opposed to force, his rhetoric, if not his intentions (which may, as most historians contend, have very well been quite close to Spenser's), argues less consistently for all-out warfare. Within this discussion, however, Beacon rejects Machiavelli's typically complex counsel, arguing for the equal efficacy of extremely generous and extremely harsh treatment of conquered peoples. Instead Beacon advises that 'such as shall contend to make continuance of their conquest' should make 'a thorough and absolute reformation'.[21]

For Spenser and Beacon, this 'thorough and absolute reformation' requires force. In the one passage in *A View* directly attributed to Machiavelli, Spenser praises the Romans' 'giving absolute power to all their consuls and governors'.[22] Like Spenser's endorsement of uncontrolled power for the Lord Deputy, Beacon's proposal to follow the Roman precedent of 'creat[ing] a Dictatorship to manage the affairs of their wars, unto whom they give an absolute power' is taken from *Discourses* II.33. Beacon's and Spenser's support for military dictatorship may have its roots in their mutual support for Lord Grey, who had been criticized for killing the Italian troops surrendering to him at Smerwick during the Desmond rebellion.[23] Grey's decision to obliterate his opponents makes sense in terms of the sudden and extreme measures that Machiavelli acknowledges are necessary to maintain power during wars, which were best made 'short and crushing', after the Roman model.[24] Indeed, Machiavelli criticizes the inadequacy of persuasion alone and defends the necessity of force in *The Prince* vi. He illustrates this point through the example of Moses's strength through forces and Savanarola's failure through lack of them, which Beacon in turn cites in *Solon* II.12. Despite Beacon's many chapters in which he theorizes about the use of persuasion, he ultimately sides with Machiavelli's approval of the severity of Lucius Junius Brutus, who ordered the execution of his own sons, and criticism of the self-destructive patience of Piero Soderini, who had sufficient forces but did not use them in time to avoid 'the overthrowe [of] his country and regiment'.[25] Machiavelli does not recommend violence against the civilian population, and Beacon, like him, seems to reserve the use of extreme force for warfare or for the punishment of treason. In recommending that an army 'should tread down all that standeth before them on foot and lay on the ground all the stiff necked people of that land', Spenser seems to recommend a completely unrestrained and indiscriminate use of military force.[26]

At times, in adapting Machiavelli's text, Spenser and Beacon lend it a violent and moralistic character, lacking in the original. In *Discourses* II.3, Machiavelli writes of how the Romans expanded their territory by conquering neighbouring cities and moving those people back to Rome in order to strengthen the centre of power:

> For in this the Roman people do as a good farmer does, who that a plant may grow big and produce and mature its fruit, cuts off the first branches that are put forth so that its roots may gather virtue and in due course may produce greener and more fruitful branches.[27]

When Beacon deploys the image of a farmer pruning a plant he does so not to express the need to move the conquered population to the metropolitan centre of the republic so that it may expand, as Machiavelli does, but to allude to the need to eliminate the evils of the Irish and the Irish themselves:

> for no doubt like as the wilde olive and figge tree, by the continuall addressing of a skillful husbandman is made at the last kindely, profitable, and fruitfull, and not inferiour to the naturall braunches; so a common-wealth overgrowne with a generall corruption of manners, and thereby become savage, barbarous, and barren, like unto the wilde olive and figge tree may by the continuall pruning and addressing of a skillful magistrate, be made obedient, civill and profitable unto that prince, whom God has constituted to be the labourer in that vineyarde.[28]

This passage alludes to the parable of the fig tree in the vineyard from Luke 13.6–9, which illustrates the judgement of God. The conclusion of this parable, 'if it bear fruit well, and if not, then after that thou shalt cut it down', is a figural way of stating the lesson of this gospel chapter: 'except ye repent, ye shall likewise perish' (Luke 13.5). Similarly, Spenser uses the metaphor of pruning to express a crusade against evil – and in language that is more directly violent than Beacon's. In response to Eudoxus's question about how the reformation of Ireland will proceed 'if not by laws and ordinances', Irenius responds:

> Even by the sword, for all those evils must first be cut away with a strong hand before any good can be planted, like as the corrupt branches and the unwholesome boughs are first to be pruned, and the foul moss cleansed or scraped away, before the tree can bring forth any good fruit.[29]

Machiavelli uses the metaphor of pruning within the context of an argument for swelling the metropolis with conquered people, following the example of

Rome, and against denying foreigners citizens' rights and forbidding inter-marriage with them, according to the example of Sparta. In contrast, Spenser uses the metaphor within the context of an argument for destroying the cor-rupt customs that have resulted from social intercourse and intermarriage with the Irish. His approach to ruling Ireland less resembles the inclusive model of Roman expansion in the *Discourses* than the violent suppression rec-ommended in *The Prince* v: 'Indeed there is no surer way of keeping posses-sion than by devastation.'[30] Echoing this passage from *The Prince*, Beacon argues that 'lenitie . . . may be commended as a way to conquere, but not a safe way to holde and keepe'.[31]

In making this distinction, drawn from *The Prince*, between the appro-priate times for 'devastating' the conquered people or letting them 'keep their own laws', Beacon has incorporated the Machiavellian sense of historical contingency as a factor in determining policy. In Machiavelli's analysis of political action, the means need to be suited to the specific ends as opposed to following an idealized and unchanging platonic sense of the good. The principle from which Machiavelli argues for 'extraordinary methods' is repeatedly cited by Beacon: 'since similar forms cannot subsist in matter which is disposed in a contrary manner'.[32] The combination of feminine *for-tuna* as matter and men's *virtù* as form in the creation of political opportunity – 'Fortune, as it were, provided the matter, but they gave it its form'[33] – underscores the Machiavellian notion that specific material conditions dic-tate particular actions. Beacon quotes *The Prince* to illustrate the role of con-tingency in determining the success of *virtù*: 'sine occasione frustra virtus, sine virtute frustra occasio sese obtulit' ['without opportunity their prowess would have been extinguished, and without such prowess the opportunity would have come in vain'].[34] 'Men's fortune', as Machiavelli writes in *Dis-courses* III.9, 'depends upon whether their behaviour is in conformity with the times'.[35] And different conditions call for different tactics, as Beacon notes, citing Plutarch's 'Life of Julius Caesar': 'The times of warre and lawe are two things'.[36] To illustrate the extreme change called for by extreme sit-uations, Beacon compares Cicero's execution without indictment of the trai-tors Lentulus and Cethegus with Sir Richard Bingham's summary execution of the rebel Burkes in Connacht.[37]

Machiavelli applies the same principle of the need for change with the times to governments as well as to individuals. He argues that the 'downfall of cities also comes about because institutions in republics do not change with the times'.[38] For Beacon, Machiavelli's example of how outmoded the laws had become with the corruption of Rome is an analogy for Salamina, or Ireland:

> without a mutation made of these auncient customes and priviledges now growne out of use, and declyned from their first institution by a general cor-ruption of the subject, the state of Salamina may never be perfitly and thor-oughly reformed.[39]

Although Beacon devotes much attention to the strict enforcement of the laws, ultimately he comes to the same conclusion as Machiavelli that when institutions have become corrupt, 'new laws are ineffectual'.[40] In calling for an 'absolute reformation' Beacon can justify 'extraordinary methods, such as the use of forces and an appeal to arms' that Machiavelli maintains are necessary when 'modifying institutions all at once'.[41] Spenser also dismisses the possibility of new laws effecting a reform in the face of corruption: 'where you think good and sound laws might amend and reform things there you think surely amiss, for it is vain to prescribe laws when no man careth for keeping them'.[42]

The goal of preserving Rome's liberty, which Machiavelli saw as the ultimate aim of strict adherence to the law, territorial expansion, and even the use of arms in extreme situations, completely drops out of Beacon's and Spenser's account of the reformation in Ireland. When Beacon turns to the praise of reform in Ireland, on the model of the return to first principles, or *ricorso*, by which Rome had renovated its institutions, his selective and skewed interpretation of *Discourses* III.1 shows how little he understands the role of severe self-criticism in maintaining justice that is the ultimate goal of such republican reform. For example, Beacon completely overlooks Machiavelli's criticism of the way the Romans conducted their war against the Gauls. The *ricorso*, in this case, was brought about when the Romans 'renewed the ordinances of their ancient religion and punished the Fabii who had fought "in contravention of the Law of Nations"'.[43] All of the examples cited by Machiavelli involve the severe punishment of Roman citizens for not upholding the justice of Rome. Beacon's examples of the 'severe discipline of laws' include Lord Grey's summary execution of Irish rebels and Sir Richard Bingham's brutality towards those who, used to supporting their local Gaelic lords, resisted the composition of taxes to the crown. In other words, whereas in Machiavelli the reformation is from within Rome, in Beacon it is unleashed against rebellious outsiders. Similarly, Beacon misconstrues Machiavelli's praise of France. Whereas Machiavelli praises the French parliament for how 'it takes action against a prince of the realm' and 'in its judgments condemns the king', Beacon simply mentions how 'the Citie of Paris severely punished offenders'.[44] Beacon omits any reference to parliament and its check on the monarchy. Machiavelli's praise for the reformation of those in power in order to maintain the integrity of institutions becomes little more in Beacon's account than the imposition of martial law, or at best the strict imposition of English law, upon the Irish. Spenser, too, calls for the strict implementation of the law following the military defeat of the Irish: 'since we cannot now apply laws fit to the people as in the first institution of commonweales as it ought to be, we will apply the people and fit them to the laws'.[45] This passage directly contradicts Beacon's description of Solon's 'reformation of particular mischiefs . . . fram[ing] the lawes to the subject and matter and not the subject and matter to the laws'.[46] Beacon, however, also rejects Solon's method of reform as useless in Ireland because it had become 'corrrupted and declyned' from its 'first institution'.[47]

If Beacon and Spenser are not concerned with republican liberty, why did they attempt to adapt elements from Machiavelli's republican *Discourses* into their proposals for how Ireland should be governed? The answer, I think, lies in the relation between republic and empire in the *Discourses*. If republican government in and of itself was not important to Beacon and Spenser, it was important in so far as it could be a means towards building an empire on the model of Rome. As Peltonen has pointed out, the aggressive Rome, well armed and devoted to glory, is Beacon's model for England, while the servile state such as Pisa, disarmed and devoted to peace, is his model for Ireland.[48] Spenser also plans to have the Irish 'unarmed utterly and stripped of all their warlike weapons' as part of the reformation.[49] In order to settle 'an eternal peace in that country and make it very profitable to Her Majesty' the country is to be ringed with English garrisons so that 'no part of all Ireland shall be able to dare so much as quinch'.[50] Machiavelli's republic was also a fit model for Beacon's and Spenser's purposes because of its capacity to conquer and expand into other territories. Indeed, according to Machiavelli, a republic is even more 'successful' than a principality in the 'conquest of the world'.[51] Beacon notes that it was the reformation effected by the republican institution of the censors, as well as the skill and discipline of the army, through which the Romans 'quietly governed at home and fortunately conquered abroad in all parts of the world'.[52] Machiavelli's 'highly virtuous rulers', made possible by the free election of the republic, become a 'succession of severe Magistrates' in Beacon's plan for the 'absolute reformation' of Ireland.[53] Republics not only produce stronger armies and civil institutions with which to build an empire but also rule subject territories even more severely than principalities do; as Machiavelli notes in *Discourses* II.2:

> Of all forms of servitude, too, that is the hardest which subjects you to a republic. First because it is more lasting, and there is no hope of escape; secondly because the aim of a republic is to deprive all other corporations of their vitality and to weaken them, to the end that its own body corporate may increase.[54]

The 'absolute reformation' of Ireland that both Beacon and Spenser propose is contrary to the practice of a prince, who, Machiavelli writes, 'will leave [conquered peoples] in possession of all their trades and all their ancient institutions'.[55] The republic's methods of subduing, disarming, exploiting, radically transforming, and maintaining power over a conquered territory were even more effective than those of a principality. Hence the appeal of republican Rome to Beacon and Spenser. Machiavelli's republican Rome becomes a way for these New English writers to translate the present state of Ireland in terms of the past and also to envision what they saw as the need for more effective rule over this colony in the future.

If both Beacon and Spenser are concerned with the Roman model of colonial expansion, Beacon needs to be credited on the whole with an understanding of the *Discourses* that is more thorough and exact than Spenser's. Beacon explicitly quotes from the Latin translation of Machiavelli's *Discourses* on every page of *Solon*, whereas Spenser echoes Machiavellian principles, largely from *The Prince* rather than from the *Discourses*, which he may not even be taking directly from Machiavelli, but from an intermediate source – perhaps even from *Solon* itself. The major difference between Beacon's and Spenser's interpretation of Machiavelli has to do, as I have tried to point out along the way, with the use of force – both against whom and when it will be used. For Beacon, the use of force is tactical, dependent upon 'the times', whereas for Spenser it is the only alternative and a matter of necessary strategy. Their attitudes toward famine and destruction of the civilian population differ in so far as Beacon sees these as contingencies to be taken advantage of, whereas Spenser sees them as plans to be carried out. For example, Beacon writes 'for the times which shall represent unto us the shew and face of publike calamities, as famine, plague, pestilence, povertie, and warres shall mightily advaunce this action of reformation'.[56] Spenser makes the forced relocation or destruction of civilians a matter of policy: 'all those subjects who border upon those parts are either to be removed and drawn away or likewise to be spoiled, that the enemy may find no succour thereby, for what the soldier spares the rebel will surely spoil'.[57] Since Spenser was writing in the midst of the Nine Years' War from Ireland, he could not prevaricate in the way that Beacon, always a lawyer and publishing his tract in the safety of Oxford before the outbreak of full-scale conflict, did. At the same time that the differences between *A View* and *Solon* may seem rhetorical, still that rhetoric makes a difference. And largely the difference is that Beacon has more fully appropriated the republican ideology and language of Machiavelli. Beacon's republican sentiments surface in his complaints against the aristocracy in Ireland: 'they oppresse where they dislike, they reward whom they favour, they perish whom they hate, and finally they make themselves judges and arbitrators of the goods, lands, life, liberty, and of all the fortunes of the subject'.[58] Even Beacon's allegory extends the force of republicanism in the service of empire; the demagogue '*Cæsar*' stands for the Old English nobles to whom power should not be granted by the defenders of the republic, 'as well *Pompey*, as the Citie of *Rome*'.[59] Beacon's more precise understanding of the role of fortune and his more explicit use of republican historical analogy are the very features of Machiavelli's work that, I want to argue, also surface in some Irish responses to the English conquest.

If the New English were reading Machiavelli and applying his political analysis of history to the conquest of Ireland, where is there evidence that the Irish were either reading or indirectly acquainted with Machiavelli, and if so, how if at all did they apply his political theory to an explanation of their defeat? The only explicit references to Machiavelli that I have discovered so far are the condemnation of New English policies in *Breve relacion de la perse-cucion de Irlanda* (1619), which I mentioned at the outset, and a similar criticism of 'a view of the State of Ireland, written dialogue-wise betweene Eudoxus and Iraeneus by an ill-wisher of Ireland Edmond Spenser' by Michael Kearney, the first translator of Keating's *Foras Feasa ar Éirinn* into English.[60] Writing in 1635, just two years after Keating completed his history and Ware published Spenser's *View*, Kearney characterizes the 'plantations, displantations, transplantations, translations, dispersions, and scattering of Ireland's poore natives' as 'Matchivilian projects' and 'a destructive platforme laid for the utter subversion of this kingdome'. These two examples show that at least some Irish intellectuals conceived of such New English proposals for the complete social, political and economic reorganization of Ireland as a form of Machiavellian innovation. Even before such early seventeenth-century Irish critiques, it is very likely, however, that Machiavelli was known by the Irish intelligentsia. In the late sixteenth century Irish political figures such as Hugh O'Neill would have read *The Prince* and the *Discourses*. Although I cannot prove conclusively that the bardic poet Eochaidh Ó hEódhusa was reading these works of political philosophy, at least two of his poems deploy concepts indirectly indebted to them: the relation between *fortuna* and *virtù*, and the *conversazione tra secolari*, or the conversation across the centuries. These Machiavellian concepts become a way of translating the traditional topoi of bardic poetry into the contemporary contexts of the accession of James I to the throne of England and the defeat of Hugh O'Neill at the end of the Nine Years' War.

Eochaidh Ó hEódhusa's 'Metamorphosis 1603' opens with the conceit that the changes occurring in this year would be a fit theme for Ovid, who 'spoke of the change of the first elements'.[61] At the start of the poem, especially in stanzas 7 and 8, the influence of Ovid is strong, with allusions to the defeat of Medusa and the Gorgons from *Metamorphoses* IV.782–802. As the poem progresses, the Ovidian conceit of a metamorphosis is revealed as a figure for the change of sovereign. The great metamorphosis of 1603 that the poem celebrates is James I's assumption of kingship, yet another change earlier that same year, which cannot be explicitly mentioned, lurks in the background: the defeat of O'Neill, who was not aware of Elizabeth's death at the time of his surrender. 'There was many a thing that changed to evil in the beginning' (stanza 3).[62] At the time of composition, the poet could not have foreseen all the ramifications of these changes for the Gaelic élite and for himself as a poet as part of that élite. Still, the poem shows an acute awareness that 1603 marks the creation of a whole new cosmos in Ireland.

Ó hEódhusa both hopes for change and is all too aware of how dramatically everything has already changed. Although he mentions that 'Cing Séamas' has banished all anxiety, still the people of Ireland are called 'troubled' ('popal imshníomhach Éirionn') / [stanza 14]. Whereas Elizabeth is referred to as the 'first brightness' ('chéadshoillse') surpassed by the even greater 'brilliance beyond measure' ('deallradh éagcoimse') / [stanza 11] of James, the poet's hopes for the new reign also entail the 'curtailment of the sovereignty of the men of London' ('Bearradh flaithis bhfear Lunndan') [stanza 12]. The poem appears to take for granted the Stuarts' claims to Gaelic sovereignty that James was thought to have embodied by virtue of his genealogy, a claim and a genealogy that Breandán Ó Buachalla has shown was taken very seriously at the symbolic and even at times on the practical level in the seventeenth century.[63] Indeed, Ó hEódhusa describes James's succession in traditional Gaelic terms. As James Carney has characterized the bardic representation of kingship: 'A king married his territory: if he was effective and behaved as a king should, according to the ethical system of the poets, his land was fertile and bore fruit.'[64] Ó hEódhusa portrays the landscape as transformed by the fertility of James's reign: 'In sum Ceres ploughs fruitful hillocks' ('Atá Seireis – as sé a shuim / ag treabhadh thulach ndíoghuinn') [stanza 9].[65] James is kin to nature who shows him 'not a stepmother's love' ('ní searc leasmháthor') because he is her 'true kin' ('dheirbhshlíocht') [stanza 30].

In addition to this traditional representation of the king as a force of Nature is the new sense of him as a man like Machiavelli's *Prince*, who has defeated fortune through his own ability. The use of the word 'Fortún' itself [see stanzas 22, 24, 31, 32, 34] in this context is remarkable, since it is clearly a loan word from the romance languages, and since the other uses of it cited in the *Royal Irish Academy Dictionary of the Irish Language* are all from the early seventeenth century, suggesting that the word came into use in Irish at this time.[66] Like Machiavelli's *fortuna*, Ó hEódhusa's *Fortún* is a woman, and beyond that she is a jealous woman who vies with her rival Nature for the king's love [stanza 24]. The portrayal of fortune as a woman can be traced back to ancient Rome, but the notion that she must be sexually subdued was an innovation on Machiavelli's part.[67] According to Ó hEódhusa, *Fortún* is 'accustomed to gain dominance [or literally, empire]' ('Impireacht . . . / gidh gnáth don Fhortún d'fhagháil'), but under the reign of Séamas she becomes a 'female slave', or 'handmaiden' ('banchumhal') [stanza 32]. What is more, the king has accomplished all this through what is referred to as his 'choicest talents' ('soibhert') [stanza 25]; Fortune would be his mortal enemy if he were without 'the grades of accomplishment' ('cheardghrádha' [stanza 26], in which the root 'ceard' means art, craft, skill, trick). The skill with which Nature has gifted the king to transform Fortune is like the *virtù* with which the Prince must control *fortuna*.[68]

So, the metamorphosis in this poem is expressed in terms of both the traditional Gaelic representation of kingship as the rebirth of the natural world and a newer Machiavellian analysis of the achievement of power as the interplay between contingency and skill. The poem is a perfect example of what Breandán Ó Buachalla has analysed as the innovative use of an inherited topos.[69] In 'Metamorphosis 1603', the king is instructed by Nature in order to subdue her dangerous and unruly rival Fortune. The poem recounts more than a change from one sovereign to another; in a sense it represents kingship itself in a new way. In the repeated harping on change, both in the sense of transformation ('cclaochládh') and translation ('athrughadh'), the poem also registers a sea change in the culture and in the understanding of politics. The final line, 'we have experienced every transformation', or literally translation ('gach athrughadh uaramar'), brings all the changes that the poem has recounted to bear upon the troubled people of Ireland ('popal imshníomhach Éirionn'). There is a sense that so much change has been undergone that no more can be endured: 'may no second change come for us soon again' ('ar n-athchruthadh go hullamh') [stanza 34]. The only hope is for a king who by the 'instruction' ('teagusc') [stanza 31] of Nature can withstand the 'reversal of Fortune' ('d'fhilltighe an Fhortún') [stanza 34].

If 'Metamorphosis 1603' represents the traditional topos of the king's union with Nature in terms that resemble Machiavelli's struggle between *fortuna* and *virtù* in *The Prince*, 'Dá ghrádh tréigfead Máol Mórdha', one of the last poems of Ó hEódhusa, represents another inherited topos in Machiavellian terms. This time the poet makes use of the Machiavellian *conversazione tra secolari*, the conversation between different historical epochs, and in particular between the present and ancient Rome.[70] In a letter to Francesco Vettori, Machiavelli describes this conversation with the ancients: 'I am not ashamed to speak with them, and to ask them about the reasons for their actions; and they in their kindness answer me.'[71] In 'Dá ghrádh tréigfead Máol Mórdha', Ó hEódhusa expresses the traditional bardic topos of the poet's relationship with his patron as a marriage in terms of an analogy with a story from Roman history. The poet compares himself to the Roman matron Cornelia, who was grieved by the thought that her love caused the demise of both her husbands, Marcus Crassus and Pompey. These two republican heroes stand for Ó hEódhusa's Irish patrons the O'Reillys, along with the O'Donnells and the O'Neills. Like Cornelia, who wished she had married Caesar so that he rather than Pompey could have suffered such ill fortune, Ó hEódhusa vows to find 'a lover amongst [his] enemies', i.e. the English.[72] Whereas in the New English text *Solon His Follie* Caesar stands for the tyranny of the Old English nobility preying upon the people, and such figures as Cato and Pompey for the strict republican integrity of the New English deputies attempting to protect the people from the overmighty nobles, in Ó hEódhusa's poem Caesar stands for the conquering New English, and his republican enemies for the defeated Irish chieftains.

The specific source for this story from Roman history is the lament of Cornelia on the return of her defeated husband Pompey in Book VIII of Lucan's *De bello civili*, or *Pharsalia*.[73] Lucan's epic had been translated into Irish as *In Cath Catharda*, and the text was recopied many times from the fifteenth through the seventeenth centuries, but the translation ends with Book VII, indicating that Ó hEódhusa must have translated Cornelia's lament from Book VIII directly from the Latin. The choice of an exemplum from Roman history to present contemporary events follows the Machiavellian practice of *conversazione tra secolari*. And within this conversation across the centuries, it is significant that the poet chooses to identify his Gaelic patrons with republican heroes. As David Quint has shown in his analysis of epic in terms of the politics of empire, narrative poems that represent the point of view of those who have been defeated by empire trace their literary genealogy back to Lucan's *Pharsalia*, in part because of its anti-imperial theme of the defence of the republic.[74] Ó hEódhusa's analogy of his Gaelic patrons to the heroes of the Roman republic points not only to their common defeat but also to their common resistance to empire. The extended historical exemplum at the centre of 'Dá ghrádh tréigfead Máol Mórdha' embodies an historical awareness of the totality of the Gaelic defeat and the subjugation to England as an incipient empire that this defeat entailed. The metaphor of a republic defeated at the hands of an empire expresses profound historical change, for which there is no political solution in sight.

The various meanings derived from the image of the Roman republic by New English and Irish writers drive home the contradictory senses of the republic in Machiavelli's *Discourses*. The republic was both a strong government capable of coercing colonies into empire and an embattled government struggling against the tendency towards tyranny within itself.[75] If Beacon and Spenser deployed the example of the Roman republic to describe the conditions that would promote the expansionist goals of the English monarchy in its colonization of Ireland, Ó hEódhusa also used the example of the Roman republic to describe the defeat of his Irish patrons at the hands of the English. Both Machiavelli and the Roman history through which he produced his political theories could be read and adapted either to promote or to criticize the emergence of empire in early seventeenth-century Ireland.[76]

2000

IRISH AND SPANISH CULTURAL AND POLITICAL RELATIONS IN THE WORK OF O'SULLIVAN BEARE

The author of the first published history of Catholic Ireland, Philip O'Sullivan Beare has not received much attention since the earlier part of this century.[1] In the seventeenth century, his *Historiae Catholicae Iberniae Compendium* (Lisbon, 1621) influenced such Irish Catholic historians as O'Mahony, Lynch, and O'Ferrall.[2] Protestant historians, such as Borlase and Cox, repeatedly cited the *Compendium* as a source but at the same time vilified its lack of reliability.[3] In the nineteenth century, just following the Famine, Matthew Kelly edited the *Compendium* as part of an emerging Irish cultural and historiographical movement, which Byrne also contributed to with his early twentieth-century translation of parts of the text.[4] Perhaps because of a tradition of judging O'Sullivan Beare's history as inaccurate and as part of an emerging Irish nationalism, the *Compendium* has not received the attention that it deserves. Now what needs to be done is to place this work within its specific early seventeenth-century historical context. The present article offers an attempt, which is in part speculative, to reconstruct the context based on a close reading of the structure of the text itself, a comparison of its historiography with early modern Spanish historiography, and a contextualization of its political aims in relation to the activities of the Irish exiles in Spain. Philip O'Sullivan Beare's relationship with the protagonists of his narrative, many of whom were members of his own family, needs to be taken into account in understanding a history that is written from the perspective of an exile. Above all the *Compendium* was an opportunistic attempt by a leading member of the Irish emigré community to influence the policy of a new king at a critical time, when the Austrian Habsburgs were about to resume the war against Holland in the West. In his history, O'Sullivan Beare witnesses the losses of recent Irish history as a tragedy that he hopes can be overturned by Spanish intervention.

i. 'The Most Egregious Liar' Versus 'the Heretics'

The seventeenth-century Anglo-Irish antiquarian Archbishop Ussher referred to Philip O'Sullivan Beare as 'the most egregious liar of any in Christendom', while the nineteenth-century Anglo-Irish antiquarian Standish O'Grady wrote of the 'sterling honesty of Philip O'Sullivan as a historian' who 'did not spare his own family when the narrative of their misdeeds was necessary to set out the true course of events'.[5] Ussher's characterization of O'Sullivan Beare as a liar locates both Protestant accuser and Catholic accused as combatants in early modern Christian polemics, which since the Reformation had been notoriously acrimonious on both sides. In early seventeenth-century English-speaking culture, Protestant authors such as Barnabe Riche symbolically associated Catholics with the whore of Babylon and all manner of corruption, while earlier a Catholic humanist such as Sir Thomas More had employed scatological vocabulary in his arguments against Luther. If Ussher's comment identifies O'Sullivan Beare against an audience of his opponents, O'Grady's identifies the Irish historian in relation to an audience of his allies, whom he was able to criticize. For O'Grady, the great merit of O'Sullivan Beare's history was that it was written 'by one who had conversed for many years with all the principal actors of the Irish war theatre'.[6] O'Sullivan Beare's reliance upon Irish soldiers' oral accounts makes him a faithful witness to their experience of warfare. Like his eye-witness informants, O'Sullivan Beare, too, was a soldier, and also, like many of them, he was living in exile in Spain.

As the dedication to O'Sullivan Beare's *Historiae Catholicae Iberniae Compendium* indicates, however, his primary audience was one of neither English Protestant enemies nor Irish Catholic allies but the Spanish king who harboured the Irish exiles: 'Don Philip of Austria, most potent Catholic king and monarch of the Spains, the Indies, of other kingdoms, and diverse dominions'.[7] Printed in 1621 at Lisbon by Peter Craesbeeck, '*impressor del rey*' (printer of the king), and bearing the arms of Spain on its title page, O'Sullivan Beare's *Compendium* presents both the polemical and military conflict between Irish and English and the English defeat of the Irish in terms that his Spanish royal audience would understand. In his address to Philip IV, O'Sullivan Beare explains why he 'commit[s]' his book to the 'patronage' of this 'Catholic majesty . . . in earnest token of a grateful spirit'. The author cites his own commission in the Spanish navy, and 'the generous and noble succours to the Irish people' granted not only by Philip, but also by the king's father and grandfather. Reminding his royal audience of this historical alliance between Spain and Ireland, O'Sullivan Beare calls for continued aid in what is styled as a holy crusade against heresy:

> Ireland has never swerved from the law which Christ our Redeemer instituted, the blessed Apostles preached, and the Roman pontiffs instructed us to cherish. You are ever a barrier to the pestilence of hellish heresy: Ireland is overwhelmed with the most violent fury of heresy. You are the refuge of Catholics: Ireland turns to you as to an asylum.

In appealing to Philip IV as a 'barrier to the pestilence of hellish heresy' and 'the refuge of Catholics', O'Sullivan Beare characterizes the Spanish monarch in terms of what J. H. Elliott has referred to as the 'governing principles of the Spanish Monarchy': 'the universalism of a global mission and the recurring identification of king and altar'.[8] O'Sullivan Beare calls upon Philip not only as the defender of Spain, 'forbidding all apostates from the Catholic faith access to your kingdoms', but also as the defender of the faith around the world, in order to enlist his defence of the faith in Ireland: 'your labours and zeal will in a short time . . . restore and re-establish it in its former splendour, authority and dignity in other realms in which, dishonoured by the crimes of impious men, it has fallen to the lowest depths'.[9] O'Sullivan Beare refers to the title granted to the Spanish kings by the papacy – 'You above other kings are most justly styled "Catholic"' – and uses the identification between the monarch and the church which unified the disparate kingdoms of Spain to fuse the alliance between Spain and Ireland – 'Ireland stands forth Catholic, amidst the monstrous confusion of the errors of the north'.[10] O'Sullivan Beare's *Compendium* repeatedly represents the English as 'heretics' ('*haeresi*'), a term that needs to be understood in its Continental Counter-Reformation and specifically Spanish context. The Irish author to whom O'Sullivan Beare can best be compared is Peter Lombard, who, writing his '*De Hibernia Insula Commentarius*' in Rome, characterized both the wars of James Fitzgerald and of Hugh O'Neill against the English as a crusade '*adversus haereticos*'.[11] In order to promote papal support for O'Neill, Lombard deploys a language designed to unite the Irish cause with the larger European Catholic opposition to Protestantism. The very presence of the word '*Catholicae*' in the title of O'Sullivan Beare's history signals the pre-eminence of religion.

To characterize the English as heretics meant, as Juan de Mariana, the chief Spanish court historian of the early seventeenth century, wrote in his *General History of Spain* (published in Latin 1592, and in Castilian 1601) of both medieval Albigensians and contemporary Lutherans, that they were 'enemies to the truth'.[12] 'Heretic' referred to those within Christianity whose theology was unorthodox, and this sense of the word can be seen in O'Sullivan Beare's address 'to the Catholic reader', which describes the ideological struggle of 'our most eloquent Orators, who have encountered the fury of infernal doctrines'.[13] His depiction of the English as 'heretics' in the sense of religious enemies can be seen as provoking a response in kind from Ussher, who vilified the Catholic historian as a liar. The very context in which Ussher makes this accusation is in a debate with O'Sullivan Beare over the state of the Pelagian heresy in medieval Ireland. In response to O'Sullivan Beare's claim that 'the error of Pelagius is reported to have found no patron nor maintainer in Ireland', Ussher quotes Egilwardus as maintaining that 'Ireland had of old been defiled with the Pelagian heresy'.[14] But what needs to be taken into account is that, however antiquarian his method, Ussher uses the Pelagian heresy to prove that 'the bishops of Ireland did not take the resolutions of the Church of Rome for undoubted oracles', as part of his larger argument that the Irish church was from ancient times Protestant and not Roman Catholic in its genealogy.[15] Both Ussher and O'Sullivan Beare approach this issue of heresy from equally partisan standpoints which are formulated polemically in ideological terms, where the past is used to endorse the present – a Protestant past for a Protestant hegemony in alliance with England, a Counter-Reformation past for a Catholic alliance with Spain.

In the wake of the Spanish Inquisition and the *Reconquista*, the term heretic had also taken on the political colouration of one who was not part of the Catholic Spanish hegemony – the Jews and the Moors who were expelled to produce this hegemony. As J. G. Casey has noted in commenting on the early seventeenth-century policy of Madrid towards the *moriscos* in Valencia, they 'presented a twofold problem: military security and religious heterodoxy'.[16] Similarly, for O'Sullivan Beare 'heretics' are not only Protestants but enemies to the body politic. He refers to the English as 'heretics' in a call for Spanish arms to aid: 'our most valiant and renowned generals and magnanimous soldiers who preferred to fall in arms fighting strenuously and devotedly, rather than to submit to heretics'.[17] Whereas Lombard could maintain that O'Neill's success up to 1600 was due to 'Divine aid . . . against the most powerful and insolent heretics of all Europe', O'Sullivan Beare had to reckon with defeat.[18] His task was to explain that defeat, to gain aid for the Irish exiles in Spain, and also to obtain Spanish support for military intervention in Ireland. The English, though victorious in the Nine Years' War and though claiming Ireland as subject to the English crown, when portrayed as heretics could be seen as an alien people who, similar to the Jews and the Moors in the Spanish Reconquest, would have to be expelled in the reconquest of Ireland by the Irish. O'Sullivan Beare was calling on the new Spanish sovereign Philip IV to aid in this crusade. Like so much else in O'Sullivan Beare's *Compendium*, this language of heresy is dictated by the author's rhetorical strategies to influence a Spanish audience, his political struggle with competing factions in the exile community, and his own ideological formation as an Irish exile.

ii. Irish History for a Spanish Audience

This strategic formulation of the Spanish alliance with the Irish as a united struggle against the heretics, in the wake of the Spanish peace with England at the end of the Nine Years' War, informs the structure of O'Sullivan Beare's *Compendium* as a narrative whole. The very first lines of the book seek to establish that the Irish are descended from Milesius, an ancient Iberian prince, by linking Irish origin myths with information from old Spanish chronicles (I.i). The organization of Irish history into four periods corresponding to the four volumes of the *Compendium*, as well as the perspective on the narrative throughout, stress the themes of Irish allegiance to and English persecution of Catholicism, and Spanish intervention in the conflict. The first volume, treating Irish geography, natural history, language, religion and customs in an almost timeless description, presents Ireland in terms reminiscent of the initial address to Philip IV as 'a barrier to the pestilence of hellish heresy': 'It is shown that Ireland is the citadel and bulwark whence heretics can be over-thrown and other kingdoms preserved' (I.i.vii). This account of early Christ-ian Ireland highlights the perspective of a Counter-Reformation Spanish Catholic through an entire chapter devoted to the pilgrimage for 'A Spanish Viscount returned from St Patrick's Purgatory' (I.ii.ii). Similarly, O'Sullivan Beare frames his critique of Stanihurst's depiction of Irish manners in terms of the judgement of the Spanish Inquisition on his *Topographia*. According to O'Sullivan Beare, the Inquisition 'having condemned the book committed it to the fires'.[19]

Stanihurst was a political as well as an intellectual opponent of O'Sullivan Beare's and had to be refuted on account of his views not only on Irish culture but also on Spanish policy. An Irish embassy seeking Spanish intervention in Ireland in 1593 had been defeated by none other than Richard Stanihurst, then serving in the court of Philip II.[20] Refuting both Richard Stanihurst's and Giraldus Cambrensis's view of the Irish as irreligious and unlearned, O'Sulli-van Beare writes his account of pre-Norman Ireland from the vantage point of its present decline, which he lays at the feet of the 'wars . . . of the English which for more than four hundred years have reduced the sacred island to a rude and uncultivated place'.[21] Later, in an unpublished manuscript, 'Vindi-ciae Hiberniae', or 'Zoilomastix' (c. 1625), O'Sullivan Beare would continue his refutation of Stanihurst, defending Irish ecclesiastics and citing English tyranny as the cause for the distress of Ireland.[22]

The second volume of the *Compendium* begins the narrative history proper with the arrival of the English in 1168 and an argument against their claim on Ireland. Unlike Geoffrey Keating, who distinguishes between the Norman con-quest of Ireland as Christian and the Elizabethan conquest as barbaric, O'Sul-livan Beare describes both conquests as unjust and destructive.[23] The reason for the invasion of 1168 was the unjust English support for the cause of an adulterer, Dermot of Leinster, who had seized O'Rourke of Connacht's wife, and the effects of the invasion were English abuse of Irish possessions and for-tunes, and cruelty and fraud towards Catholics (II.i.vii). O'Sullivan Beare claims that *Laudabiliter*, by which Pope Adrian IV granted the English licence to conquer Ireland and to collect church rents, was fraudulently obtained (II.iv). The papal decree to the English specified certain conditions – includ-ing that the boundaries of the church be extended, that souls be cared for, that church laws be served – and now these have not been extended but violated.[24]

O'Sullivan Beare's narrative of the period from the Norman Conquest to the Spanish Armada telescopes all Irish history through the lens of the Refor-mation; the *Compendium* is not antiquarian history but history necessitated by and written for the present. His historiography could be compared to that of Guicciardini, whose *Historia d'Italia* was translated by Philip IV (completed 1633) and whose historiography influenced that of Herrera y Tordesillas, 'the most influential and certainly most prolific and widely read royal chronicler of the early seventeenth century'.[25] As Richard Kagan has pointed out,

Herrera y Tordesillas took from Guicciardini the notion that history should explain why things happened, should speak to the present, and should offer political counsel to the monarch.[26] Like the Guicciardinian historiography of Herrera y Tordesillas, O'Sullivan Beare's perspective on the past is dictated by the political exigencies of the present and a greater attention to more recent events. He points to the European-wide effects of the heresies of Luther and Calvin: 'princes are incited to arms, armies are destroyed, leaders are killed, towns are levelled, states and republics overturned, reigns are toppled, and all from top to bottom is thrown into confusion'.[27] Against all this the kings of Spain 'bring aid to every part of the world including Italy, the Spanish Indies, to which lately the faith has been conveyed, and other dominions of the King of Spain'. O'Sullivan Beare appeals to the global role of the Spanish kings in the wars of religion as the 'sword in duty and faith' as a precedent for what their response to the situation in Ireland should be. The rhetoric of O'Sullivan Beare in persuading Philip IV of his commitment to Ireland would have been familiar to the king from his reading of Spain's leading historian Juan de Mariana's *De Rege et Regis Institutione*, which was dedicated to Philip III.[28] De Mariana had portrayed the king's responsibility 'to maintain large armies' and 'to engage in virtually perpetual warfare' in a 'relentless power-system of applied religion'.[29] O'Sullivan Beare's history of Ireland is a history of continual combat against the violation of the body politic by the heretics. Just as Juan de Mariana portrays the social effects of peace as debilitating and those of war as strengthening, so does O'Sullivan Beare: 'it is the custom of the English . . . in war and critical times of difficulties not to provoke the Irish with the least injustice . . . in peace and prosperous times they [the English] kill, destroy and ruin'.[30] Tracing the conflict with the English from the abuses of the papal decree to the crucible of the Reformation up to 1588, the second volume represents this period as one of continued Irish resistance to English intervention: from Shane O'Neill in Ulster, the O'Mores and O'Conors of Offaly, the Fitzgeralds of Munster, and James Eustace and Fiach O'Byrne in Leinster.

Woven throughout this history of an aggressive military defence against the English are narratives of martyrdom. The Irish are portrayed on the one hand as defenders of the faith, on analogy with the imperial cause of the King of Spain, and on the other hand as the victims of English tyranny, on analogy with the early Christians who suffered at the hands of Roman imperialism. O'Sullivan Beare's accounts of how Irish ecclesiastics were martyred conform to the pattern established in Eusebius's *Ecclesiastical History*. John Knott has analysed the elements of the early Christian narrative of martyrdom as follows:

> the readiness of the martyrs to suffer, their constancy in the face of appalling tortures, their influence in spreading the faith, the drama of the confrontation between the rage of the persecutors and the peacefulness of the martyrs, the celebration of the triumph of the martyrs over the enemies of God.[31]

The account of how Patrick O'Healy responded to interrogation, torture, and death illustrates how O'Sullivan Beare's Irish martyrs are both political heroes for the cause of Spain and religious heroes, resembling the early Christians. On being challenged to divulge information about the plans of 'the King of Spain to make war on the queen', O'Healy remained silent, even after 'his hands and feet were broken and splinters were driven into his nails'.[32] As he rose to the scaffold, the Bishop 'addressed the crowd . . . confirming the people in the Catholic faith, warning them against the errors of the English'. O'Healy's prophecy of God's vengeance upon the English viceroy as persecutor of the faithful is fulfilled when he contracts a 'horrible disease . . . accompanied by a repulsive stench', similar to the Roman tyrant Galerius, who contracted a disease with a 'deadly stench' as a result of his persecution of Christians.[33] The story of Dermot O'Hurley, Archbishop of Cashel, 'the Most Unconquerable and Illustrious Martyr', displays the same bribery and rage of the persecutors, and loyalty and constancy of the martyr.[34] When Dermot declines the rewards offered to him in return for following the 'tenets of the heretics', renouncing the Pope and submitting to the queen, 'the heretics are filled with anger'. Even when he is bound, tied to a stake, his legs encased in boots filled with pitch and boiling water, and roasted over a fire, O'Hurley 'never uttered a word but held out to the end of the torture with the same cheerfulness and serenity of countenance he had exhibited at the commencement of his sufferings'. The miracle of 'a noble lady being delivered from a wicked devil' that proceeds from this martyrdom marks O'Sullivan Beare's text as particularly Catholic. Such miraculous events as the cleansing from evil spirits and healing of the sick, recounted by Eusebius, are rejected by the Protestant martyrologist John Foxe.[35] Such miracles of the saints are a common feature of Catholic hagiography. Later O'Sullivan Beare would recount such manifestations of healing powers in the life of Saint Mochua, based on Irish sources, for Colgan's *Acta sanctorum Hiberniae* (Louvain, 1645).[36]

As victims of tyranny, the Irish are not only represented as individual exemplary martyrs but also as collective victims of English cruelty: 'The cruelty of their Princes in persecuting the Catholics was carried out by the Royalist governors and ministers . . . in Ireland, where the natives even to this day, patiently endure all extremities for Christ's sake.'[37] O'Sullivan Beare not only catalogues English cruelties towards the Irish but also defends the Spanish against English claims of their cruelty:

> The English Governors and clergy by themselves and their followers declaimed against the unheard of cruelty of the Spaniards, and unjustness of their laws in order to deter the Irish from friendship with them, but there is at this day no Irishman who does not know perfectly well that the truth is otherwise.[38]

O'Sullivan Beare's indictment of the English and defence of the Spanish could be seen as a counter-attack against the Black Legend. Spread through the many translations of Las Casas's *Brevísima relación de las destrucción de las Indias* (1552), the Black Legend was known throughout Europe.[39] Within Spain, the critique of Las Casas, beginning in the early seventeenth century with the works of Vargas Machuca and Quevedo, might lead one to believe that any reference to Las Casas would have been controversial.[40] At the same time, he was still a respected historian, the source for the official chronicler Antonio de Herrera y Tordesillas; and the *Brevísima relación* was available in Spain at the time that O'Sullivan Beare was writing.[41] A Spanish text contemporary with the *Compendium*, which complains of the laws against Catholics in Ireland, may also echo the title of Las Casas's text in order to turn the accusation of cruelty back on the English: *Breve relacion de la presente persecucion de Irlanda* (Sevilla, 1619). Although there is no way to prove conclusively that O'Sullivan Beare was imitating Las Casas, the Irish historian's account of the English persecution of the Irish closely resembles the Spanish historian's account of Spanish persecution of the Indians. While it might be argued that to create such an analogy would be an embarrassment to the text's dedicatee, the King of Spain, it could also be argued that to reveal that the English were guilty of the same sorts of cruelties that the Spaniards were being vilified for all over Europe would be a glaring revelation of the hypocrisy of the English.

O'Sullivan Beare's Irish suffer cruelties at the hands of the English similar to those suffered by the colonized and enslaved Indians in Las Casas's *Brevísima relación*. If the horrors of torture and the nemesis that falls from heaven upon the heads of the aggressors are part of a providential framework of history that both texts share with the narratives of the early Christian martyrs, such *topoi* as the treacherous parley, the sneak attack upon friendly hosts and the massacre of civilians make these texts records of colonial aggression.[42] Both Irish and Indian hospitality are met with treachery. Donough MacCarthy is murdered after entertaining the English President with 'hospitality and generosity'; Montezuma is made prisoner after presenting the Spaniards with splendid gifts.[43] Just as Fergus O'Kelly's house was set on fire when he is peacefully enjoying Christmas dinner with his family, so, too, the Indians' houses are set on fire when they are peacefully 'sleeping yet with their wives and children'.[44] O'Sullivan Beare repeatedly relates how the English killed 'the old men, women, and children'; similarly Las Casas relates how the Spanish 'commit murders . . . sparing neyther children, nor old men, neither women with child'.[45] In the massacre that occurred at his birthplace, Dursey Island, O'Sullivan Beare tells of violence against women and children: 'Some ran their swords up to the hilt through the babe and mother, who was carrying it on her breast, others paraded before their comrades little children, writhing and convulsed on their spears'; similarly, Las Casas relates 'It was a lamentable thing to beholde the women with their children stabbed with these pickes'.[46] O'Sullivan Beare tells how at Dursey the English 'binding all the survivors . . . threw them into the sea over jagged and sharp rocks'.[47] So, too, Las Casas relates how at Hispaniola the Spanish drowned innocent victims:

> They took the little soules by the heeles, ramping them from the mothers dugges, and crushed their heades against the cliftes. Others they cast in to the rivers laughing and mocking, and when they tumbled into the water, they sayde, nowe shift for thy self such a ones corpes.[48]

Such sadism in the above passage from Las Casas also appears in O'Sullivan Beare's history – for example, in the account of the English governor of Leix Francis Cosby's torture of women and children at Mullaghmast:[49]

> When women were hanging from the tree by a halter he took an incredible pleasure in at the same time hanging by the mother's long hair their infant children. It is said that when the tree was without the corpses of Catholics hanging from it, he was wont to say – 'You seem to me, my tree, shrouded with great sadness, and no wonder, for you have now long been childless. I will speedily relieve your mourning. I will shortly adorn your boughs with corpses'.[50]

The gratuitous pleasure of the invaders in mutilating, burning, hanging, and massacring the native inhabitants unites the characterization of the English heretics and the Spanish devils. The sadism of the aggressors in Las Casas's and O'Sullivan Beare's narratives justifies resistance to colonial aggression.

If the Las Casian justification of armed resistance to colonial aggression appears to contradict the Irish historian's appeal to the imperial power of the Spanish king, two other Las Casian arguments explain if not resolve the ideological rift between the dominion of Catholic empire and the rights of native inhabitants. For both Las Casas and O'Sullivan Beare, colonial conquest entails an attack upon the Catholic religion. In the *Brevísima relación*, both the clergy and the Indians are portrayed as victims of religious persecution:

> the Spaniards were never any more mindful to spread the Gospel among them, then as if they had been dogs; but on the contrary forbid religious persons to exercise their dutie, deterring them by many afflictions and persecutions from preaching and teaching among them.[51]

Similarly, in the *Compendium*, the Irish clergy are prohibited from ministering to the people:

> The holy communities of friars were for the most part scattered and banished, and in many places priests could not easily be found to baptise infants.[52]

Furthermore, just as Las Casas had objected to the forced conversion of the Indians,[53] O'Sullivan Beare objected to the forced submission of the Irish to Protestantism:

> The queen is declared head of the church in her own kingdoms, and all must admit her to be head and attest the same by an oath . . . because the chieftains

were nowise willing to conform, various artifices were devised, by means of
which they were despoiled of their property, gradually overthrown, and punished with death.[54]

Like Las Casas, who argued for the right of the Indians to political jurisdiction in their native territories, O'Sullivan Beare argues for the right of the Irish
to defend themselves against English confiscation of their land. Ironically, this
same right to political determination for indigenous inhabitants had allowed
Las Casas to justify the Spanish war against the Moors.[55] In this sense, the
Irish are analogous to the Spanish as well as the Indians.

The third volume, 'On the Fifteen Years' War', begins with the Armada of
1588, subordinating O'Neill's revolt in 1594–1603 to the larger framework of
war between Spain and England. Twice as long as the three other volumes,
and the best known because it is the sole volume to have been translated into
English, the limits of this volume mark turning points in the shifting alliances
among the Irish and in the Spanish alliance with the Irish. At the outset of the
volume the various factions are laid out according to those who 'sided with
the Queen' and 'those who took up arms for the Catholic faith' – both groups
including 'new Irish', those 'of mixed English and Spanish blood', and 'old
Irish, deriving their descent from Spain'.[56] By the end of the third volume, the
devastating effects of the defeat eliminate the need to make distinctions
among factions: 'Ireland was almost entirely laid waste and destroyed, and
terrible want and famine oppressed all.'[57] If at the outset of volume III the
Catholic Irish are divided by those who 'did not secede from the heretics'
because they 'despaired of the Catholics succeeding, as they were not assisted
by the Popes or the Kings of Spain or France', at the close of the volume they
are 'scattered . . . amongst foreign nations, and generously received by
Catholics on account of their faith'.[58] Singled out for special gratitude is the
King of Spain: 'such was his kindness and generosity that one could scarcely
find word to express or mind to conceive, all they owed him'.[59]

The third volume begins and concludes with the account of a debate that
was presented before the judicial court of the doctors of the Universities of
Salamanca and Valladolid: 'Did the Irish justly wage this war?' (III.viii.vii).
Again, the purpose of this debate, and the purpose of O'Sullivan Beare's
recounting it, is to convince a Spanish audience. Clement VIII's letter, while
only endorsed by the doctors in 1603 'at too late a stage', is presented by
O'Sullivan Beare as the Pope's immediate response to Irish factionalism at the
outbreak of the war (III.i.iii). In the account of the 1603 debate about
whether the war was just, the Irish prevail over the Anglo-Irish: 'Some Anglo-
Irish priests asserted that it was not; the Irish persuaded the Anglo-Irish that
it was.'[60] O'Sullivan Beare explains that the doctors' judgement hinged in
large part on establishing the authenticity of a letter from Pope Clement VIII
stating that it is because 'the Queen of England fights against the Catholic religion and does not permit the Irish to worship the Catholic faith' that war had

been undertaken against her.[61] Indeed, the doctors determined that the Pope had proclaimed that 'one must fight the English against the Catholic Religion no less than one must oppose the Turks'.[62] Since as late as 1596 Pope Clement VIII did not grant a papal donation freeing the Irish from English jurisdiction and granting Ireland to Spain, as O'Neill and O'Donnell as well as some of their Spanish allies had wanted, O'Sullivan Beare's account of the 1603 debate and the doctors' validation of the Pope's declaration against the English seems to be part of a propaganda war.[63] On the one hand, O'Sullivan Beare persuades his audience that the lack of papal and Spanish support in the early years of the Fifteen Years' War divided the Irish into factions. On the other hand, he retrospectively constructs papal justification for Spanish intervention in Ireland.

Framing Volume III of the *Compendium* is the judgement of God against those who have stood in the way of the Irish-Spanish alliance. The affiliation of the Catholic Irish with the English heretics is due to God's judgement upon sin. O 'Sullivan Beare begins the explanation of the Irish siding with the English in terms of divine retribution: 'In truth, I think, this must have been a punishment of God on Ireland for the crimes of Irishmen.'[64] Pope Clement is said to have commanded Irish allegiance to the King of Spain: 'Therefore those Catholics who fight against the ordained prince [*praedictum principem*] in the camp of the enemy sin most gravely.'[65]

From the defeat of Anglo-Irish opposition to Spanish intervention at the end of the third volume, O'Sullivan Beare continues to narrate the increased persecution of both new and old Irish that presents a society with little room for factionalism – a united front ready to accept aid from Spain. Covering the period from the defeat of the Irish in the Fifteen Years' War in 1603 to the Parliament of 1613, the fourth and final volume of the *Compendium* records the persecution against all sectors of Irish Catholic society in five stages:

> First, all Catholic Irish, whether the old or new, whether of the Irish or English faction, who were seen to be strong in courage and military skill, were destroyed, either submitted to the greatest torture or thrown into prison or sent away into exile. Second, the rest were prohibited from the practice of arms, the exercise of letters and the rites of the Catholic religion, since the priests were expelled. Third, with their livelihoods and fortunes spoiled, they were reduced to poverty, and they were disinherited from public duties and the administration of public affairs. Fourth, they were forced to attend the churches of the heretics and to acknowledge their ceremonies and to swear allegiance to King James as head of the church and the prince of his kingdoms. Fifth, in the assembly of the kingdom, which they call parliament, the most severe laws were introduced towards the priests and their harbourers and protectors.[66]

In Volume IV, O'Sullivan Beare reports 'The King's Proclamation against the Catholic Religion' of 1605, the confiscation of land from Catholics and its redistribution to Protestants, and the ousting of 'legitimate' Catholics from the Irish parliament and the appointment of 'illegitimate' Protestants in their place. The conclusion of the *Compendium* portrays the common religious, economic and political disenfranchisement of all Irish Catholics.[67]

The Irish response to the persecution is framed with reference to the Spanish context. First of all, such Irish nobles as Maguire are presented as flying to Spain.[68] Even the arguments made by the Irish agents in their embassy to James I can be seen as corresponding to those of Juan de Mariana, the chief Spanish constitutionalist of the early seventeenth century. In his *De Rege et Regis Institutione*, Mariana had argued that 'the Prince ought to see that the immunities and rights of the clergy remain intact'.[69] The Jesuit humanist further maintained that the king could not rule without the consent of the people and the people could not be taxed without their consent.[70] Basing their arguments on similar constitutional grounds, the Irish agents argued that the fines levied against Catholics were unjust:

> whereas it is excessive towards the subjects and an intolerable arrogance to exact any tribute without command, if collecting from the people on charge of the King's majesty, since the king does not collect any subsidy without the decree of the senate, and the free consent of the entire Republic of the kingdom; & whereas now for a long time by various edicts the King's majesty acknowledges the direct guardianship of his subjects in this kingdom, not that of the Deputy of this same kingdom and the counsel, we are not held in debt to the kingdom, since edicts have been supplied in this kingdom to protect and to render exempt, from this heavy, unjust, and onerous tribute those who seem to be made paupers by it.[71]

After translating James's English speech in which the king rejected his Irish subjects' pleas and called for their severe punishment as 'authors of sedition' (*seditionis authores*), O'Sullivan Beare translates a letter written in Spanish by Florence Conry, Archbishop of Tuam, who argues against the heretical rule of the English and their confiscation of Catholic lands.[72]

The *Compendium* progresses in a telescoping movement, with each successive book covering a shorter span and more recent period of Irish history, designed to explain the need for Spanish aid to the present plight of the Irish – both in Ireland and as exiles in Spain. This last volume brings the reader closest to the present moment and the present context of the author in Spain, where he was in communication with Archbishop Florence Conry on the eve of the publication of the *Compendium*. O'Sullivan Beare tells us that he finished his work at the Ides of December 1618, at which point he had already penned an English language document that the Archbishop presented to the Council of Spain.[73]

iii. Factions within the Exile Community: Identity, Patronage, Education, Politics

An intelligence document entitled 'A Briefe Relation of Ireland and the diversity of Irish in the same' sheds some light on O'Sullivan Beare's context and his descriptions of the various groups in Irish society in the *Compendium*. Marked in the left-hand corner of the first folio with the following heading: 'Presented to the Counsell of Spayne circum 1618 by Florence ye pretended archb. of Tuam and thought to be penned by O'Sullevan Beare',[74] this manuscript was written at roughly the same time as the *Compendium*, which though published in 1621 had already been completed by 1618. Both texts construct Irish identity in religious and political rather than what Joep Leerssen has called 'tribal or racial terms'.[75] In the *Compendium*, O'Sullivan Beare refers to the Gaelic Irish as 'veteres Iberni' and the Old English as 'novi Iberni'.[76] While Leerssen has interpreted these terms as 'exclud[ing] non-Gaelic forces from the anti-English cause', I would argue that the terms are more inclusive than discriminatory.[77] That both the Gaelic Irish and the recusant Catholic Old English are called 'Iberni', whether 'veteres' or 'novi', indicates first of all the linguistic formation of a common identity, which privileges geographic location – the '*Iberniae*' of the title – and cultural practice – the use of the Irish language and Irish customs – over ethnic origins.[78] Moreover, both this English language document attributed to O'Sullivan Beare and the *Compendium* show a more sophisticated analysis of the various groups of Irish in terms of their cultural practice, political affiliation, and changing historical circumstances. In other words, O'Sullivan Beare's conception of groups of Irish is not a matter of static essential identity but one of historical formation.

Just as in the *Compendium*, in this manuscript the 'Ancient Irish' are said to be 'descended from ye Spaniards'.[79] The author stresses the Milesian origins of the Irish to create a sense of affiliation with their Spanish hosts. But the 'Irish' are not limited to these ancient inhabitants. As the heading of the manuscript suggests, 'the diversity of Irish' includes the 'English Irish and the mixt Irish'.[80] The twelfth-century Anglo-Norman invaders whom O'Sullivan Beare refers to as 'Those English who at first past over with Dermitius' are 'divided into two sorts'.[81] Some of those who were originally 'English' have now become 'mixt Irish' through intermarriage and acculturation: 'in their language, habits, and customes [they] doe conforme themselves for the most part with the Irish'.[82] Among those whom O'Sullivan Beare considers 'mixt Irish' are 'the Earles of Kildare, Desmond, Clanrickard, Ormond, Viscount Barry, Roche'.[83] Similarly, in the *Compendium*, he comments that the New Irish 'are divided among themselves by a very well known distinction' by which some of them:

> are more favourable to the old Irish . . . than to return to the English of their own sort by origin, having Irish vernacular speech: As long as they prosper in

strength, they live by the laws and the customs of the old Irish and not the rule of the English, and thus these and the old Irish are called Ibernici.[84]

But perhaps even more important than adherence to Irish language and law is the fact that many of these New Irish have fought with the Old Irish 'for the will of the prince and the name of honour, against the will of the Kings of England'.[85] Although some of the New Irish follow English customs, habits, and language, they 'agree with the Irish in the Catholic religion and are opposed to the Heretical errors of the English'. Clearly O'Sullivan Beare can conceive of a 'a non-Gaelic and yet anti-English stance'.[86]

In both 'A Briefe Relation of Ireland' and the *Compendium*, O'Sullivan Beare describes the second group of English origin, the 'English-Irished', who 'did not marry with the ancyent Irish' in terms of their economic and social context: 'all for the most part marchants, and men of trade in all the citties and townes of Ireland'.[87] In the *Compendium* he differentiates another subset of the New Irish, the inhabitants of Fingal, as 'Anglo Irish and colonists'.[88] The crucial factor that separates this group from the other New Irish and Ancient Irish is not their religion, since all three groups are Catholic, and not their English culture, since some of the other New Irish also follow English language and customs, but their political affiliation: 'in war nevertheless they have followed the party of the English'.[89] In 'A Briefe Relation' the crucial distinction is also one of political allegiance, not of genealogy, ethnicity, or even culture:

> This difference of naturall inclinations and law did playnely appeare in the last warres which the Irish, holpen on by his Catholick Maiesty, made against the English; for the ancyent Irish and all of the best and noblest of the mixt Irish held for the King of Spayne and allmost all the English Irish held with the King of England.[90]

O'Sullivan Beare allows for contingencies that show further evidence that political allegiance is not necessarily determined by origin. In 'A Briefe Relation of Ireland', the author admits that

> as man hath free will, by which he may forsake his own inclynation, and follow the contrary, so we have seen sometymes the Englished-Irished hath followed or imitated the Auncient Irish, and aunciente Irish the English, as it fell out with Captain Whyte, who being an Englished Irish, fought against the English for the king of Spayne, and the Earle of Thomand being an ancient Irish did helpe the English.[91]

For O'Sullivan Beare, even political allegiance is a mutable thing, subject to the pressure of historical events. He views the defeat of 1603 as a pivotal moment in Irish history, which further shifted political alliances:

yet after that peace was confirmed betwixt Spayne and England great persecution was used against all these sortes of Irish without exception whetherby Englished Irish now perceive how farre they were overseen in helping the English and resisting the ancient Irish and mixt, and now at this present they repent it very much and are very desirous to get occasion to make satisfaction and to serve the Catholicke king of Spayne.[92]

That 'persecution was used against all these sortes of Irish without exception' has caused disillusionment on the part of the English Irish who now see their collaboration with the English against the Old and New Irish as a fatal political error. Because of the common persecution of all Irish following the Nine Years' War, these English Irish now perceive 'how far they were overseen', or 'betrayed into a fault or blunder' (*OED*), by the English; the English Irish, like the Ancient Irish, now seek alliance with Catholic Spain.

What this means is that the Ancient and mixt Irish are now vying for patronage in the court of Spain. It is for this reason that, while O'Sullivan Beare attempts to present the Irish as united in their grievances against the English, he must still stand by his initial distinctions. A final qualification on the English Irish reinstates their difference from the Ancient and mixt Irish: 'if they were shutt of their persecution and troubles their naturall inclynations carrieth them more towards the English king and nation'.[93] Just as the English Irish have been pushed into alliance with Spain by the recent persecution, so a further change in events could mean a further shift in English Irish political allegiance.

The list of Irish which follows 'A Briefe Relation of Ireland' is divided into 'Auncient', 'mixt', and 'Englished Irish' in order that 'his Matie may know of what Irish he may use in the kings occasions'.[94] In other words, the distinctions are made so that King Philip can know who is who in the Irish exile community, and ultimately which of them can be trusted. One of the purposes of this document appears to be to plead for the greater affinity between the Ancient Irish and the Spanish in order to make sure that the king will prefer the members of this group in choosing whom he will patronize in military and ecclesiastical office, and to whom he will listen for political counsel when it comes to Irish affairs:

> And therefore the Ancient Irish, as these are descended from the Spaniards, desire always to be governed by the kings of Spayne and his successors, and bear greater affection, and love to the Spanish nation, contrarywise greate hatred and enmity to his enemyes and in sharpness of wit and valour in warr are altogether like unto the Spaniard.[95]

Nevertheless, even within his list dividing those 'who have been bred here and speake the Spanish tongue, and serve his Maiestie in severall places of his Dominions'[96] into Ancient, mixt, and Englished Irish, there are exceptions. For example, O'Sullivan Beare identifies the Irish Jesuits, whatever their ethnic origins, as particularly English and prone to side with whomever they perceive to be more powerful:

> the Societie of Jesus . . . yea the very ancient Irish that enter into that same order, become allmost all Englished, conforming themselves to their superior not only in their rules of religion, but allso in their rules of Pollicy and government, and manner of life, procuring to conforme themselves to the tymes, and to winne the willes of the mighty.[97]

Conversely, even among the 'Englished Irish' there are those who ally themselves with the Ancient Irish, such as Father Archer:

> though alltogether Englished, yet is he of the inclynacion and condicion of the ancyent Irish, and much affected to the Spaniards and their King, and their manner of living more then to the auncient Irish whome he followed and ayded in their last warres.[98]

In 'A Breife Relation', O'Sullivan Beare ultimately casts the issue of Irish descent in terms of nobility, the chief characteristics of which are liberality, landed rather than monetary wealth, and military prowess. In contrast to the 'englished Irish' who because they 'neither use such liberality and hospitality as the auncient Irish and mixt' are 'thought . . . [to] have store of coyne gathered', 'the auncient and mixt have more lands and goods, notwithstanding that they have lost farre more then the englished in the persecution, yet are they more powerfull to make soldiers and armies'.[99] O'Sullivan Beare's intelligence document is calculated to present a united front – 'many of all three sorts do excellent services to his Maiestie'.[100] Within this united front, the historian presents an at once politically sophisticated sense of shifting alliances and a traditional Spanish sense of the greater aristocracy of the Ancient Irish, used for the very practical purpose of persuading the Spanish king that they are the most worthy of his patronage.

This concern with Spanish royal patronage and the aristocratic genealogy necessary to attain it figures in O'Sullivan Beare's own experience of exile in Spain. Philip O'Sullivan Beare was the first Irishman to enter into the Spanish order of knighthood, for which he had to be nominated by the king. The candidate for knighthood was subject to the scrutiny of the Council of Knights who required evidence of the nobility of his genealogy and 'the absence of heresy'.[101] After his own knighthood in 1607, Don Philip O'Sullivan Beare is recorded to have sponsored at least seven other of the 200 Irishmen (among these both Old and New Irish) who were admitted to knighthood in Spain. Among those whom he sponsored were his cousin's son Dermot O'Sullivan, who became Conde de Birhaven after the death of his father Donal, and 'later lord in waiting to the King of Spain'.[102] So when Don Philip writes in his intelligence document of 'such as have been bred here and speake the Spanish tongue', he is referring to a sizeable number of exiles for whom aristocratic lineage had the practical purpose of securing their place and livelihood in Spain.

Some, like O'Sullivan Beare, were educated in Spain, and the controversies among the exile Irish community concerning education have some bearing on both his political orientation and his perspective on history. Having been sent out of Ireland in 1602 just after the defeat of Kinsale, he was educated at the College of Santiago de Compostella.[103] Don Philip and eleven of his classmates were expelled from the college in 1613 for supporting Donal, Conde de Birhaven, who opposed the Jesuit takeover of the college. Donal objected to the 'obligation to become priests' that the Jesuits would have required.[104] This obligation to become priests also would have entailed a return to Ireland as missionaries, in the face of the very penal laws from which these nobles had sought refuge in Spain. Patrick Sinnott's complaints against the Franciscan administration of the college included that 'many have gone off to the war' and that the students 'give themselves over to playing the guitar, and to fencing'.[105] Donal's opposition to the Jesuit power-play for the school was not an objection to students entering the priesthood, since he claimed they had voluntarily done so. It seems rather that he wanted to preserve the status of the college as one for Irish nobles who would also have the option of pursuing the life of a warrior.[106] Strangely enough Donal's defence of the school mentions the future historian 'about to be ordained Don Felipe O Sullevan, nephew of the Lord of Berhaven, Master of the Arts and Bachelor of Canon Law'. No evidence of Philip's ordination has been found, but it is known that he entered the Spanish navy. It is notable that in his 'Breife Relation' he, too, complained against the Irish Jesuits, on account of their English sympathies. His criticism of the Jesuits may relate to an earlier controversy from 1602, when Florence Ó Conry organized a student protest against the Jesuit administration of the college. As Helga Hammerstein has pointed out, 'The Franciscans backed the Irish chiefs, the Jesuits, working in the Pale, were critical of the religious motivation of O'Neill's campaign'.[107] Among these same Jesuits, after all, were Father Archer, 'of the inclynacion and condicion of the ancyent Irish', and Patrick Sinnott, O'Sullivan Beare's esteemed teacher, letters from whom and to whom are included in the *Compendium*.[108] The quarrel over the patronage and administration of the college at Compostella appears, nevertheless, to be a quarrel between English Irish and Ancient Irish, between Franciscans and Jesuits, and perhaps even a struggle between the notion of a religious or military role for the Irish in exile.[109] Throughout the *Compendium*, O'Sullivan Beare sees priests and soldiers engaged in the common resistance to English tyranny and heresy. He is also quick to point out the dangers posed by the English affiliations of certain members of the Irish clergy.

The struggle for patronage among factions in the Irish exile community was directly tied to the attempts of the Irish exiles to influence Spanish foreign policy in support of a military solution. In 1621, for example, a letter from Bourdeux by James Tobin informs Lord Carew of:

> a petition delivered to the King of Spain; also of a Prince in this Kingdom who promised to let them have five thousand crowns in arms whensoever they were to go into Ireland; also of some in Ireland that make provision of arms for rebellion.[110]

Four years later, intelligence concerning possible plans for an Irish military expedition had been leaked by 'John Kelly . . . who had been ordered to keep these things secret but had told them to his foster-father in Ireland':

> Being in a room with Tyrconnel's son, Tyrone's sone, and O'Sullivan, he heard them plan that one of them should visit Ireland in disguise to take a view of the country. They had consulted on the landing places and mentioned Killybegs and Broadhaven. The preparations had been proceeding for two years.[111]

This same document also mentions that 'Tyrconnel's son had a commission from the King of Spain to levy 1,500 men, and went last winter with it into the Low Countries'. When Spain started up the war in the Low Countries again in 1621, at least three-quarters of the Irish exiles served in the Army of Flanders.[112] The English attempted 'to sow discord among the divergent elements within the exiled Irish community' by offering Anglo-Irish officers positions in the English army equivalent to those they held in the Irish regiment in the Low Countries.[113] O'Sullivan Beare's fears about the loyalty of the English Irish to the cause of Spain and Ireland were not unfounded. The very Anglo-Irish officers recruited by the English are mentioned in his 'Breife Relation' under the heading 'Englished Irish Seculers': 'Walter Delahyde' and 'Captain Thomas Preston'.[114] The strained diplomatic relations between Spain and England after the attack against Cadiz in 1625 granted further hope to the Irish exiles' plans for a military expedition to Ireland that would be launched by the Irish regiment. Such hopes were ended only by the Anglo-Spanish treaty of 1630.[115]

iv. The Historian as Exile and the History as Tragedy

O'Sullivan Beare underscores the precarious and uncertain position of the Irish exiles in Spain through the allusions to the Roman exile Ovid that frame the *Compendium*. In his address 'to the Catholic reader', O'Sullivan Beare describes how there is 'no leisure for writing', and 'how many calamaties deter our people from the attempt', by quoting Ovid, who had likened his position in exile to that of Socrates, banished by Anytus and the tyranny of the Thirty: 'ille senex, dictus sapiens Apolline, nullum / scribere in hoc casu sustinuisset opus' [That famous old man, called a sage by Apollo, would have had no power in this misfortune to write a single work].[116] Again, at the very conclusion of the *Compendium*, O'Sullivan Beare cites Ovid to express the desolation of the Irish in exile: 'no safe hosting from the foreigner'.[117] From the start the historian displays an awareness of his conscious choice to write for a foreign audience by mentioning his choice of the Latin over the Irish language, 'which was confined to the home circle'. He is also conscious of the power of writing not only to preserve the memory of events but even to create history, as he quotes Ovid at the close of the 'Address to the Reader':

> quis Thebas septemque duces sine carmine nosset
> et quicquid post haec, quidquid et ante fuit?
> di quoque carminibus, si fas est dicere fiunt,
> tantaque maiestas ore canentis eget.[118]

[Who would ever know of Thebes and the seven leaders, were it not for verse, of all that went before and after? Even the gods, if it is right to say this, are created by verse; their mighty majesty needs the bard's voice.]

Like Ovid, O'Sullivan Beare was an exile and a writer aware of his powerful role in creating the memory of history through his writing.

In creating the history that will be remembered he gives a prominent place to the role of his own family in the struggle against England, nowhere more so than in his account of the great march.[119] In recounting the long winter march from Cork to Connacht at the end of the Fifteen Years' War, O'Sullivan Beare inserts his first-person response, making himself the witness to the devastating event that nearly destroyed his entire family:

> They reached Leitrim fort about eleven o'clock being then reduced to 35, of whom 18 were armed, 16 were sutlers, and one was a woman. The others, who were over 1,000 leaving Bear had either perished or had deserted their leader, or lingered on the road through weariness or wounds. Some followed in twos and threes. I am astonished that Dermot O'Sullivan, my father, an old man near 70, and the woman of delicate sex, were able to go through these toils, which youths in the flower of age and height of their strength were unable to endure.[120]

This forced march was necessitated by a letter from O'Sullivan Beare swearing allegiance to and seeking aid from the King of Spain, which was intercepted by the English.[121] Unlike O'Neill and O'Donnell, O'Sullivan Beare was not pardoned by James I. Not only were his lands confiscated but he was not even allowed within forty miles of them.[122] Indeed, as the Count of Caracena wrote to Philip III in 1605, when Donal Cam and his followers were hiding in Galicia, 'he lost everything in defence of the Catholic cause and in the service of your majesty'.[123] It is from this experience of absolute defeat and total allegiance to Spain that O'Sullivan Beare writes his *Compendium*. At the core of his history for a Spanish audience is a narrative to which the author is personally bound.

His allegiance to his family and their role in the struggle against English domination gives his account of exile the cast of a tragedy on an epic scale. When O'Sullivan Beare compares the state of the Irish after the war to that of the Trojans upon their defeat, the tension between the Irish as persecuted exiles and allies of empire is set in relief by literary allusion.[124] Like the Trojans, the Irish are defeated:

> urbs antiqua ruit multos dominata per annos
> plurima perque vias sternatur inertia passim
> corpora perque domos et religiosa deorum
> limina.

> [An ancient city meets its doom;
> Its rule of ages is undone.
> The streets are strewn with silent dead,
> E'en homes, aye God's abodes, are graves.]
> (*Aeneid* II.363–6)

But also like the Trojans, the Irish in their exile will seek refuge in an empire. The *Compendium* is both the history of persecution and the search for a safe haven in a foreign land.

As I have tried to demonstrate, the importance of O'Sullivan Beare's Spanish audience can be sensed in the *Compendium*'s rhetoric, historiography, and construction of a religious-political alliance. The very practical situation of the Irish exiles as competitors for Spanish patronage and for influence upon Spanish policy towards Ireland are crucial to an understanding of O'Sullivan Beare's text. The devastating losses of his family – their suffering in the war and the confiscation of their lands – make him represent his narrative as tragedy. In 1621, when the *Compendium* was published, O'Sullivan Beare could still hope that those who suffered defeat at the hands of the emerging English empire could seek a successful alliance with the empire of Spain.

1999

CUSTOM AND LAW IN THE PHILOSOPHY OF SUÁREZ AND IN THE HISTORIES OF O'SULLIVAN BEARE, CÉITINN, AND Ó CLÉIRIGH

'Custom is king; law is a tyrant', as Giambattista Vico wrote in his *Scienza nuova*. This Vichian proverb expresses the central role of custom in early modern Irish writing about kingdom and colony. Custom constitutes the basis for Irish law and an Irish kingdom; law, when not rooted in local custom, becomes the exercise of tyranny. References to the differences between native inhabitants and colonists in seventeenth-century writing by the Irish intelligentsia show that notions of kingdom and colony are bound up with custom: the foundation of Gaelic rule in custom and the critique of English colonization as the destroyer of custom. Philip O'Sullivan Beare explicitly makes this argument in a political vocabulary that he takes from the Spanish tradition of natural law theory. Indeed, he relies on the most radical Spanish interpreter of natural law theory, Francisco Suárez.[1] O'Sullivan Beare relies on such concepts from the natural law tradition as *dominium* (the natural right of ownership or property) and *indiginae* (indigenous natives or natural inhabitants). In particular, he draws on the Suárezian understanding of *ius gentium* (the law of nations) and the role of *consuetudo* (custom) in establishing the justice of the law. Whether they were readers of natural law theory or not, his contemporaries writing in Irish, Séathrún Céitinn and Mícheál Ó Cléirigh, express the Irish equivalent of such concepts.

Natural law theory from the tradition of the school of Salamanca needs to be investigated as an influence upon – whether direct or indirect – and as a point of comparison for the early modern Irish critique of English rule in Ireland. Anthony Pagden describes the natural law concept of *dominium* as the basis for the early modern Spanish debates about the conquest of the Americas. *Dominium* was interpreted as the natural right of people over 'not only their private property, their goods (*bona*), but also over their actions, their liberty and even . . . their own bodies'. For the sixteenth-century school of Salamanca, working in the tradition of Thomas Aquinas, such natural rights were ordained by God's law. This concept of *dominium* as a natural right also played an important role in the Irish critique of the early modern English conquest of Ireland.[2] Generally, in the élite secular liberal culture of Anglo-America, appeals to natural law in public debate are shunned as a violation of the

124

doctrine of relativism and pragmatic contingency – the never-ending malleability of the individual and the community as social constructs. This contemporary prejudice against natural law theory obscures the role that it played in defending the rights of peoples subject to colonization and slavery. Natural law theory, as interpreted by the school of Salamanca, formed the philosophical foundation of the first major European argument against slavery and the colonization of indigenous peoples by Bartolomé Las Casas.[3] As Las Casas wrote in his *Brevísima relación de la destrucción de las Indias*:

> And those wretches, those Spaniards, blinded by greed, think they have the God-given right to perpetrate all these cruelties and cannot see that the Indians have cause, have abundant causes, to attack them and by force of arms, if they had weapons, to throw them out of their lands, this under all the laws, natural, human, and divine.[4]

In the case of early modern Irish history, such concepts as *imperium* (sovereignty) and *ius naturale* (natural right) found their equivalents in such Irish terms as *flaitheas* (rule, sovereignty), *cumachtae* (power) and *toich* (inherently right) as deployed in Céitinn's and Ó Cléirigh's recording of Irish political customs. Such concepts as *imperium* (sovereignty) and *civitas* (citizenship) made possible O'Sullivan Beare's critique of English colonization. One could argue, 'Isn't the history of such concepts as sovereignty and citizenship part of the "repression and violence" that Dipesh Chakrabarty has called "instrumental in the victory of the modern" in both Europe and the rest of the world?'[5] In the early modern Irish context, before the advent of the nation state but at the beginning of the death of the traditional culture – the language, the laws, the schools – the encounter with such concepts as sovereignty and citizenship was far from mystified. The analysis of sovereignty and citizenship in the writing of the native élites demonstrated the contradictions in the deployment of such terms in the colonial context.

Both the critique of the English colony and the establishment of the Irish kingdom were in a sense acts of cultural translation. For in order to unmask the injustice underneath the disguise of English legal discourse, Philip O'Sullivan Beare in his *Historiae Catholicae Hiberniae Compendium* (Lisbon, 1621) had to resort to a Latin vocabulary that would allow him both to explain what the English claimed they were doing and to judge this by a philosophical standard that would make sense to a European audience. In effect what he achieved was a philosophical translation that Alasdair MacIntyre has claimed was unavailable to both the English and the Irish in the early modern period. According to MacIntyre, there were no common terms in which the English and Irish could debate their competing political claims.[6] Reflecting on the English onslaught empirically, one might argue that this is beside the point. At any rate, in terms of the history of political thought, perhaps MacIntyre did not realize that this conceptual incommensurability had been overcome by an

Irishman writing Latin within a Spanish tradition of natural law. Another long march, this one linguistic and intellectual.

Similarly, the first historians to establish a sense of the Irish kingdom, Séathrún Céitinn and Mícheál Ó Cléirigh and his collaborators (called 'The Four Masters'), engaged in another act of translation: the creation of a national narrative in a modern prose vernacular, the conversion of Irish *senchas* into a version of Renaissance humanist history.[7] As defined in the *Royal Irish Academy Dictionary of the Irish Language*, *senchas* includes 'old tales, ancient history, tradition', especially 'genealogy' and 'traditional law'.[8] As Byrne points out:

> *Senchas* was the traditional lore of Irish culture: topographical (*dindshenchas* – an essential part of the poet's repertoire), legal (the most ambitious attempt to compile an authoritative corpus of law texts was known as the *Senchas Már*, 'the great tradition'), and genealogical.[9]

There is certainly a great deal of genealogy in Céitinn's *Foras Feasa ar Éirinn* (which literally translated means 'The foundations of knowledge about Ireland') and in the Four Masters' *Annála Ríoghachta Éireann* (*Annals of the Kingdom of Ireland*). Even more important for Céitinn's critique of English legal practice is the sense of *senchas* as traditional legal knowledge. Similarly in the work of the Four Masters, the cumulative record of Gaelic custom is a form of *senchas* in this sense of traditional legal knowledge, and the contrast between Gaelic custom and English violation of it acts as an implicit criticism of the excesses of colonial rule.[10] All three histories – the *Compendium* of O'Sullivan Beare, the *Foras Feasa* of Céitinn, and the *Annals* of the Four Masters – were acts of self-conscious historical and cultural definition that later became important for nineteenth-century Irish cultural nationalism. One thinks of the influential translations and editions of these early modern Irish texts: for example Matthew Kelly's edition of O'Sullivan Beare (1850), O'Donovan's magisterial bilingual edition of the Four Masters (1848–51), and O'Mahony's translation of the *Foras Feasa* (1857).[11]

O'Sullivan Beare chose to write in Latin rather than Irish in order to reach a wider European audience. Latin also suited his political goals. Most immediately, he sought to persuade the King of Spain that a war against the King of England's rule in Ireland would be just. The 1621 publication of the *Compendium* can be linked to a whole series of campaigns by the Irish exiles to muster Spanish support for armed intervention in Ireland that continued right up until the English peace treaty with Spain in 1630.[12] If we take O'Sullivan Beare's audience in a wider sense as the intellectual élite of Europe, then Latin also permits him to criticize English political practice in Ireland in terms of a philosophical language that would make sense to legal theorists and theologians, as well as to the political advisors of the King of Spain. O'Sullivan Beare translates his account of English rule in Ireland into the language of the most influential and systematic exponent of the natural law critique of tyranny and the right of the people to revolution: Francisco Suárez. The Jesuit theologian Suárez's radical ideas were well known to Europe's intellectual élites through his 1612 *De Legibus* and 1613 *Defensio Fidei*.[13] This last work met with disapproval from the Roman Curia and a public burning in London ordered by James I. Protected by the King of Spain, Suárez's works were available to O'Sullivan Beare.[14] The Irish exile in Spain was writing his history, published in Lisbon in 1621, at the very same time that Suárez's works were published and having their greatest impact.

One of the chief concepts from Suárez's *De Legibus* that O'Sullivan Beare deploys in order to represent and analyse the relationship between kingdom and colony is *consuetudo,* or custom. Suárez was the first European legal theorist to argue that custom was a source of law, constituted the *ius gentium* in the specific sense of the customary law of the nation, and had the power to abrogate other kinds of law.[15] O'Sullivan Beare's first mention of 'colonists' allows that they could be considered Irish according to their birth; he calls them '*Novi Hiberni*' or 'New Irish' (as opposed to 'Old English'), but he identifies them as English in their customs:

> And among these moreover are those who some time ago began to inhabit Fingall or the English province, that is the part of Ireland closest to England, and they are called colonists and they live according to the laws and customs of the English.[16]

The problem arises when these colonists impose their customs and laws upon the Irish:

> First, they observe the law with incredible care and severity by which they make sure that in Ireland those who derive their origin from the English either force Ireland to be under the sovereignty of the English or, let me speak more to the point, the new Irish produce the magistrates, perform the civil duties; and they carry the votes in the senate which they call parliament.[17]

Another concept that O'Sullivan Beare takes from Suárez is that the power of the state, whether it is a democracy or a monarchy, derives from the people as a community.[18] This notion of sovereignty deriving from the consent of the people along with the natural law theory of citizenship – that people born in their native place have a right to citizenship – help O'Sullivan Beare to explain how English law contradicts natural law:

> the old Irish do not control the government of the commonwealth otherwise than by opposing the government from without; in particular they oppose the government in terms of natural philosophy or the condition of civil justice; they must submit to the opinion of these very rulers that which by the English is called 'denization' and by the Spanish indeed is called 'naturalizacion', to me however is called 'enrolment in citizenship', or donation of civil justice.[19]

In other words, the Irish have been excluded from power in the government, and since they are outside it they must as aliens submit themselves to the requirements of those who have excluded them in order to be considered citizens in their native land. When O'Sullivan Beare translates the process of English law to which the Irish are submitted – denization into naturalization into citizenship – the contradiction and injustice of the law is revealed. He even calls English law a fiction:

> It follows by the fiction of English law that the old Irish are not indigenous but born outside and are considered enemies in their own fatherland. The law of national right and of natural right stands plainly opposed to a situation in which each citizen in his own country is held an alien within alien borders.[20]

This sense of the right of an indigenous people to jurisdiction within the territory of their birth that O'Sullivan Beare invokes here could be compared to the right that Las Casas, arguing from the principles of natural law, had claimed for the Indians:

> Hence every nation, no matter how barbaric, has the right to defend itself against a more civilized one that wants to conquer it and take away its freedom. And, moreover, it can lawfully punish with death the more civilized as savage and cruel aggressor against the law of nature.[21]

O'Sullivan Beare also expresses the notion of an indigenous constitution which bears comparison with Suárez's concept of the consonance of the *ius gentium*, which, as a form of civil law, is human in origin, and natural law, which, as divinely ordained, has universal applicability. According to Suárez, the similarity between the individual customs of nations constitutes an international law by which relations between nations should be regulated. As Reijo Wilenius puts it: 'all the customary rules of law which are common to all or nearly all nations come within *ius gentium*'.[22] For O'Sullivan Beare the constitution is just such a common custom that while human in origin agrees with the natural law of divine origin. He argues: 'by divine providence, all peoples, even the Gentiles and barbarians, defend a firm and immutable constitution'.[23] 'The eternal law' [i.e. the natural law ordained by God], according to Suárez, 'will always coincide with providence'.[24] At the same time that O'Sullivan Beare represents the notion of an indigenous constitution as a natural right, he protests against the imposition of English law as a violation of the ancient Irish constitution. For the concept of the ancient constitution I am indebted to John Pocock's study of the unwritten customary practice of the common law in the tradition of English legal theory.[25] In a Folger seminar on early modern Irish political thought, Pocock asked where the ancient Irish constitution was. It is at least in part in the record of Irish customs as recorded in the histories of O'Sullivan Beare, Céitinn, and Ó Cléirigh.

In criticizing the abuses of the English in Ireland, O'Sullivan Beare defends the customs that make up the ancient Irish constitution. He argues that the English treat citizenship as a right for sale: 'The English kings were granting this right to the Irish either in exchange for money or for rewards collected or conferred upon themselves'.[26] Viewed from the perspective of the rights of native inhabitants to the ownership and use of their land in natural law, the English practice of surrender and regrant, by which the Irish chieftains were granted English titles in exchange for surrendering their Gaelic titles and their land to the English sovereign, becomes, according to O'Sullivan Beare, a form of 'usury' [usura]: 'these contracts are indeed frauds which are celebrated as a fiduciary donation'.[27] Surrender and regrant entails lending with interest not just titles, but also land – in terms of 'ownership or use for profit'.[28] Just as O'Sullivan Beare finds the dominium of the English over Irish land to be a fraud, he also finds that the basis of English rule in Ireland obscures the role of ancient Gaelic custom and disinherits the ancient Irish:

> Thus therefore we might say that the Old Irish were not installed [in power] first by the English kings, and even the new Irish were created magnates by the custom of the Old Irish, and the Old Irish were disinherited by the right of the vote being given in the parliament or in the senate.[29]

Underlying O'Sullivan Beare's notion that the Normans (or 'the New Irish') came to power in Ireland not through the English king, but through their being recognized by Old Irish custom, is the Suárezian concept of power coming from the consent of the community. Following Suárez's notion of custom as the basis of the ius gentium, O'Sullivan Beare argues that Irish custom supercedes English law, and English law invalidates the natural rights of native inhabitants. Again toward the end of his history, He describes the English administration's packing of the 1613 Parliament as the result of not only making colonists citizens but also granting them double representation:

> They give the colonies of the English and Scots, on account of whom we suffer greater want, the name of citizenship and the right of suffrage, and other freedoms; they have transgressed the boundary of laws and of custom, so that out of a single colony they send two administrators to parliament.[30]

Here, the unequal execution of civil law comes into conflict with the stronger precedent of custom as the standard of justice.

Not only do the English colonists in Ireland transgress custom and so make a mockery of both natural and national rights with the fiction of their laws, but the seizure of property and the denial of the ius gentum that their planting and control of the government in Ireland entails makes the English king a tyrant and makes war against him just. O'Sullivan Beare's repeated description of English rule in Ireland as tyranny echoes the account of tyranny in Suárez's writing. Two of the chief causes of a just war, according to

Suárez, are 'denial of the common rights of nations' and 'the seizure by a prince of another's property'.[31] Suárez argues the justice of revolt against tyranny: 'The state as a whole. . . may rise in revolt against such a tyrant; and this uprising would not be a case of sedition in the strict sense' [since] 'the state. . . granted him his power . . . upon these conditions: that he should govern in accord with the public weal and not tyrannically; and that if he did not govern thus, he might be deposed from that position of power'.[32]

In his *Defensio Fidei*, Suárez specifically argues for the deposition of the King of England as a tyrant because he is the sort of tyrant 'who leads his subjects into heresy'.[33] O'Sullivan Beare repeatedly charges the English not only with heresy but also with the persecution of Catholics in Ireland. In his catalogue of persecutions, He includes the exile and torture of priests, the prohibition of Catholic rites, the imposition of attendance at and support for the Protestant church, the oath of allegiance to James I as the head of the church, and the laws passed in parliament against priests and their supporters.[34] The misuses of power that for Suárez constitute tyranny, such as 'oppressing subjects by corruption, plunder, and slaughter', are all part of O'Sullivan Beare's complaint against the English king.[35] Along with political disenfranchisement and confiscation of land, religious persecution is a form of tyranny that demands to be overthrown by war, according to both Suárez and O'Sullivan Beare. O'Sullivan Beare represents the numerous Irish rebellions of the late sixteenth century, culminating in the revolt of Hugh O'Neill, as just wars and the current persecution under James I as an argument for Spanish support for an Irish armed struggle.

O'Sullivan Beare's defence of the Irish nation as a community sharing a common language and customary laws has its source in Irish *senchas*. While Suárez provided O'Sullivan Beare with the theoretical language to explain the significance of Irish custom and its conflict with the law of English colonists in an international context, it is the local Irish tradition recorded by Céitinn and the Four Masters that necessitated this defence in the first place. Whereas O'Sullivan Beare writing in Latin uses the very political lexicon and arguments of Suárez, Céitinn and the Four Masters create a record of Irish custom and tradition, embedded in which is the Suárezian notion of custom as the basis of law. Céitinn and O Cléirigh and his collaborators did not produce as thoroughgoing a critique of English rule in Ireland as O'Sullivan Beare did; however, they follow him in at times referring to this rule as 'tyranny'. At the same time, apparently quite independently of direct influence from Suárez, they suggest that the limited, local, and time-honoured practices of customary law are the basis for just rule.[36]

The contrast between O'Sullivan Beare's politics and those of Céitinn comes to the fore when Céitinn discusses colonists. The word 'coilíneach' crops up as a loan word from English in an Irish translation of how Stanihurst (in Holinshed's *Chronicles*) noted that 'the most lowly of the colonists who dwell in the English province would not give his daughter in marriage to the greatest prince among the Irish'.[37] Céitinn rebuts Stanihurst by citing the many Old Irish who married into the families of the Old English – Kildare, Desmond, Clanricard. Céitinn asks rhetorically, 'which were the more noble, the more honourable, or the more loyal to the crown of England or which were better as securities for preserving Ireland to the crown of England, the colonists of Fingall or the noble earls of the foreigners?'[38] Céitinn is more concerned with the recognition of the aristocratic standing of the Gaels and the cultural effects of colonialism rather than with its economic and political consequences. Whereas O'Sullivan Beare protests against political and religious persecution, Céitinn decries what Luke Gibbons has called cultural 'ethnocide', or indeed what Pier Paolo Pasolini in describing the Americanization of Europe called 'anthropological genocide'. Céitinn rails against Stanihurst's faulting 'the colonists of the English province for that they did not banish Gaelic from the country at the time when they routed the people who were dwelling in the land before them'.[39] Céitinn makes a distinction between a 'pagan conquest' that destroys the people and a 'Christian conquest [that] extinguishes not the language'.[40] He gives the Saxon conquest of the Britons as an example of pagan conquest and the Norman conquest of the Saxons as an example of a Christian conquest. The Normans are analogous to the twelfth-century *Sean-Ghaill* (Old English) as Christian conquerors, who did not destroy the language, and the Saxons are analogous to the sixteenth-century *Nua-Ghaill* (New English) as pagan conquerors, who 'having banished everyone, banished their language with them'.[41] For Céitinn the destruction of the language means the destruction of the people as a nation; the people only exist as a nation if they exist as a living culture with their own language: 'It is not possible to banish the language without banishing the folk whose language it is.'[42]

It is from the point of view of Céitinn's understanding language as the custom that defines the people that we have to understand his defence of Gaelic customs. He defends Irish laws – particularly the customs of tanistry, gavelkind, and kin-cogish – against Sir John Davies's attacks. While Céitinn shows a humanist's awareness of the change of customs in his account of tanistry and gavelkind (as he writes 'though they are not suitable for Ireland now they were necessary at the time they were established'), change is not the only issue here.[43] He notes that not only the Gaels but also the Galls still keep up the practice of kin-cogish (paying an honour price for loss caused to a friend or relative).[44] And when it comes to the patronage of the *ollúna* (bardic poets), Céitinn hypothesizes that the French custom of holding learned men immune in times of war stems from the practice the Irish brought with them when they travelled to the west of Europe.[45] So, far from presenting Irish custom as merely a thing of the past, Céitinn presents it as part of an on-going and traditional *ius gentium* that has furthered the arts and learning not only in Ireland but throughout Europe. Although the concepts of citizenship and sovereignty are not part of his vocabulary, he calls Ireland 'a kingdom apart, like

a little world'[46] and so suggests that the ancient kingdom of Ireland is a separate entity – separate from England. This is not only because of the use of
the word 'ríoghacht' or kingdom, which Brendan Bradshaw has noted was
translated into Irish in this period from the Latin humanist *regnum*.[47] Céitinn
repeatedly stresses the integrity of Irish culture: 'that the nobles and the
learned who were there long ago arranged to have jurisprudence, medicine,
poetry, and music established in Ireland with appropriate regulations'.[48] In
Foras Feasa, Ireland is a separate civil society in no need of reformation –
indeed not even in need of reformation by the Normans at the time of Henry
II, as Céitinn argues in his defence of the state of religion and morality before
the Normans. In fact, he explains the Gaelic resistance to the Norman Conquest as a reaction to tyranny and injustice:

> It is plain from the facts we have stated above [here he is referring to spoliation
> and sacrilege of termon lands] that it was owing to tyranny and wrong and the
> want of fulfilling their own laws on the part of the Norman leaders of Ireland
> that there was so much resistance on the part of the Gaels to the Norman
> yoke.[49]

Although both Céitinn and the Four Masters accept the fact of English rule in
Ireland – perhaps even more so in the case of the Four Masters (something
the editor O'Donovan ascribes to O'Gara's patronage[50]) there is imbedded in
both narratives the history of Ireland as a kingdom, with the sovereignty of
that kingdom clearly located in the tradition of Irish custom. Hence, the Four
Masters call their history *Annala Ríghiochta*, or 'Annals of the kingdom'.

Another term associated with European humanist political thought,
'atharda', seems to fluctuate in meaning between 'patria' or 'fatherland' and a
more localized sense of 'patrimony'.[51] The 'coilínighe' or colonists of the Foras
Feasa do not appear in the Annals. Instead the words for English invaders
include 'danar' (literally 'Danes', figuratively barbarians) and 'ainfinne' (hostile or foreign tribe). The opposition between 'atharda' [*patria*] and 'ainfinne'
[foreign tribe] comes up in the description of the battle of the Yellow Ford.
The Gaelic leaders spur their men into combat by telling them 'that it was
easier to defend their patrimony against this foreign people [now] than to take
the patrimony of others by force, after having been expelled from their own
native country'.[52] O'Donovan explains this passage as referring to the Irish
custom of going off to take another territory by force after having been
expelled from their own native territory. While the particular and local meaning of 'atharda' may be operative here, it is interesting to note that 'atharda' is
set in opposition to 'ainfinne', suggesting a larger sense of the Irish patria versus the hostile English foreigner. The more local word 'dúthaigh' is used in the
phrase 'dúthaigh neich ele' to refer to 'the patrimony of another', while the
second instance of the warriors' own native territory that they are defending,
'ttír ndílis', could be translated as 'native land'.

In other instances 'atharda' occurs in the explanation of native Irish political arrangements. For instance, in the description of Owny O'More at the time of his death:

> He was by right the sole heir of his territory [of Leix] and had wrested the control of his patrimony, by the prowess of his hand and the resoluteness of his heart, from the hands of foreigners and adventurers, who had its fee-simple possession passing into a prescribed right for some time before, and until he brought it under his own sway and jurisdiction, and under the custody of his stewards and bonnaghts, according to the Irish usage.[53]

Again his local territory is referred to as 'dúthaigh', but when it is set in opposition to the foreigners and aliens ['danar agus deoradh'], the sense of possession of and authority over the patria is conveyed by 'urlámhas a atharda' [control of his patrimony].[54] Furthermore, he has brought this fatherland under his sovereignty or jurisdiction [chumachtiobh] according to Gaelic custom [do réir gnáthaighe gaoidheal], suggesting a restoration of right through native usage.

Another example of the sense of what is customary according to Gaelic custom determining what is right occurs in the description of the death of O'Donnell:

> a lord who had not coveted to possess himself of the illegal or excessive property of any other, except such as had been hereditary in his ancestors from a remote period.[55]

The word 'toich', translated by O'Donovan as hereditary, also has, according to the *Royal Irish Academy Dictionary of the Irish Language,* the meanings of 'natural hereditary right' or 'propriety', which comes very close to the natural law concept of *dominium*. O'Donnell's sense of what was properly his is neither 'illegal or excessive' but determined by a sense of what was by tradition deemed to be his hereditary right.

In contrast to this sense of O'Donnell's recognizing the proper limits of his hereditary *dominium*, the description of English law in the account of the first rescue of Hugh O'Donnell from prison indicates a sense of the repressive nature of martial law. His own friends returned him to prison because of their 'fear of the English government'.[56] O'Donovan translates the phrase 'umhan smacht chána na ngall' as 'fear of the law of the English', but 'smacht chána' could be even more literally translated as 'fear of penalty of the punishment of the English'. As in O'Sullivan Beare's *Compendium*, law as a coercive and repressive measure is associated with the English, whereas Irish authority is located in what is customary.

If Céitinn and Ó Cléirigh did not know Suárez's work, their portrayal of the Irish community as one rooted in a common language and customary laws is certainly compatible with the Spanish philosopher's notion of the *ius gentium.* O'Sullivan Beare elaborated the theoretical significance of this Irish tradition of customary law in the terms of an international theory of natural law. His deployment of natural law was a means of influencing the imperial power of Spain to side with the justice of the Irish kingdom. With Céitinn and Ó Cléirigh, O'Sullivan Beare sought to differentiate the kingdom of Irish custom from the tyranny of English colonial law.

2000

BREVE RELACION DE LA PRESENTE PERSECUCION DE IRLANDA AND THE IRISH COLLEGE AT SEVILLE

The anonymous author of *Breve relacion de la presente persecucion de Irlanda* proclaims his purpose for writing 'as much for relief of the said Catholics who clamour for assistance . . . as for the edification and gratification of the rest'.[1] This text was meant to raise money for the Irish students who had come to Spain to study for the priesthood at 'this our Irish College of the Immaculate Conception of the Virgin Mother of God, at Seville', where the author wrote his preface of May 28, 1619. In supporting these young men who had 'voluntarily exiled themselves for God', patrons of the college would be granting 'relief' to 'the Catholics of the kingdom of Ireland . . . suffering from foreign heretics'. The text was also directed toward those Irish clergymen who laboured under what were at times extremely difficult conditions 'producing good workers for the defence of the Catholic faith in that kingdom'. Written in Spanish (although of a peculiarly non-native variety) for patrons amongst local nobles and fishermen as well as merchants, soldiers, and priests in the exiled Irish community, the text presents Irish history and politics from a Catholic European perspective, as well as a national one. This perspective takes in a sense of the long and distinguished history of the Irish in Europe as well as the immediate and urgent crisis of the Catholics in Ireland. The brief account contained in the forty-nine pages of this pamphlet relies on medieval and Renaissance scholarly European sources on Irish history as well as the most recent eyewitness reports of the current situation in Ireland.

Uniting the college's patrons and the priests they supported was a sense of a shared past as well as a common present enemy. What emerges in the text is a sense of the nation forged through a common culture, and an emerging nationalism pressured into existence through the defence of that culture when under attack. As Adrian Hastings has argued in *The Construction of Nationhood*, religion is a crucial constituent of national culture in the middle ages.[2] While he acknowledges the existence of an Irish nation in the seventeenth century, precisely because of the defence of the culture from an aggressive English nationalism, he questions the existence of Irish nationalism, because of the lack of a nation state.[3] The Irish sense that their culture – religious, linguistic, and economic – was under assault from expanding English Protestant nationalism necessitated a strategy for cultural survival. To the extent that this text creates a sense of a past worth remembering and a people whose culture

– not just religious but also political and economic – is under threat, the *Breve relacion* is part of this strategy for survival. The text has a twofold strategy: to achieve unity and cooperation among the exile community in Spain in order to found institutions that would help the exiles survive and prosper there, and to direct the resources of the exiles to alleviate the plight of those suffering persecution in Ireland. This text records what could be called emerging nationalist strategies on the part of exiles in the first great Irish diaspora in Europe.

The title page of *Breve relacion de la presente persecucion de Irlanda* bears a dedication to 'Don Felix de Guzman, Archdeacon, and Canon of the Holy Church of Seville, High Chaplain of Kings, and Commissioner of the Holy Crusade' along with his coat of arms. Although the secondary literature on the Irish at Seville makes no mention of this *Breve relacion*, an early eighteenth-century manuscript history refers to the text, its author, and the circumstances under which it came to be published.[4] The manuscript history, entitled 'Breve Historia de el Origen, y Progressos de el Coll. De los Irlandeses de Sevilla', relates how 'to move the piety of the Faithful in this same year of 1619 Father Conway printed a Relacion in which he explained the state of affairs of the Faith in Ireland, and the necessity for this Seminary to have a College of grammar students'.[5] Just below this account of the publication of the 'Relacion', the margin announces the next stage of the narrative: 'Donacion de S Don Felix de Guzman', the date of which is given in the text as '11 de Octobre de 1619'. While there are repeated references in the *Breve relacion* to de Guzman's generosity – 'such exemplary liberality as that which Your Grace . . . is employing more and more each day with this Irish College of ours', and an 'honorary letter' from the king 'encouraging you to continue with this business of such great service and honour'[6] – it would appear that this book was not just dedicated to him in thanks for his past gifts to the college but actually calculated to inspire him to make yet another donation. The manuscript history informs us that in October 1619, just after the publication of this text, de Guzman gave 'four thousand ducados in principal' and 'two hundred ducados per year'.

If de Guzman was the primary patron at whom the text was aimed, there were many others. In 1619 when the Jesuits took over the college, Don Geronimo de Medina Farragut, who had already been hosting students for some time, then gave his house to the college.[7] When Father Richard Conway became the first Jesuit rector of the college in August 1619, he found the place in a miserable state, apparently 'robbed' by the former lay administrators of all its furniture and books, and with not enough food to last even for a month.[8] Directly following the account of the poverty of the college, the manuscript history mentions a 'relation drawn up by Father Conway' which 'brought the institution under the notice of people of quality'.[9] This would appear to be yet another reference to the *Breve relacion*. The manuscript history goes on to acknowledge the other patrons of the college. Among these were the Irish soldiers to whom the priests 'administered the sacraments, corrected abuses, and suppressed enmities'.[10] They volunteered part of their pay to support students at the college. Irish merchants of Cadiz and Seville also contributed to the college out of the profits that they made from exporting wine to the British Isles. Father Richard Conway asked the Pope to grant the fishermen of Seville the right to fish on six festival Sundays in order to sell their catch in support of the college, a request which Paul V granted in an indult of September 1619.[11]

The manuscript history for the early years of the college and the *Breve relacion* are written with similar ends. Both stress the material need of the college and both relate the spiritual worth and trials of its students. This similarity may be accounted for in part by the common authorship of the two texts. 'Origin, Progress and State of the Irish Seminary of Seville of the Pure Conception of the Mother of God' is a text of four folios (2v–6r) contained within the manuscript history, which tells us that it was at least edited by Richard Conway, who, I would argue, also wrote the *Breve relacion*.[12] These four folios of the manuscript history relate how one Theobald Stapleton of Tipperary, otherwise called Gall Dubh, came to Seville from Lisbon where he was a student. He approached the Duke of Braganza with the intention of 'founding a seminary of his Nation in Seville'. With the Duke's support and letters to the Archbishop of Seville, Stapleton set out to found the Irish College. But despite their approval for the founding of the college, the Irish were poor, and Stapleton had to struggle to keep it going. So poor was the college that he was reduced to begging from door to door to support the students. At one point three soldiers conspired to murder him. They subsequently died. Others beat him; 'recovering his health and recognizing the work of the devil in this, he gathered new strength to prosecute his good intentions'.[13] The reason for his founding the new college was his 'desire of increasing the number of ecclesiastics in his home country'. These, too, would be faced with hardships.

While the students originally studied grammar, three years of philosophy, and four of theology at St Hermenigild's, the English Jesuit seminary in Seville founded by Father Persons in 1586, the Irish wanted their own college.[14] The manuscript history reflects this strong sense of a separate nation. Most important in this sense of national identity was the commitment of the students, embodied in an oath that they took before entering the college that bound them to return to the mission in Ireland.[15] For example, we are told how James Carney, a teacher whom Stapleton brought from Salamanca to the students at Seville, 'did them great service for a considerable time until he determined on going to Ireland to comply with his obligation and procure the salvation of his fellow-countrymen'.[16]

Securing patronage in high places was clearly not the only purpose of the *Breve relacion de la present persecucion de Irlanda*, since that could have just as effectively been accomplished through a letter to Don Felix de Guzman. As the role of patronage recorded in the manuscript history shows, the text was most likely also intended for a larger audience of Spanish-speaking Irishmen in Spain – including soldiers and merchants. Indeed, the audience extended beyond Spain to the Low Countries and Rome, and included, for example, Luke Wadding, who had a copy of the book in his library at St Isidore's in Rome.[17] He was given this book by Patrick Comerford, O.S.A. (later bishop of Waterford and Lismore 1629–52), whose name is inscribed on the title page. The first half of the text focuses on the ecclesiastical history of Ireland, a topic that would have drawn the attention of such learned clerics as Wadding and Comerford. The second half focuses on the present persecution of Ireland as reported through contemporary documents that would have been of burning interest to all those in the exile community.

The whole first half of the text is devoted to 'the happy state of the king-dom of Ireland . . . in times past in order to compare it with the so calamitous present'.[18] History is important here in so far as it has a bearing on the present. In support of his characterization of Ireland as a learned culture and the Irish as a civilized people, the author draws on the 'testimony of many serious authors both ancient and modern, whose authority, without attributing anything solely to our own, will be the foundation and proof of whatever we say here'.[19] Among over two dozen authors cited are the classical Tacitus, Ptolemy, and Strabo. There are also medieval and Renaissance authors from England (Bede, Giraldus Cambrensis, Camden) and Scotland (Hector Boece). Among Irish texts cited are Richard Stanihurst's *De Rebus in Hibernia Gestis* (Antwerp, 1584), Henry Fitzsimon's *Britanomachia* (Douai, 1614), a Latin controversial work against Protestant theologians, and *Catalogus Praecipuorum Sanctorum Iberniae* (Douai, 1615), a calendar of Irish saints. Such medieval Spanish writers as Isidore of Seville (7th century) and Johan Gil de Camora (13th century) also appear in the marginal notes. A reference to the late antique Spanish historian Flavio Dextro's *Omniomodo historia* (c. 430) as well as a late sixteenth-century commentary on it by the Jesuit Geronimo Roman de la Higuera shows that the author of the *Breve relacion* kept abreast of the latest philological discoveries and controversies.[20] Both Spanish authors are brought in to testify on behalf of the Irish descent from the Spanish and the preaching of St James to the 'Spaniards there in Ireland'.[21] A still authoritative and reliable source because of the wealth of archival research behind it, is the *Cronica General de la Orden de San Benito* (1609–20) by Fray Antonio de Yepes, the great Spanish writer and Benedictine Renaissance humanist historian.[22] The author of the *Breve relacion* refers to Fray Antonio de Yepes's work as a source for the Irish founding of monasteries such as St Gall in Helvetia, the Luxonian in France, Bobbio in Italy, and St Gisleno in Flanders, and contributions to such universities as those of Paris and Pavia.[23]

The most frequently and extensively quoted author in the *Breve relacion*'s defence of Irish history and culture is Paolo Giovio.[24] He was a bishop, a prolific correspondent, a humanist of broad learning, and a wry social commentator who knew almost everyone of power and influence in six-teenth-century Italy. The most recent biography of Giovio maintains that he was also a conscientious, independent-minded historian.[25] Giovio had his *Descriptio Britanniae, Scotiae, Hyberniae, et Orchadum* published in Venice in 1548. The text includes an introductory essay addressed to Cardinal Alessandro Farnese, and the text as a whole is dedicated to Pope Paul III. Giovio describes the Irish as 'ignorant of luxury' [*gens ignara lux*], as well as 'uncorrupted' [*incorrupta*].[26] But what is most interesting is his distinction between '*sylvestres*' and '*barbari*'. The Irish, he points out, are '*sylvestres*', a rural or pastoral people, rather than '*barbari*', barbarians, and

> since they are in no way entirely subservient either to their Scottish allies or English enemies, either in customs or actions; rather they are recalled to equa-nimity and greatness of spirit; since they themselves are remarkable in Hibern-ian simplicity, & in a certain Roman gravity, in proven moral worth, & on account of this they lead a blameless life, & they disdain the luxury and allure-ments of foreigners.[27]

In fact, Giovio's praise of the Irish calls to mind the portrayal of the virtuous country people of Italian Renaissance pastorals who, far from being barbaric, are the standard of virtue against which the decadent city folk must be judged. What for New English authors is a mark of incivility for Giovio is a mark of 'Hibernian simplicity' [*Hibernica simplicitate*] and 'Roman gravity' [*Romana gravitate*]. Irish dress, particularly the mantle, so roundly vilified by the New English, is compared by Giovio to the Roman toga, which was a sym-bol of Roman citizenship.[28] Giovio's comparison of the mantle to the toga fuses an image of the idyllic pastoral *sylvestri* with the Roman citizen in the time of peace. His magnification of Irish virtue is a refreshing contrast to its disparagement by the New English, whom Geoffrey Keating compared to the dung beetle, since their critiques sought to stigmatize and pathologize the Irish and their culture.

The anonymous author of *Breve relacion* has his own explanation for such New English propaganda. This trenchant passage from the conclusion of the section on Spanish historiography on Ireland deserves quotation in full:

> it is easy to see what credit is deserved by those who either through ignorance or envy write otherwise [that is otherwise than these Spanish authors] imput-ing a lack of civility to the Irish holding on so tenaciously to their Catholic, salutary, and ancient customs, and shielding themselves to such a degree against the profane novelties, errors and vices and Machiavellian or Calvinistic policies that such writers would like to see introduced.[29]

The connection between the terms Machiavellian and Calvinistic here recalls Brendan Bradshaw's explanation of Spenser's notion of justice as influenced by Calvinist 'coercion as an instrument of social reform'.[30] In the *Breve relacion*, 'policia' refers both to the deficiency in civility that the English have charged the Irish with and the reform policy that the English have pursued in Ireland. The policies that the author decries – forced religious conformity, over-representation of the Protestants in Parliament, and the debarrment of Catholics from civil office – are examples of what Brendan Bradshaw has associated with English reform as social coercion.

The whole second half of the text is taken up with the documentation of the persecution of the Catholics in Ireland. In providing an eyewitness account, the text resembles Bartolomé de las Casas's *Brevíssima relación,* which had reported the torture and massacres of the Indians by the Spanish conquistadores. A *relacion* is a report. A forthcoming edition of Las Casas's famous report by José Miguel Martinez-Torrejón will show that Las Casas's report is far from rhetorical exaggeration and is founded on documentary evidence. Similarly, the author of *Breve relacion de la presente persecucion de Irlanda* provides documentary evidence. This evidence includes: 1) a letter from Ireland; 2) a copy of an edict against ecclesiastics; 3) a letter from the king forbidding recusants from holding office; 4) a copy of an edict ordering the removal of Catholics from the plantation of Ulster. These documents were then compiled by someone from the college at Seville – as I have argued, very likely the first Jesuit rector of the college, Richard Conway. He gave these documents a narrative frame, and a trenchant concluding analysis.

The first piece of evidence is in the form of a testimonial letter, addressed to the Provincial of the Jesuits in Portugal, Antonio Mascarennas, written from Ireland on 31 October 1618 by one 'N. N.' While it is perfectly possible that these initials may simply stand for *Nemo Nemo,* I think this may well be a letter by the Irish Jesuit Nicholas Nugent, as Ignatius Fennessy has suggested.[31] Nugent, who had been in the seminary in Evora, Portugal, was assigned to Dublin some time around 1615, where he was imprisoned under the harsh laws against ecclesiastics and those who protected them. He is described in the *Calendar of State Papers* as having been harboured by Incequyn.[32] As a result of 'receiving and relieving Jesuits' Incequyn was called before the King's Court of Castle Chamber, which fined him 500 pounds and committed him to the Castle of Dublin. Allison and Rogers suggest that the author of the letter was Patrick Comerford, O.S.A., whose name is inscribed on the flyleaf of Luke Wadding's copy.[33] Comerford's association with Waterford, where he later became bishop, may tie him to the letter, which makes particular mention of the political troubles of recusants there. Whoever wrote the letter from Ireland may have provided copies of the three documents that follow it in the text of the *Breve relacion* – two edicts and a letter from the King of England.

The letter from Ireland[34] to the Provincial of the Jesuits in Portugal begins with scrutiny of the conditions for the papal bull of Adrian IV granting Ireland to English rule. Since these conditions, requiring both the reform and maintenance of the church, have not only not been met but have been positively controverted by the Reformation, the bull is found null and void. The letter proceeds to tell of the means by which the 1613 parliament was packed with Protestants: four new municipal towns were created and each of these was given two votes. The Irish Catholics protested this both in the parliament and in the presence of the king, but to no avail. Their protests were only met with further disenfranchisement: the seizure of one-seventh of all the goods and the confiscation of the lands of O'Neill, O'Donnell, and McGuire, all turned into colonies of foreign heretics. Whereas in the reign of Elizabeth and at the beginning of James's reign, the English had not strictly enforced the laws against recusants in Ireland, now they execute each one with 'rigour and excess'.[35] Recusants who are elected to office and refuse to take the oath of supremacy are 'condemned to prison and harsh financial penalties, and not he alone, but also those who voted for him are punished with the same penalties for giving their vote to a Catholic man'. The result is that whole towns lose their liberties: 'if, finally, the citizens do not want to elect some heretic who will take the stated oath, then the city loses all its privileges and immunities for the same cause, as just recently happened to the very ancient and Catholic city of Waterford for not having anyone to be elected governor of it who was not Catholic'.[36] The State Papers record the trials of Waterford, where the recusant citizens were punished with 'forfeiture of their liberties'.[37]

In addition to confiscation of land and of political disenfranchisement, the letter complains of the laws barring Catholics from inheritance unless they take the 'stated impious oath of the king's ecclesiastical primate'. The strictures against recusants also include a new form of penalty – 'wishing in this to imitate the style of the holy canon law' – enforced through excommunication:

> By virtue of this they, the pseudo-bishops, et al., seize and detain them in prison until they are ready to agree with them; or at least they will always be forced to go about in hiding, fleeing from them and their ministers. And while this excommunication lasts the Catholic is not able to exercise his trade or office nor even less is he permitted to avail himself of any favour of the laws, to demand or to defend the fairness of his cause against anyone, nor to cover his debts even though he can be summoned and harassed by all. And, finally, having to be redeemed and reconciled with them to pardon him will cost the Catholic a great sum of money, if he does not lose everything.[38]

The author notes that some sixty Catholic gentlemen, sons of the principal lords, are currently 'litigating against this point'.

The letter concludes with a description of the terror unleashed by the edict of October 1617 punishing both priests and those who harbour them. Half of the huge fines on these recusants are given to their accusers. The majority of the people are without priests to minister to their needs, and those wealthy recusants who risk protecting priests in their houses dare not allow large numbers to attend their masses for fear of informers. Even those who comply with the heretics are treated badly. Those who comply 'either in order to collect their patrimonies or to achieve the honours to which they pretend . . . without intending to persevere in it' are compelled to remain Protestants 'on pain of losing all their lands and goods'.

The second piece of evidence provided is a complete copy of this edict against priests and their supporters, the disastrous effects of which had been described at the end of the letter from Ireland. This edict 'by order of the King of England, his Viceroy in Ireland published against the Ecclesiastics and Catholics in the year 1617 and returned to proclaim again in 1618'[39] corresponds to the edict of 13 October 1617, described in the *Bibliography of Proclamations of the Tudor and Stuart Sovereigns* as 'enforcing the proclamation against popish bishops' and citing 'former proclamations banishing all Papist ecclesiastics within 10 days'.[40] Yet another piece of evidence is 'a copy of the letter written by the King of England to his Viceroy in Ireland harshly commanding that the Irish Catholics be deposed from their Offices and the Cities and Towns deprived of their ancient Privileges, for not being willing to follow the Anglican sect, refusing the impious oath of ecclesiastical Primacy of the King'.[41] The author's commentary on this letter also describes how the elected officials of Waterford refused to take the oath of supremacy, for which the city was deprived of its 'ancient privileges and of being a city'.[42]

The fourth and final document provided is an edict for the confiscation of land from the Catholics of Ulster. Described in the *Breve relacion* as 'A New Edict of the Viceroy of Ireland, by special order of the King of England, commanding that all of the natives depart the Province of Ulster in Ireland and leave it solely for the foreign heretics, English and Scots, dated the first of October 1618', this text corresponds in all its details to the edict of the same date described in *Proclamations of the Tudor and Stuart Sovereigns*: 'The British undertakers are bound by the terms of their letters patent not to plant a mixed plantation of Irish and English, but only of English and inland Scots. As there are a large number of Irish who still reside upon the lands given to planters, His Majesty commands that before this 1st of May next ensuing they shall remove with all their belongings.'[43] The author's analysis of the motivation for this legislation zeroes in not only on the greed for land but on the competition for survival as a nation:

> The inhumanity and insolence of these heretics was able to come to such as this, to plan a thing never ever seen nor heard of among Christians, despite the enemies there may have been among themselves, but it was [as if] they were among infidels and unjust usurpers of our lands, much less than among legitimate natives and vassals, submissive and peaceful, from whom, openly and tyrannically, they want to make off with so much land and estates, to deprive the natives of them, who have possessed them for more than three thousand years, and to little by little banish everyone from all of Ireland in order to extend their sect and nation, introducing them in place of the Catholic nation and religion, which they plan to completely extinguish by this approach.[44]

This is an account not only of religious persecution but also of an attempt to destroy an entire culture – indeed an entire people. Here the author emphasizes the revolutionary sectarianism that the reformation brought to bear on Ireland. Calvinism was a doctrine based on an election that was nearly racist in its exclusivity and permitted its adherents to employ ruthless tactics of violent exclusion and dispossession that were unfettered by any common Christian identity or standard of justice. The convertible identification of the sect and nation in the construction of the Ulster plantation is ironically a source for the role of religious confession in the Irish nationalist tradition, for which that tradition has often been vilified. It is precisely this sense of a culture under attack, described here in the analysis of the consequences of the Ulster plantation in the *Breve relacion*, that Adrian Hastings has pointed to as the source of the seventeenth-century Irish sense of the nation.

The detailed economic and political analysis in the final 'summary of the persecutions against the Catholics'[45] gives the lie to Joep Leerssen's assertion that the early modern Catholic response to English colonization was articulated merely in terms of religion. If this text has something to do with Counter-Reformation ideology, it has as much to do with resource acquisition and national survival. The argument against the impoverishment of the natives through control of capital by the metropolitan centre that is the cornerstone of any post-colonial economic critique is made forcefully here. Complaints against English rule in the *Breve relacion* include the monopolization of trade and the prohibition against trade with other kingdoms except England. As a specific example of this, the author points to Sir George Carew:

> advocating for and reserving for foreigners almost all of the principal commerce of the kingdom, as Sir George Carew did more than others, to the extent that he was able to send ahead of himself to England the sum of 50 thousand pounds silver, which amounts to 200 thousand pieces, in addition to the great sums that he dispatched by other means; prohibiting Catholic merchants so that without his licence they would be unable to contract with other kingdoms except England; imposing new and heavy customs fees on them each time they leave and return from abroad.[46]

The author's critique of the English devaluation of Irish currency also lends weight to this as an economic analysis.[47] And when it comes to cultural matters, he sees the clear intersection between cultural practice and material domination. He outlines how the institutions of English law were used in order to dispossess people of their property, and how the printing press only allowed for the dissemination of Protestant catechisms and bibles.[48] He also points out that people were forced to pay for the rebuilding of churches that in other times the English had destroyed.[49] The need for the seminaries in Spain is made clear in his description of how Catholics were prohibited from reading and teaching in public. And the very risks that those who came to the

Irish colleges on the Continent were taking are brought home to the audience when he relates how parents were forbidden to send their children to study abroad unless it be in England, and that those children who remained in seminaries in Catholic lands were declared 'traitors'.[50]

This is a cultural war: 'such battle do these seminaries do with them that by means of the many good individuals who are brought up in them in letters and virtue, they have been the principal means of preserving this kingdom in the Catholic faith'.[51] On a similarly militant note, the author commends the 'invincible squadrons' (and here the militancy of the Jesuits is everywhere in the military resonance of the language) and 'most faithful guards' who will be brought up in these Irish seminaries and who will 'complete our liberation from this our hard pressed siege in which we are held by the foreign heretics, enemies of God and of your homeland'.[52] In a sense that homeland was a Catholic European homeland shared by Spanish patrons, Irish merchants, soldiers, and clerics in Spain, as well as persecuted Catholics back in Ireland. But even more, this is a national homeland from which those Irish émigrés in Spain were exiled and which they had to work hard to support – whether through their religious vocation, financial assistance, or the cultural work of writing history and spreading the news of conditions in Ireland, as the author of the *Breve relacion* did. The text both develops strategies for national survival and documents the conditions that necessitated these strategies in the development of a defensive nationalism, which could be compared to contemporary defensive nationalisms such as that of the Palestinians. *Breve relacion de la presente persecucion de Irlanda* was intended for a general audience for what I might like to call an educated Irish public in exile. It is a text that shows little or no divide between the general and the learned reader. Indeed we might take it as a kind of model for current history, which should be urgent and topical rather than merely antiquarian and academic in order to appeal to that wider public who might want to understand the history of the Irish in Europe.

NOTES

Introduction

1. See Stanihurst, 'A Treatise Conteining A Plaine and Perfect Description of Ireland', in *Holinshed's Chronicles of England, Scotland, and Ireland*, 6 vols. (New York, 1976), 6, p. 69; Sir John Davies, 'A Discovery of the True Causes Why Ireland Was Never Entirely Subdued', in *Ireland under Elizabeth and James the First*, ed. Henry Morley (London, 1890), p. 297. The classical source for the image of Circe's cup is Ovid, *Metamorphoses* XIV, 250–311.

2. *Dánta do chum Aonghus Fionn Ó Dalaigh*, ed. and trans. Rev. L. McKenna, S.J. (Dublin and London: Maunsel and Company, 1919), pp. 73, 75.

3. T. F. O'Rahilly, 'On the origin of the names *Érainn* and *Ériu*', *Ériu* xiv (1946), p. 19, where he cites the image of Ireland as a harlot in poems by Keating and Ó Rathile. See *Dánta Amhráin is Caointe Seathrúin Céitinn* (Dublin, 1900), ll. 1373–6; 1380–96; 'Créachta crích Fódla', in *The Poems of Egan O'Rahilly*, ed. Patrick S. Dinneen, Irish Texts Society III (London, 1900), pp. 2–5; R. A. Breatnach, 'The Lady and the King', *Studies* 42 (1953), pp. 321–36.

4. See T. F. O'Rahilly, 'On the origin of the names *Érainn* and *Ériu*', pp. 14–21; R. A. Breatnach, 'The Lady and the King', pp. 321–36; and Máire Herbert, 'Goddess and King: the Sacred Marriage in Early Ireland', in L. O. Fradenburg (ed.), *Women and Sovereignty* (Edinburgh, 1992), pp. 264–75.

5. T. F. O'Rahilly, 'On the origin of the names *Érainn* and *Ériu*', p. 14.

6. See Brendan Bradshaw, 'Robe and Sword in the Conquest of Ireland', in *Law and Government under the Tudors*, ed. Claire Cross et al. (Cambridge, 1988); and 'Edmund Spenser on Justice and Mercy', in *The Writer as Witness: Literature as Historical Evidence,* ed. Tom Dunne (Cork: Cork University Press, 1987).

7. Andrew Hadfield, *Spenser's Irish Experience: Wilde Fruit and Savage Soyl* (Oxford: Clarendon Press, 1997); Willy Maley, *Salvaging Spenser: Colonialism, Culture, and Identity* (New York: St Martin's Press, 1997). On Spenser's misogyny, see Sheila Cavanagh, *Wanton Eyes and Chaste Desires: Female Sexuality in the 'Faerie Queene'* (Bloomington: Indiana University Press, 1994); and for a contrasting view of Spenser as a proto-feminist, see Lauren Silbermann, *Erotic Knowledge in Books III and IV of the 'Faerie Queene'* (Berkeley: University of California Press, 1995).

8. Nicholas Canny, 'Edmund Spenser and the Development of an Anglo-Irish Identity', *Yearbook of English Studies* 13 (1983), pp. 1–19.

9. On the limits of Spenser's knowledge of Irish, and that of the New English generally, see Pat Palmer, 'The Grafted Tongue: Linguistic Colonisation and the Native Response in Sixteenth-Century Ireland', D.Phil. dissertation, Oxford University, 1998, forthcoming from Cambridge University Press.

10. Mícheál Mac Craith, 'Gaelic Courtly Love Poetry: A Window on the Renaissance', in *Celtic Languages and Celtic Peoples: Proceedings of the Second North American Congress of Celtic Studies* (Halifax, Nova Scotia, 1989), and *Lorg Na hIasachta Ar Na Dánta Grá* (Baile Átha Cliath: An Clóchomhar, 1989), pp. 100–14.

11.   David Armitage, *The Ideological Origins of the British Empire* (Cambridge: Cambridge University Press, 2000); Vincent Carey, 'The Irish Face of Machiavelli: Richard Beacon's *Solon His Follie* (1594) and Republican Ideology in the Conquest of Ireland', in Hiram Morgan (ed.), *Political Ideology in Ireland 1541–1641* (Dublin: Four Courts Press, 1999), pp. 83–109; Andrew Hadfield, *Spenser's Irish Experience: Wild Fruit and Savage Soyl*, pp. 73–8; Markku Peltonen, *Classical Humanism in Republicanism in English Political Thought 1570–1640* (Cambridge: Cambridge University Press, 1995).

12.   Breandán Ó Buachalla, *Aisling Ghéiar, Na Stíobhartaigh agus an tAois Léinn 1603–1788* (Dublin, 1996); 'Poetry and Politics in Early Modern Ireland', *Eighteenth Century Ireland/Iris an Dá Chultúr* 7 (1992), pp. 149–75; '*Annála Ríoghachta Éireann* is *Foras Feasa ar Éirinn*: An Comhthéacs Comhaimseartha', *Studia Hibernica* 22–3 (1982–3), pp. 59–105.

13.   Bernadette Cunningham, *The World of Geoffrey Keating* (Dublin: Four Courts Press, 2000); 'Representations of King, Parliament and the Irish People in Geoffrey Keating's *Foras Feasa ar Éirinn* and John Lynch's *Cambrensis Eversus* (1662)', in *Political Thought in Seventeenth-Century Ireland*, ed. Jane Ohlmeyer (Cambridge: Cambridge University Press, 2000).

14.   See Hiram Morgan, ' "Un pueblo unido . . .": The Politics of Philip O'Sullivan Beare', forthcoming in a collection of the proceedings for the 'Congresso Internacional: Kinsale 1601–2001'. In addition to the plans for an armed invasion of Ireland that I mention in my article, Morgan draws out the importance of the *praesidio* scheme which O'Sullivan Beare proposed for his patrimony of Dursey Island after the English attack on Cadiz in 1625. See *Affaires Étangères, Espagne* 264, for this document written to Philip IV by Philip O'Sullivan Beare.

15.   Brendan Bradshaw, 'The English Reformation and Identity Formation in Ireland and Wales', in Brendan Bradshaw and Peter Roberts (eds.), *British Consciousness and Identity: The Making of Britain, 1533–1707* (Cambridge: Cambridge University Press, 1998), pp. 43–111.

16.   Ibid., p. 58.

17.   Marc Caball, 'Faith, Culture and Sovereignty: Irish Nationality and its Development, 1558–1625', in Brendan Bradshaw and Peter Roberts (eds.), *British Consciousness and Identity*, pp. 112–39, 137.

18.   Jane Ohlmeyer, 'Introduction: For God, King or Country?' in Jane Ohlmeyer (ed.), *Political Thought in Seventeenth-Century Ireland* (Cambridge: Cambridge University Press, 2000), p. 2.

19.   See John Bossy, *The English Catholic Community, 1570–1850* (New York: Oxford University Press, 1976). For an account of the vibrancy of late medieval English Catholicism and the sense of this as a continued hidden tradition in sixteenth-century England, see Eamon Duffy, *The Stripping of the Altars* (New Haven: Yale University Press, 1992). For another reinterpretation of England's relation to its own Catholic past, as well as to the rest of the British Isles, see Susan Brigden, *New Worlds, Lost Worlds: the Rule of the Tudors 1485–1603* (London: Allen Lane, 2000).

20.   Thomas O'Connor describes the various types of exchanges between Ireland and the Continent and gives an account of the areas of research that still need to be explored in his 'Introduction' to *The Irish in Europe 1580–1815* (Dublin: Four Courts Press, 2001).

21.   J. G. A. Pocock, 'The Third Kingdom in its History: An Afterword', in Jane
      Ohlmeyer (ed.), *Political Thought in Seventeenth-Century Ireland*, p. 280. See also
      John Pocock, 'The Atlantic Archipelago and the War of Three Kingdoms', in
      Brendan Bradshaw and John Morrill (eds.), *The British Problem* c. *1534–1707:
      State Formation in the Atlantic Archipelago* (Basingstoke: Macmillan, 1996), pp.
      172–91. This entire collection of essays is an excellent introduction to the lim-
      its as well as the applicability of the British model to Irish history.
22.   For a detailed review of the various misuses of the term 'British' and 'Britain'
      with respect to Irish, Scots and English history, see Norman Davies, *The Isles: A
      History* (New York: Oxford University Press, 1999), pp. xxiii–xli.
23.   Marc Caball, *Poets and Politics: Reaction and Continuity in Irish Poetry, 1558–1625*
      (Cork: Cork University Press, 1998), p. 12. See also Mícheál Mac Craith,
      'Litríocht an 17ú hAois: Tonnbhriseadh an tSeanghnáthaimh nó Tonnchruthú
      an Nuaghnáthaimh', *Léachtaí Cholm Cille* XXVI (1996), pp. 50–82.
24.   For an overview of the Irish diaspora in early modern Europe, see John J. Silke,
      'The Irish Abroad, 1534–1691', in T. W. Moody, F. X. Martin, and F. J. Byrne
      (eds.), *New History of Ireland, vol. 3: Early Modern Ireland 1534–1691* (Oxford,
      1976). On Irish aristocratic families abroad, see Micheline Kerney Walsh, *The
      O'Neills in Spain* (Dublin, 1957), *The MacDonnells of Antrim on the Continent*
      (Dublin, 1960), *Spanish Knights of Irish Origin*, 4 vols. (Dublin, 1960–78), *An
      Exile of Ireland: Hugh O'Neill, Prince of Ulster* (Dublin, 1996); Hector McDonnell,
      The Wild Geese of the Antrim McDonnells (Dublin, 1996). On Irish diplomatic
      connections, see Declan Downey, 'Culture and Diplomacy: The Spanish Habs-
      burg Dimension in the Irish Counter-Reformation Movement, c. 1529–1629'
      (PhD thesis, Cambridge, 1994). On Irish soldiers in European armies in the
      seventeenth century, see Gráinne Henry, *The Irish Military Community in Spanish
      Flanders 1586–1621* (Dublin, 1992); Robert A. Stradling, *The Spanish Monarchy
      and Irish Mercenaries: The Wild Geese in Spain 1618–68* (Dublin, 1994); and John
      McGurk, 'Wilde Geese: The Irish in European Armies (Sixteenth to Seventeenth
      Centuries)', in John Patrick O'Sullivan (ed.), *The Irish World Wide, History Her-
      itage Identity*, 6 vols. (Leicester, London, New York, 1992–7). On Irish clerics
      abroad, see Benignus Millett, 'Irish Exiles in Catholic Europe', in P. J. Corish
      (ed.), *A History of Irish Catholicism* (1971), iv, 3, *The Irish Franciscans* (Rome,
      1964) and 'Irish Literature in Latin, 1550–1700', in T. W. Moody, F. X. Martin,
      and F. J. Byrne (eds.), *New History of Ireland, vol. 3*, pp. 561–86; Donald Cregan,
      'The Social and Cultural Background of a Counter-Reformation Episcopate,
      1618–60', in Art Cosgrove and Donal McCartney (eds.), *Studies Presented to R.
      Dudley Edwards* (Dublin, 1979). On the influence of European texts upon Irish
      literature in the seventeenth century, see Tadgh Ó Dúshláine, *An Eoraip agus
      litríocht na Gaeilge 1600–1650* (Baile Átha Cliath: An Clóchomhar, 1987).
25.   For the view that nationalism precedes the nation and that nationalism only
      begins in the late eighteenth century, see Benedict Anderson, *Imagined Commu-
      nities* (London: Verso, 1983); Ernest Gellner, *Nations and Nationalism* (Oxford:
      Blackwell, 1983); E. J. Hobsbawm, *Nations and Nationalism since 1780* (Cam-
      bridge: Cambridge University Press, 1990). For a very different view of the
      nation as the basis for nationalism and as a concept rooted in the experience of
      a common culture, especially a common religion, customs, language and ver-
      nacular literature, see Adrian Hastings, *The Construction of Nationhood: Ethnicity,*

Religion, and Nationalism (Cambridge: Cambridge University Press, 1997). Hastings would place a cultural sense of the Irish nation to as far back as the eleventh century, while he would date the development of Irish nationalism from the late sixteenth century through to the seventeenth century, when Ireland was under assault from English colonial expansion (pp. 69, 82–95).

26.   O'Sullivan Beare's *Compendium* was partially translated by Matthew Byrne, as *Ireland under Elizabeth* (Dublin, 1903).

27.   See for example the nineteenth-century editions of O'Sullivan Beare's *Compendium* edited by Matthew Kelly (Dublin, 1850) and of Peter Lombard's *Commentarius* edited by P. F. Moran (Dublin, 1868).

28.   For a list of the Hiberno-Latin texts that are in the process of being translated or considered for translation, see the website of the Centre for Neo-Latin Studies at University College Cork, http://www.ucc.ie/acad/classics/CNLS/

29.   Royal Irish Academy Manuscript 24G 16, fol. 34v.

Barbarous Slaves and Civil Cannibals

1.   Denis Donoghue, 'Fears for Irish Studies in an Age of Identity Politics', *Chronicle of Higher Education*, 21 November 1997, B4–B5.

2.   Homi K. Bhabha, 'Signs Taken for Wonders', in *The Post-Colonial Studies Reader*, ed. B. Ashcroft, G. Griffiths, and H. Tiffin (London: Routledge, 1995), pp. 34–5.

3.   Homi K. Bhabha, 'Sly Civility', *October* 34, pp. 71–8.

4.   Gerald of Wales, *The History and Topography of Ireland* (London: Penguin, 1982), pp. 115–6.

5.   D. Denoon, *Settler Capitalism* (Oxford: Oxford University Press, 1983), p. 27.

6.   Raymond Crotty, *Ireland in Crisis: A Study in Capitalist Colonial Underdevelopment* (Dingle: Brandon, 1987), pp. 37, 40.

7.   Jane Ohlmeyer, 'Seventeenth-Century Ireland and the New British and Atlantic Histories', *American Historical Review*, vol. 104, no. 2 (April 1999), pp. 446–62.

8.   D. B. Quinn, 'Ireland and Sixteenth-Century European Expansion', *Historical Studies* 1 (1958), pp. 20–32; Nicholas Canny, *The Elizabethan Conquest of Ireland: A Pattern Established 1565–76* (New York: Harper & Row, 1976); 'Identity Formation in Ireland: The Emergence of an Anglo-Irish Identity', in *Colonial Identity in the Atlantic World*, ed. N. Canny and A. Pagden (Princeton: Princeton University Press, 1987). Two more recent articles comparing English colonialist representations of North America and Ireland include: James E. Doan, '"An Island in the Virginian Sea": Native Americans and Irish in English Discourse, 1585–1640', *New Hibernia Review* I, 1 (Spring 1987), pp. 79–99, and Rolf Loeber, 'Preliminaries to the Massachusetts Bay Colony: The Irish Ventures of Emmanuel Downing and John Winthrop, Sr.', in T. Barnard, D. Ó Cróinín, and K. Simms, eds., *'A Miracle of Learning': Studies in Manuscripts and Irish Learning* (Aldershot, 1998).

9.   Hiram Morgan, 'Mid-Atlantic Blues', *Irish Review* 11 (1991), pp. 50–1.

10.   The alliance of the Incas with the Spanish in the sixteenth century, and of the North American Indian tribes with the English and the French during the eighteenth-century French and Indian War, would be examples of such

alliances. Needless to say, the Indians were the tools of European conquest in such alliances, but one could argue that the Irish, too, were pawns in Spain's rivalry with England.

11.   *H.M.C., Egmont*, i, pt.i, 35, as cited in John McCavitt, 'Veni, Vidi, Vici: Sir John the Conqueror', paper delivered at the Folger Library in September 1995. John McCavitt, *Sir Arthur Chichester* (Belfast: Institute of Irish Studies, 1998), pp. 104–5.

12.   Andrew Hadfield, 'Rocking the Boat: A Response to Hiram Morgan', *Irish Review* 12 (1992), pp. 15–19.

13.   Walter Mignolo, *The Darker Side of the Renaissance: Literacy, Territoriality, and Colonization* (Ann Arbor: University of Michigan Press, 1995), pp. 332–4.

14.   Sir John Davies, *A Discovery of the True Causes why Ireland was Never Entirely Subdued* (Shannon, 1969), 266; *Cal.S.P. Ire., 1603–6*, pp. 464–5; *Cal.S.P. Ire., 1608–10*, pp. 224–5; *Cal.S.P. Ire., 1608–10*, p. 17; *H.M.C. Egmont*, i, pt. i, p. 35. Garrett Fagan of Trinity College Dublin has pointed out to me that jurors in England were also fined.

15.   *Cal. S.P. Ire., 1608–10*, p. 17.

16.   Geoffrey Keating, *The History of Ireland*, vol. I, trans. David Comyn (London: Irish Texts Society, 1902), pp. 65–71; Philip O'Sullivan Beare, *Historiae Catholicae Hiberniae Compendium*, ed. Matthew Kelly (Dublin, 1850), II.i.viii, p. 68.

17.   Enrique Dussel, 'Eurocentrism and Modernity', *Boundary 2*, vol. 20, no. 3 (1993), p. 66.

18.   John Gillingham, 'The Beginnings of English Imperialism', *Journal of Historical Sociology*, vol. 4, no. 4 (December 1992), pp. 392–409.

19.   See D. B. Quinn, 'Sir Thomas Smith and the Beginnings of English Colonial Theory', *Proceedings of the American Philosophical Society* 89, 4 (1945), pp. 543–6, and 'Ireland and Sixteenth-Century Expansion', *Historical Studies* 1 (1958), pp. 20–32.

20.   Joep Leerssen, *Mere Irish and Fíor-Ghael: Studies in the Idea of Irish Nationality, and Its Development and Literary Expression Prior to the Nineteenth Century* (Cork: Cork University Press, 1996). See in particular, 'The Vindication of Irish Civility in the Seventeenth Century', pp. 254–93, where Leerssen describes the Irish defence of their civility as a 'counter-claim' of 'tradition' versus 'the English taunt that Ireland had no civility' (p. 259).

21.   Michel Foucault, 'What is an Author?', in *Language, Countermemory, Practice*, trans. Donald F. Bouchard and Sherry Simon (Ithaca: Cornell University Press, 1977), pp. 131–6.

22.   Leerssen, *Mere Irish and Fíor-Ghael*, pp. 34–7.

23.   Gerald of Wales, *Topography*, pp. 31–2.

24.   Ibid., p. 124.

25.   On ethnography versus history, see Michel de Certeau, 'Ethnography: Speech, or the Space of the Other: Jean de Léry', in *The Writing of History*, trans. Tom Conley (New York: Columbia University Press, 1988), pp. 209–37. Also see Johannes Fabian, *Time and the Other: How Anthropology Makes Its Object* (New York: Columbia University Press, 1983).

26.   Edward Said, *Orientalism* (New York: Pantheon Books, 1978). See Hiram Morgan's comment in *Political Ideology in Ireland 1541–1641* (Dublin: Four Courts Press, 1999), p. 24.

27.   Gerald of Wales, *Topography*, p. 31.
28.   Ibid., pp. 101, 104.
29.   Ibid., p. 112.
30.   Ibid., pp. 72–6.
31.   Ibid., p. 103.
32.   Ibid., p. 100.
33.   John Derricke, *The Image of Ireland with A Discoverie of Woodkarne* (1581), ed. David B. Quinn (Blackstaff Press, 1985).
34.   R. Dudley Edwards, *Ireland in the Age of the Tudors: The Destruction of Hiberno-Norman Civilization* (London: Croom Helm, 1977). See Kenneth Nichols, 'Worlds Apart? The Ellis Two-Nation Theory of Late Medieval Ireland', *History Ireland*, vol. 7, no. 2 (Summer 1999), pp. 22–6, where he presents a mixed culture, characterized by both the adoption of Irish law, language and custom by the descendants of the Normans and the acceptance by the Gaelic Irish of the authority of the English king, outside whose control they and their English contemporaries largely existed.
35.   David Edwards, 'Beyond Reform: Martial Law and the Tudor Reconquest of Ireland', *History Ireland*, vol. 5, no. 2 (Summer 1997), pp. 16–21. Edwards provides even more detailed evidence in 'Ideology and Experience: Spenser's View and Martial Law in Ireland', in *Political Ideology in Ireland 1541–1641*, ed. Hiram Morgan (Dublin: Four Courts Press, 1999), pp. 127–57.
36.   Vincent Carey, 'John Derricke's *Image of Ireland*, Sir Henry Sidney, and the Massacre at Mullaghmast, 1578', *Irish Historical Studies*, vol. 32, no. 123 (May 1999), pp. 305–27; Nicholas Canny, *The Elizabethan Conquest of Ireland: A Pattern Established, 1565–76* (New York: Harper & Row, 1976), chapter 4.
37.   Derricke, *Image of Ireland*, pp. 187–8, for quotations in this paragraph.
38.   Ibid., p. 193.
39.   Ibid., p. 193.
40.   Ibid., pp. 83, 88, 92.
41.   Ibid. p. 88.
42.   Seamus Deane, 'Civilians and Barbarians', in *Ireland's Field Day* (Notre Dame: Notre Dame University Press, 1986).
43.   Richard Stanihurst, 'Description of Ireland', in *Holinshed's Chronicles of England, Scotland, and Ireland*, vol. 6 (New York: AMS Press, 1976; reprint of 1808 edition, London: J. Johnson), p. 67.
44.   Ibid., see Chapters 3, 5, 6, and 7, which respectively treat 'Cities', 'Lords Spirituall', 'Lords Temporall', and 'Learned Men and Authors'.
45.   Ibid., p. 4.
46.   For a similar use of 'savage' to describe 'barbarians' close to home, see James I's description of the highland Scots as 'suche wild savageis voide of Godis feare and our obedience' in a letter of 1608, quoted in Jenny Wormald, *Court, Kirk, and Community*, New History of Scotland 4 (Toronto: University of Toronto Press, 1981), p. 108.
47.   Not published until 1633, the text of *A View* circulated in manuscript in the late 1590s.
48.   Edmund Spenser, *A View of the Present State of Ireland*, ed. W. L. Renwick (Oxford: Clarendon Press, 1970), pp. 84–5, for all quotations in this paragraph.
49.   Spenser, *A View*, p. 63; subsequent quotations in this paragraph, pp. 67–8.

50. Ibid., p. 56.
51. For a discussion of these sources, see Andrew Hadfield, *Spenser's Irish Experience: Wilde Fruit and Savage Soyl* (Oxford: Clarendon Press, 1997), pp. 102–3.
52. Spenser, *A View*, p. 62.
53. Ibid., p. 104.
54. Ibid., p. 104.
55. See *The Faerie Queene* (VI.viii.35–6).
56. Canny, *The Elizabethan Conquest of Ireland*, p. 126.
57. For a genealogy of 'cannibal' in sixteenth-century European writing, see Frank Lestringant, 'Le nom des cannibales de Christophe Colomb à Michel de Montaigne', *Bulletin de la Société des Amis de Montaigne* 17–18 (1984), pp. 51–74.
58. *The Diario of Christopher Columbus 1492–1493*, trans. Oliver Dunne and James E. Kelly Jr. (Norman: University of Oklahoma Press, 1989), pp. 329, 133, 217.
59. André Thevet, *Cosmographie Universelle*, t. II, f. 956 r, as cited in Lestringant, 73.
60. Bartolomé de Las Casas, *In Defense of the Indians,* trans. Stafford Poole (DeKalb: Northern Illinois University Press, 1992), pp. 29–30; Aristotle, *Politics* I. ii.
61. In Part 2 of Mignolo's *The Darker Side of the Renaissance*, 'The Colonization of Memory', he discusses how 'New World historians . . . were unable to accept that past events could have been recorded without necessarily having letters' (p. 140).
62. Las Casas, *In Defense of the Indians*, pp. 42–3.
63. Ibid., p. 222.
64. Ibid., p. 222.
65. Ibid., p. 225.
66. Ibid, p. 225.
67. Ibid., p. 47.
68. Ibid., pp. 54–5.
69. Ibid., p. 47.
70. Enrique Dussel, *The Invention of the Americas: Eclipse of 'The Other' and the Myth of Modernity*, trans. Michael D. Barber (New York: Continuum, 1995), p. 72. Also see Dussel's 'Eurocentrism and Modernity', *Boundary 2*, vol. 20, no. 3 (Fall 1993), pp. 65–76.
71. *In Defense of the Indians*, p. 33.
72. Ibid., p. 33.
73. David Lloyd, *Anomalous States* (Durham: Duke University Press, 1993), p. 127.
74. Jean de Léry, *History of a Voyage to the Land of Brazil*, trans. Janet Whatley (Berkeley: University of California Press, 1990), p. 132.
75. Ibid., p. 246, note 14.
76. Ibid., p. 132.
77. Jean de Léry, *History of a Voyage to the Land of Brazil*, p. 133.
78. Ibid., p. 41.
79. For a more extended discussion of this text, see chapter 7, which is a reprint of my article 'Irish and Spanish Cultural and Political Relations in the Work of O'Sullivan Beare' in *Political Ideology in Ireland*, ed. Hiram Morgan (Dublin: Four Courts Press, 1999), pp. 229–53.
80. Compare Las Casas, 'Chapter Fifty-Nine: Refutation of Sepulveda's claim that Alexander VI approved war against the Indians in his bull *Inter Caetera*', in *In*

Defense of the Indians, and Philip O'Sullivan Beare, *Historiae Catholicae Hiberniae Compendium* II.I.iv: 'The Letters of Pope Adrian are set down'.

81. O'Sullivan Beare, *Compendium* II.II.iii: 'How Henry, King of England, having fallen into heresy . . . tried to attack the Catholic faith in Ireland'.

82. Bartolomé de las Casas, *The Devastation of the Indies: A Brief Account*, trans. Herma Briffault (Baltimore: Johns Hopkins University Press, 1992), pp. 33–4; Philip O'Sullivan Beare, *Ireland under Elizabeth, being chapters towards a history of Ireland in the reign of Elizabeth being a portion of the history of Catholic Ireland by Don Philip O'Sullivan Beare*, trans. and ed. Matthew J. Byrne (Dublin, 1903), p. 8. For more examples of similarities in the accounts of violence against civilians in Las Casas and O'Sullivan Beare, see chapter 7.

83. Geoffrey Keating, *The History of Ireland*, vol. I, pp. 43–5.

84. Ibid., p. 37.

85. Peter Walsh, *A Prospect of the State of Ireland* (London, 1682), p. 8.

86. Ibid., p. 10.

87. John Lynch, *Cambrensis Eversus*, trans. Matthew Kelly (Dublin, 1851–2), vol. III, xxvii, p. 75.

88. Sir Roger Boyle, First Earl of Orrery, *The Irish colours displayed, in a reply of an English Protestant to a late Letter of an Irish Roman Catholique. Both address'd to . . . the Duke of Ormond* (n.p., 1662).

89. As quoted in Breandán Ó Buachalla, *Aisling Ghéar* (Dublin, 1996), p. 197.

The Construction of Gender

1. See the discussion of Spenser's last days by Judson where he cites the following disputed testimony: that Spenser died 'because of neglect and want' (*The Return from Parnassus* [1602], ed. Edward Arber [London, 1879]), and 'for lack of bread in King Street' (*Ben Jonson*, ed. C. H. Herford, Percy Simpson, and Evelyn Simpson, 11 vols. [Oxford: Oxford University Press, 1925–52], 1, p. 137), quoted in Alexander Judson, *Life of Edmund Spenser* (Baltimore: Johns Hopkins University Press, 1945), 202–3. For evidence that Spenser did not die in poverty, see Josephine Waters Bennett, 'Did Spenser Starve?' *Modern Language Notes* 52 (1937), pp. 400–1; Herbert Berry and E. K. Timings, 'Spenser's Pension', *Review of English Studies* 11 (1960), pp. 254–9.

2. On Spenser's precarious relationship with the centre of power in the Elizabethan court, see Louis Adrian Montrose, 'The Elizabethan Subject and the Spenserian Text', in *Literary Theory/Renaissance Texts*, ed. Patricia Parker and David Quint (Baltimore: Johns Hopkins University Press, 1986), p. 318: 'Spenser . . . always remained on the social and economic as well as the geographical margins of that community of privilege whom he addressed and presumed to fashion in his poetry.'

3. Spenser's characterization of the opposition between English and Irish in part resembles the opposition between imperialist and colonized, European and Oriental, that Edward Said has demonstrated was used to constitute and control the cultural other (*Orientalism* [New York: Random House, 1978]). Said's method has recently been used by cultural critics of Ireland such as Jennifer Todd, 'The Limits of Britishness,' *The Irish Review* 5 (1988), pp. 11–16.

4. Edwin Greenlaw, *Studies in Spenser's Historical Allegory* (Baltimore: Johns Hopkins University Press, 1932); C. S. Lewis, *The Allegory of Love* (Oxford: Oxford University Press, 1936); Angus Fletcher, *The Prophetic Moment* (Chicago: University of Chicago Press, 1971); Stephen Greenblatt, *Renaissance Self-Fashioning* (Chicago: University of Chicago Press, 1980).

5. See the opposing views of Nicholas Canny, who describes Spenser as a 'political theorist', 'Edmund Spenser and the Development of an Anglo-Irish Identity', *Yearbook of English Studies* 13 (1983), pp. 1–19, and Ciaran Brady, who argues that this description is 'one Spenser would surely have found strange', 'Reply to Nicholas Canny', *Past and Present* 120 (1988), p. 210. Whether or not Spenser would have found this description strange seems a moot point. Dante never refers to himself as a political theorist, yet Italian historians and literary critics see no contradiction in discussing Dante as political theorist with respect to both the *Commedia* and *De monarchia*. I shall indicate in the following notes where I stand in relation to the opposing views Canny and Brady have taken in the debate over *A View*. See also Brady, 'Spenser's Irish Crisis: Humanism and Experience in the 1590s', *Past and Present* 111 (1986), pp. 16–49; Canny, 'Debate: Spenser's Irish Crisis: Humanism and Experience in the 1590s', *Past and Present* 120 (1988), pp. 201–9.

6. Edwin Greenlaw, C. G. Osgood, F. M. Padelford, eds., *The Works of Edmund Spenser: A Variorum Edition*, 9 vols. (Baltimore: Johns Hopkins University Press, 1932–49), 5, p. 280.

7. Greenlaw, *Studies in Spenser's Historical Allegory*, pp. 142–3.

8. Quoted in *Variorum*, 5, p. 280.

9. Chris Baldick, *The Social Mission of English Criticism* (Oxford: Clarendon Press, 1983).

10. Ibid., p. 86.

11. Greenlaw, *Studies in Spenser's Historical Allegory*, p. 135.

12. Greenlaw, 'Spenser and British Imperialism', *Modern Philology* 9 (1912), pp. 347–70, reprinted in *Studies in Spenser's Historical Allegory*, p. 138.

13. Greenlaw, *Studies in Spenser's Historical Allegory*, 154.

14. Ibid., p. 144.

15. For an informative discussion of social levels in England at this time, see David Cressy, 'Describing the Social Order of Elizabethan and Stuart England', *Literature and History* 3 (1976), pp. 29–44. His comment on the tension between the legal and status system, based on ownership of land, and the increasing importance of non-landed skills is relevant to an understanding of Spenser's position in the social order: 'The clergy and professions, merchants, and office-holders, were never adequately "placed" in Elizabethan or Jacobean social theory' (p. 29).

16. C. S. Lewis, *The Allegory of Love*, p. 321.

17. Ibid., p. 321; Mathew Arnold, *Culture and Anarchy*, ed. J. Dover Wilson (Cambridge: Cambridge University Press, 1971), p. 69. Although Lewis admits that 'Spenser was the instrument of a detestable policy in Ireland, and in his fifth book the wickedness he had shared begins to corrupt his imagination' (p. 349), he does not investigate the connection between Spenser's policy and his poetry. Both Lewis's background and affiliations suggest an ideological sympathy with Spenser. As Tolkien said of Lewis's conversion to Christianity, 'taking it up again

he would also take up or reawaken the prejudices so sedulously planted in childhood and boyhood. He would become again a Northern Ireland protestant' (Humphrey Carpenter, *Tolkien* [New York: Ballantine, 1977], p. 168). Even as an adult he showed a distaste for 'papists' that, as a recent biographer puts it, made him 'still very much a Belfast man' (George Sayers, *Jack: C. S. Lewis and His Times* [San Francisco: Harper & Row, 1988], p. 138).

18. C. S. Lewis, *The Allegory of Love*, pp. 306, 310, 308.

19. Ibid., p. 310.

20. Walter Benjamin, *The Origins of German Tragic Drama*, trans. John Osborne (London: New Left Books, 1977), p. 175.

21. Walter Benjamin, *Schriften*, ed. T. W. Adorno and Gretel Adorno (Frankfurt: Suhrkamp Verlag, 1955), 1, p. 308, quoted in Fredric Jameson, *Marxism and Form* (Princeton: Princeton University Press, 1977), pp. 71–2.

22. Benjamin, *The Origins of the German Tragic Drama*, pp. 176, 175.

23. *Ben Jonson*, 8, p. 618.

24. C. S. Lewis, *The Allegory of Love*, p. 348.

25. Suzanne W. Hull, *Chaste, Silent & Obedient: English Books for Women 1475–1640* (San Marino: Huntington Library, 1984).

26. Kipling's 'The Phantom 'Rickshaw', for example, relates the story of how a man who spurns a married Englishwoman, a 'memsahib', with whom he has had a relationship, is later haunted by nightmares that picture her in a rickshaw drawn by Indian servants (*The Phantom Rickshaw* [Boston: The Greenock Press, 1903]).

27. In *Icons of Justice* (New York: Columbia University Press, 1969), Jane Aptekar claimed that Spenser's policies 'are "political" while his poem is philosophical' (p. 8). See also Michael Murrin, *The Veil of Allegory* (Chicago: University of Chicago Press, 1969); T. K. Dunseath, *Spenser's Allegory of Justice in Book Five of 'The Faerie Queene'* (Princeton: Princeton University Press, 1968). At least Dunseath admits the 'disquieting critical implications' (p. 4) of the footnotes he argues are inimical to poetry.

28. Dunseath, p. 136.

29. John Erskine Hankins, *Source and Meaning in Spenser's Allegory* (Oxford: Clarendon Press, 1971), pp. 154–5.

30. Angus Fletcher, *The Prophetic Moment*, p. 147.

31. Pauline Henley, *Spenser in Ireland* (Dublin and Cork: University of Cork Press, 1928), pp. 148–9; Edmund Spenser, *A View of the Present State of Ireland*, ed. W. L. Renwick (Oxford: Clarendon Press, 1970), p. 144.

32. Fletcher, p. 156.

33. Ibid., p. 247.

34. The term 'Hiberno–Norman' is taken from R. Dudley Edwards, *Ireland in the Age of the Tudors: The Destruction of Hiberno–Norman Civilization* (London: Croom Helm, 1977).

35. *A View*, pp. 107, 185.

36. Fletcher, p. 247.

37. Stephen Greenblatt, 'To Fashion a Gentleman: Spenser and the Destruction of the Bower of Bliss', in *Renaissance Self-Fashioning* (Chicago, 1980), pp. 157–92.

38. Ibid., p. 173.

39. Ibid., p. 173.

40. Marguerite Waller, 'Academic Tootsie: the Denial of Difference and the Difference It Makes', *Diacritics* 17.1 (1987), p.3.

41. Ibid., p. 3.

42. Vincent Crapanzano, 'Hermes' Dilemma: The Masking of Subversion in Ethnographic Description', in *Writing Culture: The Poetics and Politics of Ethnography*, ed. James Clifford and George E. Marcus (Berkeley: University of California Press, 1986), p. 74.

43. All quotations are from Edmund Spenser, *The Faerie Queene*, ed. Thomas P. Roche Jr. with C. Patrick O'Donnell Jr. (New Haven: Yale University Press, 1981).

44. Greenblatt, pp. 190–1.

45. See Andrew Hadfield, *Spenser's Irish Experience: Wilde Fruit and Savage Soyl* (Oxford: Clarendon Press, 1997), and Willy Maley, *Salvaging Spenser: Colonialism, Culture, and Identity* (New York: St Martin's Press, 1997).

46. Ibid., p. 186. For a Marxist analysis which explains the importance of Spenser's politics for his poetry (passages from *The Shepheardes Calendar*, *Colin Clouts Come Home Again*, and *The Faerie Queene* 1–6 are discussed), see Simon Shepherd, *Spenser* (London: Harvester Wheatsheaf, 1989). Ciaran Brady dissents from the view that the politics of Spenser's tract inform the entire epic and sees Book 5 as a 'fall from prophecy into politics' ('Spenser's Irish Crisis', p. 46).

47. Kenneth Gross, *Spenserian Poetics* (Ithaca: Cornell University Press, 1985).

48. Ibid., p. 81.

49. *A View*, pp. 141–2.

50. Brady, 'Spenser's Irish Crisis', p. 47.

51. *A View*, pp. 94–5.

52. Whereas Brady (cited in note 5) interprets Spenser's policy of the sword as 'power unconstrained by convention' ('Reply to Nicholas Canny', p. 214), and suggests that this called for the complete extermination of the native population ('Spenser's Irish Crisis', pp. 32, 36), Canny stresses that Spenser rejected complete extermination and gave the Irish opportunities to submit, both before the military conquest he proposed and just after it ('Debate', pp. 202–3). Although Brady's analysis of the unrestrained violence symbolized by the sword is convincing, it is also clear that Spenser wanted a docile population, who could be put to work and taxed, to survive. That this sword would continue to hang over the population after the military campaign does not really contradict Spenser's plan for 'reformation', as Brady asserts, since Spenser's reorganization of Irish society would involve 'martial law' (*A View*, p. 160). If this seems to 'rob [Spenser's] argument of its reform credentials', as Brady contends (ibid., p. 36), this is simply because those credentials are suspect to begin with.

53. Quoted in Gross, p. 78.

54. Seamus Deane, 'Civilians and Barbarians', in *Ireland's Field Day* (Notre Dame: Notre Dame University Press, 1986).

55. Greenblatt, p. 186. Like Greenblatt, I am indebted to the work of historians David Beers Quinn, *The Elizabethans and the Irish* (Ithaca: Cornell University Press, 1966), and Nicholas Canny, *The Elizabethan Conquest of Ireland: A Pattern Established: 1565–76* (New York: Harper & Row, 1976). I have also drawn on the important more recent work of both Nicholas Canny and Ciaran Brady (cited in note 5). While Canny reads *A View* as a straightforward political tract and Brady reads it as an ambiguous humanist dialogue, both have attempted to

contextualize *A View* and to compare it to other contemporary texts on Ireland. For the sociopolitical context of sixteenth-century Ireland see also: K. P. Andrews, N. P. Canny, and P. E .H. Andrews, eds., *The Westward Enterprise* (Detroit: Wayne State University Press, 1979); Nicholas Canny and Anthony Padgen, eds., *Colonial Identity in the Atlantic World* (Princeton: Princeton University Press, 1987); Ciaran Brady and Raymond Gillespie, eds., *Natives and Newcomers: Essays on the Making of Irish Colonial Society, 1534–1641* (Dublin: Irish Academic Press, 1986). I am particularly indebted to Helena Shire, with whom I first read *The Faerie Queene*. She did extensive research in Ireland for her book *A Preface to Spenser* (London: Longman, 1978).

56. Quoted in Jameson, *Marxism and Form*, p. 71.
57. W. B. Yeats, *The Cutting of an Agate* (London: Macmillan, 1919).
58. Commonwealth Book, A/28 [P.R.O.], quoted in Henley, *Spenser in Ireland*, pp. 206–7.
59. Canny, 'Edmund Spenser and the Development of an Anglo-Irish Identity', pp. 16–19.
60. Here I follow Canny's outline of *A View* (ibid., pp. 3–4). Brady outlines the text differently: '[1] the chief causes of Ireland's lawless and barbarous condition . . . [2] proposals for military subjugation . . . [3] recommendations for the reconstruction of civil society' ('Spenser's Irish Crisis', p. 27). Brady downplays Spenser's antagonism towards the Old English and stresses what he calls the 'reformation of manners' (p. 320), which for Canny is rather 'a drastic programme in social engineering' ('Reply to Nicholas Canny', p. 203).
61. Canny, *The Elizabethan Conquest of Ireland: A Pattern Established 1565–76* (New York: Harper & Row, 1976), p. 26.
62. *A View*, p. 66.
63. Michael Richter, *Medieval Ireland: The Enduring Tradition* (New York: St Martin's Press, 1988), p. 129.
64. See for example Ralph Church, ed., *Faerie Queene* (1758), cited in *Variorum 5*, p. 161.
65. See John W. Draper, 'Spenser's Linguistics in the Present State of Ireland', *Modern Philology* 17 (1919–20), pp. 471–86. He comments on 'cummericke', or 'cummnerreeih', 'I can find no Irish word or cry to be compared with it' (p. 482). I am grateful to Catherine McKenna for confirming Draper's tracing of 'cummericke' to the Welsh 'cummeraig'. See the Irish noun 'commairge', meaning 'protection' or 'refuge'.
66. See Greenlaw, 'Fairies and Britons', in *Studies in Spenser's Historical Allegory*, pp. 193–9: 'By Fairy Spenser means Welsh, or more accurately, Tudor' (p. 198).
67. *A View*, p. 84. In order to save space, the page references for the quotations from *A View* in this paragraph are given in note 68.
68. *A View*, pp. 56, 83, 66, 77, 56, 61. Spenser's *View* demonstrates a mode of acquiring knowledge within what Foucault calls the classical 'episteme' based upon identity and difference (Michel Foucault, *The Order of Things* [New York: Random House, 1973], p. 57). As Cairns and Richards argue: 'In the case of later sixteenth- and seventeenth-century England, the conjunction of shifts in ways of acquiring knowledge with colonial expansion, in Ireland and elsewhere, requires that we be aware that writing by Englishmen about Ireland and the Irish may not only have served to broaden English knowledge of the neigh-

bouring inhabitants, but also to define the qualities of "Englishness," by simultaneously defining "not Englishness" or "otherness"' (David Cairns and Shaun Richards, *Writing Ireland: Colonialism, Nationalism, and Culture*, Cultural Politics [Manchester: University of Manchester Press, 1981], p. 2).

69. Canny, *The Elizabethan Conquest of Ireland*, pp. 113–36; Giraldus Cambrensis, *The Irish History*, trans. John Hooker, in Raphael Holinshead, *Chronicles of England, Scotland and Ireland* (London: J. Johnson, 1807–8).

70. See Mary O'Dowd, 'Gaelic Economy and Society', in *Natives and Newcomers*, pp. 120–47: 'The belief that Gaelic society was rigidly and simply divided between two classes, the landowners and the cultivators, has been convincingly disproved by Kenneth Nicholls who has described a much more complex society in his 'Land, law and society in sixteenth-century Ireland' [O'Donnell lecture (Dublin, 1972)]…There were prosperous tenants who rented substantial amounts of land and acted as middlemen. There were also smaller tenants who rented land directly for their own use, either from a larger tenant or directly from a landlord' (pp. 128–9).

71. Canny demonstrates that this 'radical programme of reform' was endorsed by other English-born writers in Ireland of this period ('Edmund Spenser and the Development of an Anglo-Irish Identity', pp. 7–14). I am not convinced by Brady's objections to Canny's contextual approach: that the views towards the Irish in state papers 'can hardly be said to form an ideology' (one, of course, wants to ask, why not?); and that Spenser's treatise can only be compared to 'other formally constructed political tracts' (i.e. 'humanist' political dialogues) ('Spenser's Irish Crisis', p. 23).

72. *A View*, p. 149.

73. Henley, *Spenser in Ireland*, pp. 61–2.

74. Ibid., p. 139.

75. Judson, *Life of Edmund Spenser*, p. 128.

76. See *Variorum*, 5, pp. 336–47.

77. Lauren Silberman, 'Singing Unsung Heroines: Androgynous Discourse in Book 3 of *The Faerie Queene*', in *Rewriting the Renaissance*, eds. Margaret W. Ferguson, Maureen Quilligan, and Nancy Vickers (Chicago: University of Chicago Press, 1986), p. 384.

78. *A View*, p. 46.

79. See *Royal Irish Academy Dictionary*, Compact Edition (Dublin: Royal Irish Academy, 1983), where the seventeenth-century Geoffrey Keating's *History of Ireland* is cited under the entry for 'Saxain'.

80. *A View*, p. 66.

81. *Variorum*, 9, p. 346.

82. Renwick does not give 'puttockes' as a possible reading for 'patchocks' in his edition of *A View* (p. 64). However, as the editors of the Variorum edition explain, 'patchocks' is found only in this context. In any case the reading 'patchocks' is uncertain, and 'puttockes' is suggested as a possible reading (*Variorum*, 9, p. 346).

83. *A View*, p. 70.

84. See *Dictionary of the Royal Irish Academy*: 'radaid . . . rad* perfective stem of *dobeir* gives' (p. 499). See also Niall Ó Dónaill, ed., *Foclóir Gaeilge-Béarla* (Dublin: Richview, Browne & Nolan, 1977), pp. 679, 979.

85. *A View*, pp. 50, 73.

86. Ibid., p. 153.

87. Ibid., p. 61.

88. Ibid., pp. 123–4.

89. *Variorum*, 9, p. 328. See Brady's discussion of what he sees as the difference between the more outspoken and less disguised arguments of *A Briefe Note* and the dialogue in *A View* ('Spenser's Irish Crisis', pp. 48–9).

90. For a discussion of both agricultural and medical metaphors in *A View* see Eamon Grennan, 'Language and Politics: A Note on Some Metaphors in Spenser's *A View of the Present State of Ireland*', *Spenser Studies* 3 (1982), pp. 99–110.

Representations of Women

1. David Beers Quinn, *The Elizabethans and the Irish* (Ithaca, 1966). Amongst important books on early modern Ireland are: Nicholas Canny, *The Elizabethan Conquest of Ireland: A Pattern Established 1565–76* (New York, 1976); T. W. Moody, F. X. Martin, and F. J. Byrne, *A New History of Ireland: Vol. III: Early Modern Ireland 1534–1691* (Oxford, 1976); Dudley Edwards, *Ireland in the Age of the Tudors* (New York, 1977); Brendan Bradshaw, *The Irish Constitutional Revolution in the Sixteenth Century* (Cambridge, 1979); Steven G. Ellis, *Tudor Ireland* (London, 1985). On Irish women of this period, see Margaret MacCurtain and Mary O'Dowd, eds., *Women in Early Modern Ireland* (Dublin, 1991).

2. For the debate, see Nicholas Canny, 'Edmund Spenser and the Development of an Anglo-Irish Identity', *Yearbook of English Studies* 13 (1983), pp. 1–19; idem, 'Debate: Spenser's Irish Crisis: Humanism and Experience in the 1590s', *Past and Present* 120 (1988), pp. 201–9; Ciaran Brady, 'Spenser's Irish Crisis: Humanism and Experience in the 1590s', *Past and Present* 111 (1986), pp. 16–49; idem, 'Reply to Nicholas Canny', *Past and Present* 120 (1988), pp. 210–15; Brendan Bradshaw, 'Robe and Sword in the Conquest of Ireland', in *Law and Government under the Tudors*, ed. Claire Cross et al. (Cambridge, 1988); and Patricia Coughlan, ed., *Spenser and Ireland* (Cork, 1989). On gender in the tracts, see Ann Rosalind Jones and Peter Stallybrass, 'Dismantling Irena: The Sexualizing of Ireland in Early Modern England', in *Nationalisms and Sexualities*, ed. Andrew Parker et al. (New York, 1992), pp. 157–71.

3. Giraldus Cambrensis, *Topographia Hibernia* in *Giraldi Cambrensis Opera*, vol. 5, ed. J. F. Dimock (Rolls Series, 1867). For the effects of these stereotypes on English writing on Ireland, see Anne Laurence, 'The Cradle to the Grave: English Observations of Irish Social Customs in the Seventeenth Century', *Seventeenth Century* 3.1 (1988), pp. 63–84.

4. Edmund Spenser, *A View of the Present State of Ireland*, ed. W. L. Renwick (Oxford, 1970), p. 61 (hereafter cited as *A View*).

5. *A View*, p. 62.

6. See Steven Greenblatt's chapter on Spenser in *Renaissance Self-Fashioning* (Chicago, 1980); and chapter 2, reprinted from 'The Construction of Gender, Class and the Political Other in *The Faerie Queene V* and *A View of the Present State of Ireland*', *Criticism* (Spring 1990), pp. 163–92.

7. Richard Stanihurst, 'A Treatise Conteining A Plaine and Perfect Description of Ireland,' in *Holinshed's Chronicles of England, Scotland, and Ireland*, 6 vols. (New York, 1976), 6, pp. 1–69 (hereafter referred to as 'Description of Ireland').

8. Other Old English tracts include: Sir Nicholas Walsh, *The Office and Duety in Fighting for Our Country* (London, 1545); D. B. Quinn, ed., 'Conjectures on the State of Ireland, 1552', *Irish Historical Studies* 5 (1947), pp. 303–22; Rowland White, ' "Discourse Touching Ireland" *c.* 1569', ed. Nicholas Canny, *Irish Historical Studies* 20 (1976–7), pp. 451–83.

9. Louis Montrose, 'The Work of Gender in the Discourse of Discovery', *Representations* 33 (Winter 1991), p. 1; Joan Scott, *Gender and the Politics of History* (New York, 1988), p. 42.

10. Scott, *Gender and the Politics of History*, pp. 43–4.

11. Richard Beacon, *Solon His Follie, or A Politique Discourse, Touching the Reformation of common-weales conquered, declined or corrupted* (Oxford, 1594). Vincent Carey and I are editing this text for Medieval and Renaissance Texts & Studies. Sir William Herbert, *Croftus Sive de Hibernia Liber*, ed. and trans. Arthur Keaveney and John A. Madden (Dublin, 1992). For comparison of Herbert and Beacon with Spenser, see note 2 above. On Beacon's life, see *DNB* and Michael McCarthy-Morrogh, *The Munster Plantation* (Oxford, 1986).

12. *A View*, p. 66.

13. Barnabe Riche, *A New Description of Ireland* (London, 1610), p. 34.

14. Mary O'Dowd, 'Gaelic Economy and Society', in *Natives and Newcomers*, ed. C. Brady and R. Gillespie (Dublin, 1986), p. 129.

15. For Stanihurst's life, see Colm Lennon, *Richard Stanihurst, the Dubliner 1547–1618* (Dublin, 1981).

16. Stanihurst, 'Description of Ireland', p. 4.

17. Ibid., pp. 4–5.

18. Ibid., p. 67; *A View*, pp. 67–8.

19. Riche, *A New Description of Ireland*, pp. 33–4.

20. Ibid., p. 34.

21. Ibid., p. 90.

22. Ibid., p. 15.

23. *A View*, pp. 84–5.

24. Riche, *A New Description of Ireland*, p. 31.

25. Ibid., pp. 45–6.

26. Barnabe Riche, *The Irish Hubbub, or The English Hue and Crie* (London, 1617), p. 51.

27. Ibid., pp. 51–2.

28. Riche, *A New Description of Ireland*, p. 71.

29. Barnabe Riche, *A True and Kinde Excuse, written in Defence of that Booke, intituled A New Description of Irelande* (London, 1612), p. 6 (sig. C 1).

30. Barnabe Riche, *My Ladies Looking Glasse* (London, 1615). Barbara Bowen and Susan Gushee O'Malley introduced me to this text, which will appear in their forthcoming edition of tracts on women.

31. Riche, *My Ladies Looking Glasse*, p. 16; *A New Description of Ireland*, pp. 90–1.

32. Riche, *My Ladies Looking Glasse*, p. 52.

33. *A View*, p. 53.

34. Fynes Moryson, 'A Description of Ireland', in *Ireland Under Elizabeth and James the First*, ed. Henry Morley (London, 1890), p. 425.

35.   Riche, *A New Description of Ireland*, p. 40.
36.   Moryson, 'Description of Ireland,' p. 430.
37.   Michel de Certeau, *The Writing of History*, trans. Tom Conley (New York, 1988), p. 233.
38.   Beacon, *Solon His Follie*, 'The Epistle Dedicatorie', fol. 3r.
39.   Ibid., 'The booke vnto the Reader', jv.
40.   Sir John Davies, 'A Discovery of the True Causes Why Ireland Was Never Entirely Subdued', in *Ireland Under Elizabeth and James the First*, p. 247 (hereafter referred to as 'A Discovery'.
41.   Davies, 'A Discovery', p. 249.
42.   *A View*, pp. 95–6.
43.   'Dr. [Leonel] Sharp to the Duke of Buckingham', printed in *Cabala, Mysteries of State, in Letters of the Great Ministers of K. James and K. Charles* (London, 1656), p. 259.
44.   *A View*, p. 104.
45.   Ibid., p. 105.
46.   Ibid., p. 106.
47.   Beacon, *Solon*, 'The booke vnto the Reader', jv.
48.   Stanihurst, 'Description of Ireland', p. 69.
49.   Davies, 'A Discovery', p. 297.
50.   Beacon, *Solon*, pp. 3–4.
51.   Edmund Spenser, *The Faerie Queene*, ed. Thomas P. Roche, Jr. with C. Patrick O'Donnell Jr. (New Haven, 1981), p. 16.
52.   See Roy Strong, *The Cult of Elizabeth* (Berkeley, 1977), pp. 46–50, for descriptions of Elizabeth as a type of Diana–Venus.
53.   John King, *Tudor Royal Iconography: Literature and Art in an Age of Religious Crisis* (Princeton, 1989), plate 11a, pp. 182–267.
54.   Beacon, *Solon*, p. 4. I would like to thank Betty Travitsky and the members of the Society for the Study of Women in the Renaissance for their responses to a version of this paper that I presented to our seminar at the CUNY Graduate Centre.

Spenser's Relation to the Irish Language

1.   All quotations of *A View* are from the edition edited by W. L. Renwick (Oxford: Clarendon Press, 1970). The quotations in this paragraph are taken from pp. 67–8.
2.   *A View*, pp. 158–9.
3.   One notable exception is my tutor the late Helena Shire who, in her lectures and tutorials at Cambridge in the 1970s, stressed Spenser's context in Ireland and speculated about his knowledge of Irish. Philologists of the first half of this century were interested in Spenser's knowledge of Irish; see John W. Draper, 'Spenser's Linguistics in the Present State of Ireland', *Modern Philology* 17 (1919), pp. 471–86; F. F. Covington, 'Another View of Spenser's Linguistics', *Studies in Philology* 19 (1922), pp. 244–8; Roland M. Smith, 'The Irish Background of Spenser's "View"', *JEGP* 42 (1943), pp. 499–515; and Roland M. Smith, 'Irish Names in the *Faerie Queene*', *MLN* 61 (1946), pp. 27–38.

4. On the connection between Spenser's use of Middle English and the dialect of Wexford and Fingall described in Stanihurst's 'Description', see Willy Maley, 'Spenser's Irish English: Language and Identity in Early Modern Ireland', *Studies in Philology* (1994), pp. 417–31.

5. For the importance of patronage connections to Spenser's appointment in Ireland, see Vincent Carey and Clare Carroll, 'Factions and Fictions: Spenser's Reflections of and on Elizabethan Politics', in Judith Anderson, Donald Cheney, and David Richardson (eds.), *Spenser's Life and the Subject of Biography* (Amherst: University of Massachusetts Press, 1996).

6. Spenser, *Shepheardes Calender*, in *The Yale Edition of the Shorter Poems of Edmund Spenser*, ed. William A. Oram, Einar Bjorvand, Ronald Bond, Thomas H. Cain, Alexander Dunlop, and Richard Schell (New Haven: Yale University Press, 1989).

7. Richard Stanihurst, 'Description of Ireland', in Raphael Holinshed, *The Chronicles of England, Scotlande, Irelande*, ed. John Hooker et al., 3 vols. (London: H. Bynneman for J. Harrison, 1577, 1587), reprint, ed. Henry Ellis, 6 vols. (London: J. Johnson, 1807–8), 6, p. 67.

8. Stanihurst, 'Description of Ireland', 6, p. 68.

9. John Derricke, *The Image of Ireland with A Discoverie of Woodkarne*, with an introduction, transliteration and glossary by David B. Quinn (Belfast: Blackstaff Press, 1985), p. 219.

10. See Brian Ó Cuív, 'The Irish Language in the Early Modern Period', in T. W. Moody, F. X. Martin, and F. J. Byrne (eds.), *A New History of Ireland*, 9 vols. (Oxford: Clarendon Press, 1976), 3, pp. 509–13.

11. See Reg Hindley, *The Death of the Irish Language* (London and New York: Routledge, 1990), pp. 5–8.

12. Stanihurst, 'Description of Ireland', 6, p. 6.

13. Ibid., 6, p. 4.

14. On the use of Irish in official state correspondence, see Brian Ó Cuív, 'The Irish Language in the Early Modern Period', pp. 514, 521.

15. See Raymond Jenkins, 'Spenser with Lord Grey in Ireland', *PMLA* 52 (1937), pp. 338–9.

16. See Roland M. Smith, 'The Irish Background of Spenser's "View"', pp. 502–6, and 'Spenser's Scholarly Script and "Right Writing"', in Don Cameron Allen (ed.), *Studies in Honor of T. W. Baldwin* (Urbana: University of Illinois Press, 1958), pp. 102–3.

17. See State Papers 63/85/5 and 'Spenser's bill against Roche', State Papers 63/147/16.

18. See Smith, 'Spenser's Scholarly Script', p. 103, n. 54; *Calendar of Carew Manuscripts, 1513–74*, p. 352, no. 239: 'this said Lord O'Neyll to have all the preeminence, jurisdiction, and dominion . . . over the Lords subject to him commonly called "wrrachadh" [urraghs]'.

19. Ó Cuív, 'The Irish Language in the Early Modern Period', p. 511, n. 1.

20. *A View*, p. 40. All quotations in this paragraph are from pp. 39–40. I found myself in the same position when responding to a talk by an Irish-born academic on early modern English representations of Ireland at the 1993 City University of New York conference on Shakespeare and the Nation.

21. Ibid., p. 75.

22. Ibid., p. 42.

23. Ibid., p. 42.

24. Roland M. Smith was the first to recognize that Spenser had to have known an Irish version of the Milesian invasion story in 'Spenser, Holinshed, and the *Leabhar Gabhála*', *JEGP* 43 (1944), pp. 390–401.

25. Roland M. Smith was the first to speculate on the Irish intertexts for *The Faerie Queene* 5.4 in 'Spenser's Tale of the Two Sons of Milesio', *MLQ* 3 (1942), pp. 547–57.

26. All quotations are from Edmund Spenser, *The Faerie Queene*, ed. Thomas P. Roche Jr and C. Patrick O'Donnell Jr (New Haven and London: Yale University Press, 1981).

27. See *Lebor Gabála Érenn, the Book of the Taking of Ireland*, Part V, edited with an introduction and notes by R. A. Stewart Macalister (Dublin: Irish Texts Society, 1956), pp. 54–5.

28. Ibid., pp. 54–5.

29. Ibid., pp. 114–15.

30. Ibid., pp. 64–5, 126–7.

31. Ibid., pp. 160–1.

Ajax in Ulster and Ariosto in Ireland

1. *The Letters & Epigrams of Sir John Harington*, ed. Norman Egbert McClure (Philadelphia: University of Pennsylvania Press, 1930), p. 108 (hereafter referred to as '*L & E*').

2. *L & E*, p. 79.

3. *L & E*, p. 12. For the requirements of settlers on the plantation, see Michael MacCarthy-Morrogh, *The Munster Plantation* (Oxford: Clarendon Press, 1986).

4. *Orlando Furioso* 29.55, p. 331.

5. *Ludovico Ariosto's 'Orlando Furioso' translated into English Heroical Verse by Sir John Harington* (1591), ed. Robert McNulty (Oxford: Clarendon Press, 1972), p. 22.

6. See Johannes Fabian, *Time and the Other: How Anthropology Makes Its Object* (New York: Columbia University Press, 1983).

7. Chapter 1 of this book, and Walter Mignolo, *The Darker Side of the Renaissance*, p. xi.

8. See chapter 4 of this book, and Roland M. Smith, 'Spenser, Holinshed, and the *Leabhar Gabhála*', *JEGP* 43 (1944), pp. 390–401.

9. Spenser, *A View of the Present State of Ireland*, ed. W. L. Renwick (Oxford: Clarendon Press, 1970), pp. 43–5.

10. See, for example, among many others, the anonymous 'A Good Ship's Company' and Eoghan Ruadh Mac an Bhaird, 'The Sorrows of Éire', in *The Life of Aodh Ruadh Ó Domhnaill*, ed. Paul Walsh, Part II, pp. 118–19, pp. 140–140. On the use of this trope in the work of the historian Philip O'Sullivan Beare, see chapter 7.

11. See Gerald of Wales, *The History and Topography of Wales*, trans. John J. O'Meara (Harmondsworth: Penguin, 1982), pp. 100–1; Barnabe Riche, *A New Description of Ireland* (London, 1610), p. 40; Fynes Morison, *An Itinerary*, 4 vols. (Glasgow, 1907–8), 4: pp. 197, 237–338. Also see chapter 3.

12. *A View*, pp. 50–3.
13. For another discussion of this passage, which emphasizes the idealized character of Oberto in Ariosto but does not comment on the further idealization of the hero by Harington, see Eric G. Haywood, 'Is Ireland Worth Bothering About? Classical Perceptions of Ireland Revisited in Renaissance Italy', *International Journal of the Classical Tradition*, vol. 2, no. 4, (1996), pp. 467–86, 470–1.
14. Harington (1591), *Orlando Furioso*, p. 131.
15. Ibid., p. 286.
16. On Harington's translation of the *Orlando Furioso* and the allegorical tradition, see Susannah McMurphy, *Spenser's Use of Ariosto for Allegory* (Seattle: University of Washington Press, 1924); Townsend Rich, *Harington and Ariosto: A Study in Elizabethan Verse Translation* (New Haven: Yale University Press, 1940), and Daniel Javitch's chapter on Harington in *Proclaiming a Classic: The Canonization of 'Orlando Furioso'* (Princeton: Princeton University Press, 1991), especially n. 17, p. 195.
17. 'To Master Thomas Combe, Aug. 31, 1599', in *L & E*, p. 74.
18. See Dáithí Ó hÓgáin, *Myth, Legend & Romance: An Encyclopedia of the Irish Folk Tradition* (New York: Prentice Hall Press, 1991), pp. 407–9.
19. Harington (1591), *Orlando Furioso*, p. 140.
20. 'Notes for Lodovick Briskett for the court', 1 July 1578, in *Letters and Memorials of State . . . written and collected by Sir Henry Sidney, Sir Philip Sidney and his brother, Sir Robert Sidney*, ed. Arthur Collins (vols. 2 London, 1746), 2, p. 263. I am grateful to Vincent Carey for this reference.
21. 'To Sir Anthony Standen, Athlone, Ireland, 1599', in *L & E*, p. 70.
22. C. Falls, *Elizabeth's Irish Wars* (London, 1950), p. 225; *L & E*, pp. 68, 47; Steven G. Ellis, *Tudor Ireland*, p. 306.
23. For an account of this, see 'Journal of the L. Lieutenants procedinges from the xxviiith Aug. tyll the viiith of Spet. 1599', in *Nugae Antiquae*, ed. Thomas Park (London, 1804), vol. 1, pp. 293–301.
24. 'The Queene to the Erl of Essex, in answer to his Lettre with his Journall', in *Nugae Antiquae*, vol.1, pp. 302–8.
25. 'To Justice Carey [i.e. Carew], Ireland, October 1599', in *L & E*, p. 77.
26. *L & E*, p. 78.
27. See Hiram Morgan, *Tyrone's Rebellion* (London: Royal Historical Society, 1993), pp. 97, 108.
28. Katharine Simms, *From Kings to Warlords: The Changing Political Structure of Ireland in the Later Middle Ages* (Woodbridge, Suffolk: Boydell Press, 1987), p. 115.
29. *L & E*, p. 78.
30. Harington (1591), *Orlando Furioso*, p. 541.
31. *L & E*, p. 77.
32. Ibid., pp. 74, 77.
33. Ibid, p. 74.
34. *Nugae Antiquae*, vol. 1, p. 290.
35. 'A Short View of the State of Ireland Written in 1605 by Sir John Harington', ed. W. Dunn Macray (Oxford: James Parker, 1879); *Anecdota Bodleiana: Gleanings from Bodleian MSS*, p. 10.
36. The three MSS are: T.C.D. 1399 (formerly T.C.D. H. 5. 28), T.C.D. 1335 (formerly T.C.D. H. 3. 16), and British Museum, Egerton 106. T.C.D. 1339 is the

source of the other two manuscripts. There are two modern editions of the text: Máire Mhac an tSaoi (ed.), *Dhá Sgéal Artúraíochta. Mar atá Eachtra Mhelóra agus Orlando, agus Céilidhe Iosgaide Léithe* (Dublin, 1946), and A. M. E. Draak (ed.), 'Orlando agus Melora', *Béaloideas*, vol. 16 (1946), pp. 2–48.

37.   Draak (ed.), 'Orlando agus Melora', pp. 11, 14.

38.   Ibid., p. 45.

39.   Robin Flower and Standish Hayes O'Grady (eds.), *Catalogue of Irish Manuscripts in the British Museum*, vol. II (London: British Museum, 1926; reprint: Dublin: Dublin Institute for Advanced Studies, 1992), p. 339.

40.   See, for example, Draak (ed.), 'Orlando agus Melora', pp.35, 46; *Orlando Furioso* 32.79.

41.   *The Pursuit of Gruaidh Ghriansholus*, ed. and trans. Cecile O'Rahilly (London: Irish Texts Society, 1924), p. viii.

42.   See Alan Bruford, *Gaelic Folk-Tales and Mediaeval Romances* (Dublin: Folklore of Ireland Society, 1969), p. 49.

43.   See Townsend Rich, *Harington and Ariosto*, pp. 50–69. I am indebted to Antonio Ricci of the University of Toronto who has written a dissertation on the illustrations to the *Orlando Furioso* and who confirmed my judgement of the close correspondence between the illustrations to the Irish *Orlando agus Melora* and the Porro engravings.

44.   See the discussion of Sir John Harington's *Epigrams* in the context of lyric love poetry in Irish, and, in particular, the indebtedness of Riocard do Búrc's *Fir na Fódla ar ndul d'éag* in Mícheál Mac Craith, 'Gaelic Courtly Love Poetry: A Window on the Renaissance', in *Celtic Languages and Celtic Peoples: Proceedings of the Second North American Congress of Celtic Studies* (Halifax, Nova Scotia, 1989), and Mac Craith's *Lorg Na hIasachta Ar Na Dánta Grá* (Baile Átha Cliath: An Cló-chomhar, 1989), pp. 100–14.

45.   Bruford, *Gaelic Folk-Tales and Mediaeval Romances*, p. 28.

46.   Recently Caoimhín Breatnach has suggested that the Irish romantic prose tales based on the heroic, mythological and king cycles need to be read allegorically: 'the equating of contemporary events and persons with past events and persons figures prominently in our tales' (*Patronage, Politics, and Prose: Ceasacht Inghine Guile Sgéala Muice Meic Dhá Thó Oidheadh Chuinn Chéadchathaigh* [Maynooth: An Sagart, 1996], p. 13). But see the review by Máirín Ní Dhonnchadha (*Éigse* 30 (1997), pp. 216–29) in which she doubts his particular allegorical readings, as well as the possibility of allegory in these tales at all, since there is no explicit indication in these texts that they are allegorical. The tradition of allegorical readings of European romances, particularly of the *Orlando Furioso* as interpreted by Harington in his translation, which as we have seen was known in Ireland, suggests at the very least the possibility of an allegorical reading for *Orlando agus Melora*.

47.   Quoted in Henry Thomas, *Spanish and Portuguese Romances of Chivalry* (Cambridge: Cambridge University Press, 1920), p. 257.

48.   Quoted in Thomas, p. 259.

49.   Kaarina Hollo, 'Eachtra Ridire na Leomhan ina comhthéacs Eorpach', in *Nua-Léamha: Gnéithe de Chultúr, Stair agus Polaitíocht na hÉireann c. 1600–c. 1900*, ed. Máirín Ní Dhonnchadha (Baile Átha Cliath: An Chlóchomhar, 1996), pp. 60–1.

50.   Charles Wilson, *Select Irish Poems Translated into English* (Dublin, 1782), quoted in Andrew Carpenter and Alan Harrison, 'Swift's "O'Rourke's Feast" and

Sheridan's "Letter": Early Transcripts by Anthony Raymond', in Herman Real and Heinz Vienken (eds.), *Proceedings of the First Munster Symposium on Jonathan Swift* (Munich, 1985), pp. 40–1; also quoted in Hollo, p. 61.

51.   The fourth unnumbered leaf of T.C.D. 1335 contains this note: 'In the end some particular notes by Mr. Lhuyd'.

52.   'A Translation of the Irish Preface, to Mr. Lhuyd's Irish Dictionary', in William Nicolson, *The Irish Historical Library* (Dublin: Aaron Rhames, for R. Owen, Bookseller), 1724, p. 192.

53.   Ibid., p. 192.

54.   Ibid., p. 192.

55.   Ibid., p. 208; Lhuyd, *Archaeologica Brittanica* (1707), p. 314.

56.   Ibid., pp. 208–9.

57.   Draak (ed.), 'Orlando agus Melora', pp. 28, 29, 36, 37 (fols. 138 v, 139 r, 139 v, 145 r, 145 v).

58.   Draak (ed.), 'Orlando agus Melora', p. 37 (fol. 145 v).

59.   Joep Leerssen, *Mere Irish and Fíor-Ghael* (Cork: Cork University Press, 1996), pp. 288–9, 291–3, 340.

60.   On the myth of the Scythian origins of the Irish, see Andrew Hadfield, *Spenser's Irish Experience: Wilde Fruit and Savage Soyl* (Oxford: Clarendon Press, 1997), pp. 101–8.

61.   Nicolson, p. 209.

62.   Ibid., p. 210.

The Janus Face of Machiavelli

1.   *Breve relacion de la present persecucion de Irlanda* (Sevilla, 1619), pp. 15–16: 'imputando a falta de policia elaferrarse tan tenazmente los Irlandeses a sus Catholicas, sanas, y antiguas costumbres, y ferrarse tanto a las porphanas novedades, errores, vicios, y Machiavellistica o Calvinistica policia que ellos que sierá vèr introduzida'. Thanks to Cyrus Moore for the translation.

2.   Felix Raab, *The English Face of Machiavelli: A Changing Interpretation 1500–1700* (London: Routledge & Kegan Paul, 1964), esp. pp. 56–7, 69; Mario Praz, *Machiavelli in Inghilterra ed altri sagii* (Rome: Tumminelli, 1942); 'Machiavelli and the Elizabethans', in *The Flaming Heart* (New York, 1968).

3.   Brendan Bradshaw, 'Edmund Spenser on Justice and Mercy', in *The Writer as Witness: Literature as Historical Evidence*, ed. Tom Dunne (Cork: Cork University Press, 1987), p. 86.

4.   Sydney Anglo, 'A Machiavellian Solution to the Irish Problem: Richard Beacon's *Solon His Follie* (1594)', in *England and the Continental Renaissance*, ed. Edward Chaney and Peter Mack (Woodbridge: Boydell Press, 1990).

5.   Markku Peltonen, 'Classical Republicanism in Tudor England: The Case of Richard Beacon's *Solon His Follie*', *History of Political Thought* 15, 4 (1994), pp. 469–503, and *Classical Humanism and Republicanism in English Political Thought 1570–1640* (Cambridge: Cambridge University Press, 1995), pp. 73–102, 73, 77.

6.   See my 'Introduction: The Text, Its Sources, and Traditions', in Richard Beacon, *Solon His Follie, or A Politique Discourse Touching the Reformation of common-*

weales conquered, declined, or corrupted, ed. C. Carroll and V. Carey (Binghamton, N.Y.: Medieval & Renaissance Texts & Studies, 1996), pp. xxvi–xlii, esp. pp. xxxviii–xxxix. This is the edition of the text referred to in this article as *Solon His Follie*.

7.   Andrew Hadfield, *Spenser's Irish Experience: Wild Fruit and Savage Soyl* (Oxford: Clarendon Press, 1997), pp. 73–8.

8.   Edwin Greenlaw, 'The Influence of Machiavelli on Spenser', *Modern Philology* 7 (1909), pp. 187–202.

9.   Vincent Carey, 'The Irish Face of Machiavelli: Richard Beacon's *Solon His Follie* (1594) and Republican Ideology in the Conquest of Ireland', in Hiram Morgan (ed.), *Political Ideology in Ireland 1541–1641* (Dublin: Four Courts Press, 1999), pp. 83–109.

10.   In this respect their interpretation of Machiavelli resembles the reconciliation of *The Prince* with the *Discourses* in the earlier sixteenth-century manuscript of Stephen Gardiner; see *A Machiavellian Treatise by Stephen Gardiner*, ed. Peter Samuel Donaldson (Cambridge: Cambridge University Press, 1975), p. 20.

11.   Marc Caball, *Poets and Politics: Reaction and Continuity in Irish Poetry, 1558–1625* (Cork: Cork University Press, 1998). See also Vincent Carey, ' "Neither good English nor good Irish": Bi-lingualism and Identity Formation in Sixteenth-Century Ireland', in Morgan (ed.), *Political Ideology in Ireland, 1541–1641*, pp. 45–61.

12.   Niccolò Machiavelli, *The Prince*, trans. George Bull (Harmondsworth: Penguin, 1961), p. 36. For the influence of Machiavelli, whether direct or indirect, on the New English, see D. B. Quinn, 'Renaissance Influences on English Colonization', *Transactions of the Royal Historical Society* 26 (1976), pp. 73–93.

13.   *Solon His Follie*, p. 144; *A View*, pp. 141, 153.

14.   *A View*, p. 3. See Greenlaw, 'The Influence of Machiavelli on Spenser', p. 9.

15.   *A View*, p. 12. See Greenlaw, p. 10.

16.   *Solon His Follie*, p. 104; *A View*, against Hugh O'Neill, pp. 113–15; *The Prince* iii, p. 39; vii; xix. See Greenlaw, p. 12.

17.   Lisa Jardine, 'Mastering the Uncouth: Gabriel Harvey, Edmund Spenser and the English Experience in Ireland', in *New Perspectives on Renaissance Thought: Essays in the History of Science, Education and Philosophy*, ed. John Henry and Sarah Hutton (London: Duckworth, 1990).

18.   *Discourses* II.16, 30; *Solon His Follie*, pp. 129, 116.

19.   *Discourses* II.23; *Solon His Follie*, p. 71.

20.   *Discourses* II.23; *Solon His Follie*, pp. 70–1.

21.   *Solon His Follie*, p. 70.

22.   *Discourses* II.33; *A View*, p. 169.

23.   *Solon His Follie*, pp. 34–5; *A View*, pp. 106–7.

24.   *Discourses* II.6.

25.   *Solon His Follie* II.12, p.63; *Discourses* III.3.

26.   *A View*, p. 96.

27.   Niccolò Machiavelli, *The Discourses*, ed. Bernard Crick and trans. Leslie J. Walker, S.J. (Harmondsworth: Penguin, 1970), p. 282.

28.   *Solon His Follie*, p. 75.

29.   *A View*, p. 95.

30.   *The Prince* v, p. 48.

31.   *Solon His Follie*, p. 122.

32.   Ibid., pp. 40, 76; *Discourses* I.18, p. 163.

33.   *The Prince* vi, p. 50

34.   *Solon His Follie*, p. 98; *The Prince* vi, p. 50.

35.   *Discourses*, p. 430.

36.   *Solon His Follie*, p. 35.

37.   Ibid., pp. 34–5.

38.   *Discourses* III.9, p. 432.

39.   *Solon His Follie*, p. 41.

40.   *Discourses*, I.18, p. 163.

41.   Ibid., p. 163.

42.   *A View*, p. 94.

43.   *Discourses* III.1, p. 386.

44.   Ibid., p. 390; *Solon His Follie*, p. 23.

45.   *A View*, pp. 141–2.

46.   *Solon His Follie*, p. 19.

47.   Ibid., pp. 18–19.

48.   Peltonen, *Classical Humanism and Republicanism in English Political Thought*, pp. 101–2; *Solon His Follie*, p. 64; *Discourses* II.3.

49.   *A View*, p. 123. Greenlaw compares this passage to *The Prince* xx, where Machiavelli recommends disarming a newly conquered state ('The Influence of Machiavelli on Spenser', pp. 9–10).

50.   Ibid., p. 140.

51.   *Discourses* I.20, p. 168; J. Patrick Coby, *Machiavelli's Romans: Liberty and Greatness in the Discourses on Livy* (Lanham, Maryland, New York, Oxford: Lexington Books, 1999), p. 120.

52.   *Solon His Follie*, p. 72.

53.   *Discourses* I.20, p. 168; *Solon His Follie*, p. 75.

54.   *Discourses* II.2, p. 280.

55.   Ibid., p. 280.

56.   *Solon His Follie* II.19.

57.   *A View*, p. 105.

58.   *Solon His Follie* III.5.

59.   *Solon His Follie* II.3.

60.   Royal Irish Academy MS 24G16, fol. 33r. See Bernadette Cunningham's discussion of Kearney's translation in *The World of Geoffrey Keating* (Dublin: Four Courts Press, 2000), pp. 182–7.

61.   'Metamorphosis 1603', ed. Pádraig A. Breatnach, *Éigse* 17 (1977–8), pp. 167–80, p. 171, stanza 2: 'Óibhid . . . ag labhradh / ar cclaochládh na ccéadadhbhar'. See the account of this poem in Marc Caball, *Poets and Politics: Reaction and Continuity in Irish Poetry, 1558–1625* (Cork: Cork University Press, 1998), pp. 88–91. For the influence of Ovid on early modern Irish poetry, see Mícheál Mac Craith, 'Gaelic Ireland and the Renaissance', in *The Celts and the Renaissance: Tradition and Innovation*, ed. Glenmore Williams and Robert Owen Jones (Cardiff: University of Wales Press, 1990), pp. 57–69, esp. pp. 63–7.

62.   'Ar dtús a n-olc do iompó.'

63.   'James Our True King: The Ideology of Irish Royalism in the Seventeenth Century', in G. Boyce et al., *Political Thought in Ireland* (London, 1993), pp. 1–35.

64. James Carney, *The Irish Bardic Poet* (Dublin: Dolmen Press, 1967), p. 11. See also Pádraig A. Breatnach 'The Chief's Poet', *Proceedings of the Royal Irish Academy*, vol. 83, C, no. 3 (1983), pp. 37–79; R. A. Breatnach 'The Lady and the King', *Studies* XLII (1953): pp. 321–36; T. F. O'Rahilly, 'The Names Érainn and Ériu', *Ériu* XIV (1946), pp. 7–28.

65. 'Atá Seireis – as sé a shuim / ag treabhadh thulach ndíoghuinn' [stanza 9].

66. Among the instances of *fortún* listed in the *Royal Irish Academy Dictionary of the Irish Language* are the following: *Flight of the Earls* 180.32; *Leabhar Cloinne Aodha Buidhe* 211.16; Keating, *Three Shafts of Death*, 7086; Mac Aingil, *Scáthán shacramuinte na haithridhe* 61.16. It is interesting to note that the medieval translation of Lucan's *De bello civili* into Irish as *In Cath Catharda* uses *toici* rather than *fortún* to render the Latin *fortuna* into Irish.

67. See Hanna Fenichel Pitkin, *Fortune is a Woman: Gender and Politics in the Thought of Niccolo Machiavelli* with a New Afterword (Chicago: University of Chicago Press, 1999), p. 144.

68. On the sense of *virtù* as craft or art, see Joseph A. Mazzeo, 'Machiavelli: The Artist as Statesman', in *Renaissance and Seventeenth-Century Studies* (New York: Columbia University Press, 1964), pp. 145–65.

69. Breandán Ó Buachalla, 'Poetry and Politics in Early Modern Ireland', *Eighteenth Century Ireland* 7 (1992), pp. 149–75.

70. See Marc Caball's discussion of the poem in his *Poets and Politics*, pp. 116–17. The poem is printed in James Carney (ed.), *Poems on the O'Reillys* (Dublin: Dublin Institute for Advanced Studies, 1950), pp. 121–7.

71. The translation is by Brian Richardson, 'Appendix: Machiavelli's Letter to Francesco Vettori, 10 December 1513', in *Niccolò Machiavelli's The Prince: New Interdisciplinary Essays*, ed. Martin Coyle (Manchester and New York: Manchester University Press, 1995), p. 198.

72. The translation of ll. 2913–17 is by Carney (1950), p. 229: '"Since what has befallen me is customary with me," said Cornelia, "my heart regrets that Caesar is not my husband so that he might meet with misfortune." Just like her must I hope to find a lover amongst my enemies; that descendant of Conn will not be our beloved one of the Irish seeing that the one I love is not destined to endure.'

73. See Myles Dillon et al., *Catalogue of Irish Manuscripts in the Franciscan Library Killiney* (Dublin: Dublin Institute for Advanced Studies, 1969), p. 35: *An Cath Catharda*, 17th century, Irish translation of Lucan's *Pharsalia*; see W. Stokes (ed.), *Irische Texte* IV, pt. ii (1909).

74. David Quint, *Epic and Empire: Politics and Generic Form from Virgil to Milton* (Princeton: Princeton University Press, 1993).

75. See Willy Maley's account of the continuity of English colonial theory on Ireland from Spenser through to Milton, 'How Milton and some contemporaries read Spenser's *View*', in *Representing Ireland*, ed. B. Bradshaw, A. Hadfield, and W. Maley (Cambridge: Cambridge University Press, 1993), pp. 191–208.

76. Later, following the rebellion of 1641, the conflicting interpretations of Machiavelli can be seen, for example, in the accusation of Machiavellianism made against Strafford, an extension of the Machiavelli of force and deception in *The Prince* (see Thomas Crant, *The plott and progresse of the Irish rebellion: wherein is discovered the machavilian policie of the Earle of Straford, Sir George Ratcliffe and*

others, etc. [London, 1644]), and in the influence of the Machiavellian republicanism of the *Discourses* upon the English Revolution, see J. G. A. Pocock, *The Machiavellian Moment: Florentine Political Thought and the Atlantic Republican Tradition* (Princeton: Princeton University Press, 1975).

Irish and Spanish Cultural and Political Relations

1. Two recent articles that deal at least in part with O'Sullivan Beare are: Hiram Morgan, 'Faith and Fatherland in 16th Century Ireland', *History Ireland*, vol. 3, no. 2 (Summer 1995), pp. 13–20; Bernadette Cunningham and Raymond Gillespie, '"The most adaptable of saints": The Cult of Saint Patrick in the Seventeenth Century', *Archivium Hibernicum* XLIX (1995), pp. 82–104. See Aubrey Gwynn, 'An Unpublished Work of Philip O'Sullivan Bear', *Analecta Hibernica* 6 (1934), pp. 1–11; Denis J. O'Doherty, 'Domnaill O'Sullivan Beare and his Family in Spain', *Studies* xix (March 1930), pp. 211–26; W. F. Butler, 'The Identity of Philip O'Sullivan Beare "the Historian"', *Royal Society of Antiquaries of Ireland Journal*, series 6, xv (1925), pp. 95–8; Denis O'Connor, 'The Retreat of O'Sullivan Beare to the North', *Irish Ecclesiastical Record*, 4th series, xii (Oct. 1902), pp. 320–34; Matthew J. Byrne (trans.), 'Philip O'Sullivan Beare, Soldier, Poet, and Historian', *Cork Historical and Archaeological Society Journal*, series 2, ii (1896), pp. 392–7, 423–8, 457–67, 516–23; iii (1897), pp. 26–30, 182–8.

2. Conor O'Mahony, *Disputatio Apologetica de Iure Regni Hiberniae pro Catholicis Hibernis adversus haereticos Anglos. Accessit eiusdem authoris ad eosdem Catholicos exhortatio* (Frankfurt, 1645); Richard O'Ferrall, 'Ad Sacram Congregationem de Propaganda Fide. 5 Martii 1658'; John Lynch, *Alithinologia* (1664). See Patrick Corish, 'Two Contemporary Historians of the Confederation of Kilkenny: John Lynch and Richard O'Ferrall', *Irish Historical Studies* 9 (1952–3), pp. 271–36, and Tadhg Ó hAnnracháin, ' "Though Heretics and Politicians should Misinterpret their Good Zeale": Political Ideology and Catholicism in Early Modern Ireland', in *Political Thought in Seventeenth-Century Ireland*, ed. Jane Ohlmeyer (Cambridge: Cambridge University Press, 2000), pp. 155–75.

3. Edmund Borlase, *The History of the Execrable Irish Rebellion* (London, 1680); Richard Cox, *Hibernia Anglicana* (London, 1689). I am grateful to Jane Ohlmeyer for these references.

4. *Historiae Catholicae Hiberniae Compendium*, ed. Matthew Kelly (Dublin, 1850); *Ireland Under Elizabeth, being chapters towards a history of Ireland in the reign of Elizabeth being a portion of the history of Catholic Ireland by Don Philip O'Sullivan-Bear*, trans. and ed. Matthew J. Byrne (Dublin, 1903). Byrne translated only the dedicatory epistles and *Compendium* II.1v–III.vi.

5. Ussher, *Works* (Dublin, 1847), iv, p. 334; Standish O'Grady, Appendix to *Ulrick the Ready, A Romance of Elizabethan Ireland* (London, 1896), quoted by the Editor, *Cork Historical and Archaeological Society Journal*, series 2, vol. 2 (1896), p. 516.

6. Quoted in 'Don Philip O'Sullivan; the Siege of Dunboy and the Retreat and Asassination of the O'Sullivan Beare', *Waterford and Southeast of Ireland Archaeological Society*, 7 (1901), p. 118.

7. Philip O'Sullivan Beare, *Historiae Catholicae Iberniae Compendium*. Domino Philip Austriaco IIII. Hispaniarum, Indiarum, aliorum regnorum, atque multarum ditionum regi Catholico, monarquaesque potentissimo dicatum. (Lisbon, 1621). *Ireland Under Elizabeth, being chapters towards a history of Ireland in the reign of Elizabeth being a portion of the history of Catholic Ireland by Don Philip O'Sullivan-Bear*, trans. and ed. Matthew J. Byrne (Dublin, 1903), p. xxiii (all quotations in this paragraph). Byrne translated only the dedicatory epistles and *Compendium* II.lv–III.vi. All other translations from the *Compendium* are my own.

8. J. H. Elliott, *Spain and Its World 1500–1700* (New Haven and London, 1989), pp. 170, 171.

9. O'Sullivan Beare, *Ireland Under Elizabeth*, p. xxiv.

10. Ibid., p. xxiii.

11. Published as *De Regno Hiberniae Sanctorum Insula Commentarius* (Louvain, 1632), the manuscript 'De Hibernia Insula Commentarius Stromaticus' was written in Rome in 1600. See *Irish Historical Documents, 1, The Irish War of Defence 1598–1600, Extracts from 'De Hibernia Insula Commentarius' of Peter Lombard*, ed. Matthew J. Byrne (Cork, 1930), especially pp. 6, 40.

12. Juan de Mariana, *The General History of Spain from the first Peopling of it by Tubal, till the Death of King Ferdinand, Who United the Crowns of Castile and Aragon, To which are added Two Supplements, The First by F. Ferdinand Camargo y Salcedo, the other by Basil Varn de Soto, bringing it down to the present reign*, trans. John Stevens (London, 1699) vol. 1, pp. 5–6, 192, Supplement, p. 14.

13. O'Sullivan Beare, *Ireland Under Elizabeth*, p. xxvi.

14. Ussher, *Works* (Dublin, 1847), iv, p. 334.

15. See Alan Ford, *The Protestant Reformation in Ireland, 1590–1641* (Frankfurt, 1985), pp. 221–2.

16. J. G. Casey, 'Patriotism in Early Modern Valencia', in *Spain, Europe, and the Atlantic World: Essays in Honour of John H. Elliot* (Cambridge, 1995), p. 203.

17. O'Sullivan Beare, *Ireland Under Elizabeth*, p. xxvi.

18. *Irish Historical Documents*, 1, p. 41.

19. *Compendium*, fol. 36v.

20. Hiram Morgan, *Tyrone's Rebellion* (Woodbridge, Suffolk, 1993), pp. 142–3.

21. *Compendium*, fol. 55.

22. *Selections from the Zoilomastix of Philip O'Sullivan Beare*, ed. Thomas J. O'Donnell (Dublin, 1960), pp. 47–97; Aubrey Gwynn, 'An Unpublished Work of O'Sullivan Bear', *Analecta Hibernica* (1934), 6, pp. 1–11.

23. *Foras Feasa*, I, 34–7. For analysis of this distinction, see Brendan Bradshaw, 'Geoffrey Keating: Apologist of Irish Ireland', in *Representing Ireland*, ed. Brendan Bradshaw, Andrew Hadfield, and Willy Maley (Cambridge, 1993), pp. 183, 189–90.

24. *Compendium*, fol. 62r–62v.

25. Richard L. Kagan, 'Clio and the Crown: Writing History in Habsburg Spain', in *Spain, Europe and the Atlantic World* (Cambridge, 1995), p. 80. See also R. A. Stradling, *Philip IV and the Government of Spain, 1621–1665* (Cambridge, 1988), pp. 310–11; Antonio de Herrera y Tordesillas, *Historia general de los hechos de los castellanos en las islas & terra firme del mar oceano* (Madrid 1601–15), and *Primera-tercera parte de las historia general del mundo* (Madrid, 1601–12).

26. See Kagan, 'Clio and the Crown: Writing History in Habsburg Spain', citing Antonio y Tordesillas, 'Discurso y tratado de la historia', BNM, MS 3011, fo. 151.

27. *Compendium*, fol. 68v, for all quotations in this paragraph.

28. *De Rege et Regis Institutione* (Toledo, 1599). *The King and the Education of the King*, trans. George Albert Moore (Washington, D.C., 1948).

29. For this characterization of Juan de Mariana's political theory, see Stradling, *Philip IV and the Government of Spain*, pp. 63–4. See Juan de Mariana, *The King and the Education of the King*, III.v: 'The Military Art'; III.vi.: 'The Prince Personally Ought to Carry on Warfare'.

30. O'Sullivan Beare, *Ireland Under Elizabeth*, p. 56.

31. John Ray Knott, *Discourses of Martyrdom in English Literature, 1563–1694* (Cambridge, 1993), p. 42.

32. O'Sullivan Beare, *Ireland Under Elizabeth*, pp. 15–16.

33. Eusebius, *Ecclesiastical History*, 2 vols., with an introduction and translation by Kirsopp Lake (Cambridge, Massachusetts, 1928), VIII.16.

34. O'Sullivan Beare, *Ireland Under Elizabeth*, p. 33. The quotations which follow are taken from pp. 34–6.

35. See Eusebius, *Ecclesiastical History*, V.6; Knott, *Discourses of Martyrdom*, p. 40.

36. 'Vita S. Mochuae Ex Hibernicis MSS. Interprete PH. Osuileuano' in the *'Acta sanctorum Hiberniae'* of John Colgan, with introduction by Brian Jennings (Dublin, 1948), pp. 789–92. See Paul Grosjean, 'Un Soldat de fortune Irlandais au service des "Acta Sanctorum": Philippe O'Sullivan Beare et Jean Bolland (1634)', *Anal. Boll.* 81 (1963), pp. 418–46.

37. O'Sullivan Beare, *Ireland Under Elizabeth*, p. 33.

38. Ibid., p. 56.

39. See, for example, *Histoire des horribles insolences, cruautez, & tyrannies exercees par les Espagnoles en Indes Occidentales* (Paris, 1582); *The Spanish Colonie* (London, 1583); *Narratio Regionum Indicarum Per hispanos quosdam demonstrandum verissima* (Frankfort, 1598); *Den spiegel der Spaensche tyrannye* (Amsterdam, 1620); *Le miroir de la tyrannie espagnole perpetree aux Indes occidentales* (Amsterdam, 1620); *Tears of the Indians* (London, 1656). For a full list, see Joseph Sabin, *A List of the Printed Editions of Fray Bartolomé de las Casas* (New York, 1870).

40. Bernardo de Vargas Machuca, *Apologias y discursos de las conquistas occidentales*, ed. M. L. Martinez de Salinas Alonso (Junta de Castilla y Leon, 1993); Quevedo, *España defendida* (1609).

41. *La Destruction des Indes de Bartolome de las Casas* (1552), translated by Jacques de Miggrode (1579), ed. Alain Milhou and Jean-Paul Duviols (Paris: Editions Chandeigne, 1995), 'Introduction' by Alain Milhou, pp. 68–9. Las Casas's *Brevisima relacion* was not banned by the Spanish Inquisition until 1659.

42. On the providential interpretation of history in early modern Irish texts, see Marc Caball, 'Providence and Exile in early Seventeenth-Century Ireland', *Irish Historical Studies*, vol. 29, no. 114 (Nov. 1994), pp. 174–88.

43. O'Sullivan Beare, *Ireland Under Elizabeth*, p. 39; Las Casas, *The Spanish Colonie*, D3v.

44. *Ireland Under Elizabeth*, p. 38; *The Spanish Colonie*, C2r.

45. *Ireland Under Elizabeth*, p. 7, see also pp. 8, 156; *The Spanish Colonie*, A3v.

46. *Ireland Under Elizabeth*, p. 156; *The Spanish Colonie*, C3v.
47. *Ireland Under Elizabeth*, p. 156.
48. *The Spanish Colonie*, A3v.
49. See Vincent Carey, 'John Derricke's *Image of Ireland*, Sir Henry Sidney, and the Massacre at Mullaghmast, 1578', *Irish Historical Studies*, vol. 32, no. 123 (May 1999), pp. 305–27.
50. O'Sullivan Beare, *Ireland Under Elizabeth*, p. 8.
51. The translation is taken from *Tears of the Indians* (1656), 132, which in this passage is closer to the Spanish.
52. O'Sullivan Beare, *Ireland Under Elizabeth*, p. 43.
53. Bartolomé de Las Casas, *In Defense of the Indians*, trans. and ed. Stafford Poole, C.M. (DeKalb, 1992), Chapter 49: 'Reasons why unbelievers, in contrast to heretics, cannot be compelled', pp. 304–8.
54. O'Sullivan Beare, *Ireland Under Elizabeth*, p. 2.
55. Las Casas, *In Defense of the Indians*, p. 47.
56. O'Sullivan Beare, *Ireland Under Elizabeth*, pp. 51–2.
57. O'Sullivan Beare, *Ireland Under Elizabeth*, p. 181.
58. Ibid., pp. 54, 181.
59. Ibid., p. 182.
60. *Compendium*, fol. 202r.
61. Ibid., fol. 202v.
62. Ibid., fol. 202v.
63. See Hiram Morgan, *Tyrone's Rebellion*, p. 209, and J. J. Silke, *Ireland and Europe 1559–1607* (Dublin, 1966), p. 22.
64. O'Sullivan Beare, *Ireland Under Elizabeth*, p. 54.
65. *Compendium*, fol. 202v.
66. Ibid., fol. 205v–206r.
67. Ibid., IV.I.II, fol. 206v–208v; IV.I.X, fol. 216r; IV.II.II, fol. 238r–238v.
68. Ibid., IV.i.iv, fol. 209v.
69. *The King and the Education of the King*, I.x: 'The Prince should Determine Nothing About Religion', p. 172.
70. Ibid., I.viii: 'Whether the Authority of the Commonwealth or King is Greater'; I.ix: 'The Prince Is Not Free from the Laws'. See Pierre Mesnard, *L'essor de la philosophie politique au XVIe siècle* (Paris, 1936), pp. 555–7; C. J. Jago, 'Taxation and Political Culture in Castile', in *Spain, Europe and the Atlantic World*, pp. 58–9.
71. *Compendium*, fol. 248r. O'Sullivan Beare quotes from the following text: Datum ex regio Castello Dubhinnensi non die Iulii anno 1613. Typis mandatum Dubhinnae a Iohanne Francktone excellentissima Regiae Majestatis typographo anno 1613 (fol. 249r). Despite allegations of O'Sullivan Beare's unreliability, here he provides otherwise unavailable documentary evidence. This proclamation is not extant according to the *STC* and *Bibliotheca Lindesiana* (Vol. II). At least two other documents are faithfully translated into Latin in the *Compendium*: 'Proclamation against Toleration in Ireland by the King', July 1605, in *Cal. S.P. Ireland*, pp. 301–3 (*Compendium* 206–8); and Cox ii, p. 25 (*Compendium* 249–50).
72. *Compendium*, fol. 249v. IV.ii.vii; IV.ii.ix.
73. Ibid., fol. 263v: 'Ego facio finem feribendi Idibus Decembris anno redemptionis humanae millesimo sexcentesimo decimo ocatavo'.

74. Trinity College MS 580, fo. 94r–98r.
75. Joep Leerssen, *Mere Irish and Fíor Ghael* (Cork, 1996), p. 274.
76. *Compendium*, fol. 34v.
77. Leerssen, *Mere Irish and Fíor Ghael*, p. 273.
78. For a comparison of similarities between the new ideology of O'Sullivan Beare and that of Céitinn (Keating), see Breandán Ó Buachalla, *Aisling Ghéar, Na Stíobhartiagh agus an tAois Léinn 1603–1788* (Dublin, 1996), pp. 79–80.
79. Trinity College MS 580, fo. 95r.
80. Ibid., fo. 95r.
81. Ibid., fo. 95r.
82. Ibid., fo. 95r.
83. Ibid., fo. 95r.
84. *Compendium*, fol. 34v.
85. Ibid., fol. 34v.
86. Joep Leerssen claimed that O'Sullivan Beare's 'genealogical view of history and its implied Manicheism makes a non-Gaelic and yet anti-English stance unthinkable' (*Mere Irish and Fíor-Ghael*, p. 273).
87. 'A Briefe Relation of Ireland', fo. 94r; *Compendium*, fol. 34v.
88. Ibid., fol. 35r.
89. Ibid., fol. 35v.
90. Trinity College MS 580, fo. 96r.
91. Ibid., fo. 95v.
92. Ibid., fo. 96r.
93. Ibid., fo. 96r.
94. Ibid., fo. 95r.
95. Ibid., fo. 95v.
96. Ibid., fo. 96r.
97. Ibid., fo. 97r.
98. Ibid., fo. 97v.
99. Ibid., fo. 97v.
100. Ibid., fo. 97v.
101. Micheline Walsh (ed.) *Spanish Knights of Irish Origin: Documents from Continental Archives*, vol. I (Dublin, 1960), p. v.
102. Walsh, vol. i, pp. 4, 7, 11, 13, 15, 17; vol. ii, p. 97.
103. 'Students of the Irish College, Salamanca', *Archivium Hibernicum* III (1914).
104. Pat O'Connell, 'The Irish College, Santiago de Compostella: 1605–1767', *Archivium Hibernicum* (1996), p. 23.
105. O'Connell, pp. 20–1.
106. See Gareth Davies, 'The Irish College at Santiago de Compostella: Two Documents about Its Early Days', in *Catholic Tastes and Times* (Leeds, 1987), pp. 96–101.
107. Helga Hammerstein, 'Aspects of the Continental Education of Irish Students in the Reign of Queen Elizabeth', *Historical Studies* 8 (1971), p. 150.
108. Trinity College MS 580, fo. 97v; *Compendium*, fol. 270r–279r.
109. See Hammerstein, 'Aspects of the Continental Education of Irish Students', p. 50, where she mentions 'a basic disagreement between the traditional practical political orientation of the Franciscans and the more theoretical unconventional approach to the Irish problem adopted by the Irish Jesuits'.

110. 'James Tobin to the Lord Carew', 27 February 1621, in *Calendar of State Papers, Ireland 1615–25*, vol. 236, 4, item 732 (London, 1880), pp. 316–17.

111. 'The description of John Gardiner of Russen in Mayo, regarding Hugh Kelly, page in Spain to one Bourke, styled there the Marquis of Mayo', 2 June 1625, in *Calendar of State Papers, Ireland 1625–32*, vol. 241, item 60.6, p. 16.

112. R. A. Stradling, *The Spanish Monarchy and Irish Mercenaries: The Wilde Geese in Spain 1618–68* (Dublin, 1994), p. 17.

113. Jerrold I. Casway, *Owen Roe O'Neill and the Struggle for Catholic Ireland* (Philadelphia, 1984), p. 29. Also see Gráinne Henry, *The Irish Military Community in Spanish Flanders 1586–1621* (Dublin, 1992), ch. 6.

114. Trinity College MS 580, fo. 97r.

115. Casway, *Owen Roe O'Neill*, pp. 28–36.

116. O'Sullivan Beare, *Ireland Under Elizabeth*, xxv; Ovid, *Tristia*, V.xii.15–16. The translation is that of Arthur Leslie Wheeler, second edition revised by G. P. Gould (Cambridge, Mass., 1988), p. 253.

117. *Compendium*, 'Historiae totus Epilogus', fol. 262v: 'non hospes ab hospite tutus'.

118. Ovid, *Ex ponto*, IV.viii, pp. 53–6.

119. Aodh de Blacam, 'The Story of the Fight for the Southern Irish Ports and the Great Retreat of O'Sullivan Beare' (from the *Capuchin Annuals* 1946/47), foreword by Donal O'Siodhachain (Cork, 1987).

120. O'Sullivan Beare, *Ireland Under Elizabeth*, p. 173.

121. Aodh de Blacam, 'The Great Retreat', p. 23, citing *Pacata Hibernia*.

122. Micheline Kerney Walsh, 'O'Sullivan Beare in Spain: Some Unpublished Documents', *Archivium Hibernicum* 45 (1990), p. 50. See also R. Breatnach, 'Donal O'Sullivan Beare to King Philip III, 20th February, 1602', *Éigse* XI (1964–6), pp. 314–25.

123. La Coruña, 8 January 1605. Letter from the Count of Caracena, gove·nor of Galicia, to King Philip III, quoted in Micheline Kerney Walsh, 'O'Sulliva.1 Beare in Spain: Some Unpublished Documents', p. 49.

124. *Aeneid* II.361–9, quoted in *Ireland Under Elizabeth*, 181. *Compendium* III.viii.vi.

Custom and Law in the Philosophy of Suárez

1. Guillermo Malavassi Vargas, 'Ideas Politicas de Francisco Suárez (1548–1617)', in *Acta Academica* (October 1989 and May 1990), pp. 14–18. On the constitutionalist character of Suárez's political ideas, see J. P. Sommerville, 'From Suarez to Filmer: A Reappraisal', *Historical Journal* 25, 3 (1982), pp. 525–40.

2. Anthony Pagden, 'Dispossessing the Barbarian: The Language of Spanish Thomism and the Debate over the Property Rights of the American Indians', in *The Languages of Political Theory in Early-Modern Europe*, ed. Anthony Pagden (Cambridge, 1987), pp. 80–1.

3. Bartolomé de Las Casas, *In Defense of the Indians*, trans. Stafford Poole (De Kalb: Northern Illinois University Press, 1992).

4. Bartolomé de Las Casas, *The Devastation of the Indies: A Brief Account*, trans. Herma Briffault (Baltimore, 1992), pp. 78–9.

5. Dipesh Chakrabarty, 'Postcoloniality and the Artifice of History: Who Speaks for "Indian" Pasts?' in Bill Ashcroft, Gareth Griffiths, and Helen Tiffin (ed.) *The Post-Colonial Studies Reader* (London and New York: Routledge, 1995), p. 386.

6. Alasdair MacIntyre, 'Relativism, Power and Philosophy' in *Proceedings of the American Philosophical Association*, vol. 59, no. 1 (1985), pp. 5–22, especially pp. 15–17.

7. Breandán Ó Buachalla, '*Annála Ríoghachta Éireann* is *Foras Feasa ar Éirinn*: An Comhthéacs Comhaimseartha', *Studia Hibernica* 22–3 (1982–83), pp. 59–105.

8. *Dictionary of the Irish Language* (Royal Irish Academy, Dublin, 1990), S, p. 177.

9. Francis J. Byrne, '*Senchas*: the nature of Gaelic historical tradition' in J.G. Barry (ed.), *Historical studies* IX (Belfast, 1974), pp. 137–59, p. 138.

10. Indeed Declan Kiberd has compared Céitinn's seventeenth-century critique of colonialism to Edward Said's late twentieth-century critique of imperialism. See *Inventing Ireland* (London, 1995), p. 14.

11. Philip O'Sullivan Beare, *Historiae Catholicae Hiberniae Compendium*, ed. Matthew Kelly (Dublin, 1850); *Annals of the Kingdom of Ireland, by the Four Masters*, 6 vols., ed. John O'Donovan (2nd edition, Dublin, 1856); Geoffrey Keating, *History of Ireland from the Earliest Period to the English Invasion*, trans. John O'Mahony (New York, 1857).

12. See my article 'Irish and Spanish Cultural and Political Relations in the Work of O'Sullivan Beare', in Hiram Morgan (ed.), *Political Ideology in Ireland 1541–1641* (Dublin, 1998), pp. 229–53. See also Brian Ó Cuiv, 'An Appeal to Philip III of Spain by Ó Súilleabháin Béirre, December 1601', in *Éigse* 30 (1997), pp. 18–26; Jerrold I. Casway, *Owen Roe O'Neill and the Struggle for Catholic Ireland* (Philadelphia, 1984), p. 29; Gráinne Henry, *The Irish Military Community in Spanish Flanders 1586–1621* (Dublin, 1992), ch. 6.

13. Francisco Suárez, *De Legibus, ac Deo Legislatore* (Coimbra, 1612); *Defensio Fidei Catholicae, et Apostolicae adversus Anglicanae Sectae Errores* (Coimbra, 1613).

14. For the reception of Suárez's work in Rome and England, see Reijo Wilenius, 'The Social and Political Thought of Francisco Suárez', in *Acta Philosophica Fennica*, Fasc. XV (1963), pp. 21, 79, and Raoul de Scoraille, S.J., *François Suárez de la Compagnie de Jésus*, 2 vols. (Paris, 1912), 2, pp. 194 ff. Inventories of the libraries at the Irish Colleges in Spain indicate that Suárez's works were available.

15. *De Legibus*, VII, xiii–xviii, especially VII, xviii.2, summarized by Wilenius: 'custom can abrogate human law, both canon and civil' (p. 48). For the medieval understanding of the relation between political unity and common customs, see Susan Reynolds, 'Medieval *Origines Gentium* and the Community of the Realm', *History* 68 (1983), pp. 375–90.

16. 'Ex his adhunc illi, qui Finegaldam, vel Anglicam provinciam, id est particulam Iberniae proximam Angliae olim incolere caeperunt, ab Ibernis disjuncti, genus Anglicum, vel Anglo Iberni et coloni nuncupantur, et Anglorum moribus et legibus vixerunt' (*Compendium*, p. 37).

17. 'Principio, incredibili cura, et severitate jus illud observabant, quo caverunt ut in Ibernia ii tantum, qui ex Anglis ducebant originem, vel sub Anglorum imperio Iberniam adierunt, aut ut brevius dicam, novi Iberni, magistratus gererent, civilibus officiis fungerentur; et suffragia in senatu, quod parliamentum nuncupatur ferrent' (*Compendium*, p. 68).

18. *Selections from Three Works of Francisco Suárez, S.J. De Legibus, ac Deo Legislatore, 1612. Defensio Fidei Catholicae, adversus Anglicanae Sectae Errores, 1613. De Triplici Virtute Theologica, Fide, Spe, et Charitate, 1621*. Translated by Gwladys L. Williams, Ammi Brown, and John Waldron, with revisions by Henry Davis

(Oxford, 1944): 'such power, in the nature of things, resides immediately in the community; and therefore, in order that it may justly come to reside in a given individual, as in a sovereign prince, it must necessarily be bestowed upon him by the consent of the community' (*De legibus* III, iv, p. 384).

19. 'Veteres autem Iberni non aliter rerum publicarum gubernacula regerent, quam accedente extrinseca quadam denominatione physica seu civilis juris qualitate, ipsorum regum placito concedenda, quae Anglis quidem "Denization" Hispanis vero "Naturalizacion," mihi autem, "adscriptio in civitatem," seu municipalis juris donatio nominatur' (*Compendium*, p. 68).

20. 'Igitur quadam juris Anglici fictione, antiqui Iberni non indigenae sed exteri nasci, et hospites in sua patria esse reputabantur. Quae lex juri gentium et naturali apertissime adversatur, cum contrariam, ut in sua quisque patria civis, in alienis vero finibus hospes habeatur' (*Compendium*, p. 68).

21. Bartolomé de Las Casas, *In Defense of the Indians*, trans. Stafford Poole (De Kalb: Northern Illinois University Press, 1992), p. 47.

22. *De Legibus* II, xix; Wilenius, p. 65.

23. 'Divina quadam providentia constitutam omnes gentes, etiam Gentiles et barbarae firmam, immutabilemque custodiant' (*Compendium*, p. 68).

24. *Selections from Three Works of Francisco Suárez, S.J. De Legibus* II, iii, p. 167.

25. J. G. A. Pocock, *The Ancient Constitution, and the Feudal Law: A Study of English Historical Thought in the Seventeenth Century* (Cambridge, 1957).

26. 'Dabant autem Angli reges hoc jus Ibernis vel praetio commutatum vel pro meritis in se collatis, vel conferendis' (*Compendium*, p. 68).

27. 'Coeterum contractui fraus inesse videtur, quia fiduciaria donatione celebrata' (*Compendium*, p. 69).

28. 'Dominium, vel usufructum' (*Compendium*, p. 69).

29. 'Hinc ut dicebamus, veteres Iberni primores ab Anglis regibus non inaugurati, et novi etiam Iberni magnates veterum Ibernorum more creati, jure ferendorum in senatu vel parlamento, suffragiorum abdicabantur' (*Compendium*, pp. 68–9).

30. 'Anglorum atque Scotorum colonias, de quibus superius egimus, nomine civitatis ornant, et suffragiorum jure, et aliis immunitatibus donant, legum atque consuetudinis metam transgressi, ut singulae coloniae procuratores duos ad parlamentum mittant' (*Compendium*, p. 308).

31. *Selections from Three Works of Francisco Suárez, S.J.*, 'The three theological virtues', XIII: On War, p. 817. *De Fide, Spe et Caritate* (Coimbra, 1621) is a posthumous work, but many of the principles in it are already contained in *Defensio Fidei* (1613); see especially *Defensio Fidei* VI.iv: 'Does the Oath of King James exact more than Civil Obedience?'

32. *Selections from Three Works of Francisco Suárez, S.J.*, 'The three theological virtues', XIII: On War, p. 855.

33. Ibid., p. 706; *Defensio Fidei* IV.1.

34. O'Sullivan Beare, *Compendium*, pp. 266–7.

35. Wilenius, p. 83; *Defensio Fidei* VI.iv.i.

36. Bernadette Cunningham argues that Céitinn did at least know Suárez's theological works (*The World of Geoffrey Keating* [Dublin: Four Courts Press, 2000], pp. 32–5.

37. *Foras Feasa ar Éirinn* (*The History of Ireland*), vol. I, trans. David Comyn, Irish Texts Society (London, 1902), p. 33: 'An tí is ísle do na coilínibh d'á n-áitigheann

i san gcúigeadh Gallda, ní thiubhradh a inghean féin pósda do'n "phrionnsa" is mó d'Éireannchaibh' (p. 32). See T. F. O'Rahilly, 'Notes, Mainly Etymological', in *Éigse* 13 (1942), pp. 207–11, for the claim that Comyn mistranslated 'coilíneach' as colonist, when it actually means something closer to 'husbandman' (p. 209).

38.   Ibid., p. 33: 'cia budh honóraighe, budh huaisle, nó budh dísle do choróin na Sacsan, nó cia budh feárr do bharántaibh re cosnamh na hÉireann do choróin na Sacsan, coilínighe Fhine Gall 'nárd na hiarlaidhe uaisle atá i n-Éirinn do Ghallaibh' (p. 32).

39.   Ibid., p. 35: 'ar choilíneachaibh Fhine Gall tré n'ár dhíbirsiod an Ghaedhealg as an tír an tan do ruaigriod an fhoireann do bhí ag áitiughadh na tíre rómpa' (p. 34).

40.   Ibid., p. 37: 'gabháltas pagánta' . . . 'gabháltas Críostamhail, ní mhúchann an teanga' (p. 36).

41.   Ibid., p. 37: 'agus iar ndíbirt cháich go hiomlán dó, do dhíbir a dteanga leo' (p. 36).

42.   Ibid. p. 37: 'óir ní féidir an teanga do dhíbirt, gan an lucht d'ár teanga í do dhíbirt' (p. 36).

43.   Ibid., p. 71.

44.   Ibid., p. 71.

45.   Ibid., p. 73.

46.   Ibid., p. 39: 'bhí Éire 'na ríoghacht ar leith léi féin, amhail domhan mbeag' (p. 38).

47.   Brendan Bradshaw, 'Geoffrey Keating: Apologist for Gaelic Ireland', in *Representing Ireland*, ed. B. Bradshaw, A. Hadfield, and W. Maley (Cambridge, 1993), p. 168.

48.   *Foras Feasa*, pp. 39–41: 'agus na huaisle agus na hollamhain do bhí innte i n-allód, gur chumadar breitheamhnas, legheas, filidheacht agus ceol agus riaghlachaibh cinnte riu do bheith ar bun i n-Éirinn' (pp. 38–40).

49.   *Foras Feasa*, pp. 367–9: 'Is follus ar na neithibh do luaidheamar anuas gurab d'anfhlaitheas is d'éagcóir is da neamhchoimhéad ar a ndlighe féin ag uachtaránaibh Gall i nÉirinn, táinig iomad do neamhumhla na nGaedheal do smacht Gall' (pp. 366–8).

50.   *Annals of the Kingdom of Ireland by the Four Masters*, ed. John O'Donovan (Dublin, 1856); see for example vol. V, p. 1796, note g.

51.   Bradshaw, 'Geoffrey Keating,' p. 168.

52.   *Annals*, 1598, p. 2071: 'Atbertsat friú beos gur bó husa doibh cosnamh a nathardha friss in ainffine neachtaircheneoil sin oldas dúthaigh neich ele do ghabhail ar eiccin iar na monnarbadh somh ar a ttír ndílis budhein' (p. 2070).

53.   *Annals*, 1600, p. 2179: 'Duine eisidhe baí ina aén oidhre o chert ar a dúthaigh, agus do bhen urlámhas a atharda a los a lamha, agus a cruas a croidhe a dornaibh danar, agus deóradh ag a mbaoí a remhdísle ag dol i rudhrachus re hathaidh roimhe sin go ttardromh í fó a smacht, agus fo a chumachtoibh budein, fo breith a maor, agus a bhuannadh do reir ghathaithghe gaoidheal' (p. 2178).

54.   See Peter McQuillan's forthcoming article on '*Dúthaigh* and *Dúchas* in Irish', which he presented at the Conference on Folklore at University College Cork on June 23, 2001.

55.   *Annals*, 1616, p. 2375: 'Tighearna ná ro shanntaigh forbann ná fairbrígh neich oile do beith occa, acht in ro badh toich dia shinnseraibh ó chein mhair' (p. 2374).

56.   *Annals*, 1590, pp. 1901–3: 'umhan smacht chána na ngall' (pp. 1902–4).

Breve relacion de la presente persecucion de Irlanda

1. *Breve relacion de la presente persecucion de Irlanda* (Sevilla, 1619), p. 1. The two copies of the text that I have examined are in the National Library of Ireland and at the Franciscan Library at Killiney. I have been assisted throughout in the translation of the text by Cyrus Moore.

2. Adrian Hastings, *The Construction of Nationhood: Ethnicity, Religion, and Nationalism* (Cambridge: Cambridge University Press, 1997), pp. 35–53.

3. Ibid., pp. 80–95.

4. I am grateful to Hugh Fenning, O.P., for drawing my attention to National Library of Ireland MS 16,236, 'Breve Historia de el Origen, y Progressos de el Coll. De los Irlandeses de Sevilla'. Compiled in the eighteenth century, starting in 1720, the text spans from the beginnings of the college at Seville from 1612–19 until the closing of the college in 1770. This manuscript is clearly the unacknowledged source for the articles by William McDonald, 'Irish Colleges Since the Reformation', *Irish Ecclesiastical Record* VIII (1872), pp. 465–73, and 'Irish Ecclesiastical Colleges Since the Reformation: Seville', *Irish Ecclesiastical Record* IX (1873), pp. 208–21. See also T. J. Walsh, *The Irish Continental Movement* (Dublin: Golden Eagle Books, 1973), pp. 53–61; Francis Finegan, S.J. 'Irish Rectors at Seville 1619–1687', *Irish Ecclesiastical Record* CVI (July/Dec 1966), 5th series, pp. 45–63; Rev. John J. Silke, 'The Irish College, Seville', *Archivium Hibernicum* XXIV (1961), pp. 103–47. What Father Silke refers to as 'Salamanca records which are apparently now missing' (p. 103) are actually documents included in this manuscript history, parts of which McDonald translated in his articles.

5. National Library of Ireland MS 16, 236, fol. 9r.

6. *Breve relacion*, p. 2.

7. NLI MS 16, 236, fol. 4v.

8. Ibid., fol. 5v; William McDonald, 'Irish Colleges Since the Reformation', *Irish Ecclesiastical Record* IX (1873), p. 209.

9. NLI MS 16, 236, fol. 5v; *Irish Ecclesiastical Record* VIII (1872), p. 468.

10. NLI MS 16, 236, fol. 5v; *Irish Ecclesiastical Record* IX (1873), p. 210.

11. NLI MS 16, 236, fol. 9v–10r; *Irish Ecclesiastical Record* IX (1873), p. 211.

12. NLI MS 16, 236, fol. 2v.

13. Ibid., fol. 3r; *Irish Ecclesiastical Record* VIII (1872), p. 469.

14. NLI MS 16, 236, fol. 1r–1v.

15. For the oath, see NLI MS 16, 236, fol. 1v–2r.

16. NLI MS 16, 236, fol. 3r; *Irish Ecclesiastical Record* VIII (1872), p. 469.

17. Ignatius Fennessy, 'Printed Items Among the Wadding Papers', *Collectanea Hibernica*, nos. 39–40 (1997–8), pp. 32–95, 36. The copy of this text in the collection at Killiney shows many marks in the margins, which suggests that Wadding found much to take note of in it.

18. *Breve relacion*, p. 3.

19. Ibid., p. 4.

20. In 1594 Jerónimo Román de la Higuera thought he had found fragments of Flavio Dextro's *Omnimodo da Historia* in the monastery at Fulda. This was later shown to be apocryphal by Juan Bautista Pérez. See *Enciclopedia Universal Ilustrada Europeo-Americana* (Madrid: Espasa-Calpe, 1915).

21. *Breve relacion*, p. 15.
22. Fray Antonio de Yepes, *Crónica General de la Orden de San Benito* (ed. Fray Justo Pérez de Urbel, O.S.B.), Biblioteca de Autores Español (Madrid: Atlas, 1959–60).
23. *Breve relacion*, pp. 7, 4.
24. *Breve relacion*, pp. 12–16, see notes 56, 59, 61, 71, 72.
25. T. C. Price Zimmermann, *Paolo Giovio: The Historian and the Crisis of Sixteenth-Century Italy* (Princeton: Princeton University Press, 1995).
26. Compare *Breve relacion*, p. 12, and Paolo Giovio, *Descriptio Britanniae, Scotiae, Hyberniae, et Orchadum* (Venice, 1548), 34r.
27. 'Sane sylvestres hi non usque adeo barbari videntur . . . quando quidem nihil omnino vel Scotis sociis, vel Anglis hostibus concedant, si mores actionesque; omnes ad aequtatem atque animi magnitudinem revocentur; quum ipsi Hibernica simplicitate, & Romana quadam gravitate mirabiles, spectatae frugis, & ob id inoxiam ducant vitam & peregrini luxus illecebras aspernentur.' Compare *Breve relacion*, p. 16, and Giovio, *Descriptio Britanniae*, 4r.
28. 'Quippe illis amictus toga Romanae in humerum reiectae persimilis' [Their manner of dress is similar to the Roman toga thrown back over the shoulder]. Compare *Breve relacion*, p. 16, and Giovio, *Descriptio Britanniae*, 4r.
29. 'Siendo pues, todo lo dicho tan cierto, como authentico, facil es de veer, que credito merecen, y que poca reputacion con ello ganan, los que por ignorancia, o por invidia dizen o escriven otra cosa differente; imputando a falta de policia, el aferrarse tan tenazemente los Irlandeses a sus Catholicas, sanas, y antiguas costumbres, y ferrarse tanto a las porphanas nonedades, errors, vicios, y Machiavellisstica o Calvinistica policia que ellos que fieran ver introduzida.' *Breve relacion*, pp. 15–16.
30. Brendan Bradshaw, 'Edmund Spenser on Justice and Mercy', in *The Writer as Witness: Literature as Historical Evidence*, ed. Tom Dunne (Cork: Cork University Press, 1987), p. 86.
31. See Ignatius Fennessy, 'Printed Items Among the Wadding Papers', p. 36, where Fennessy cites George Oliver, *Collections towards Illustrating the Biography of the Scotch, English, and Irish Members of the Society of Jesus* (London, 1845), p. 260.
32. *Calendar of State Papers Ireland. James I 1615–1625* (London, 1880), 25 April 1616, 'Lord Justices to the Privy Council', vol. 234, 16, no. 241, pp. 122–3.
33. A. F. Allison and D. M. Rogers, *The Contemporary Printed Literature of the English Counter-Reformation between 1558 and 1640* (Aldershot: Scolar Press, 1989), vol. i, 1074, p. 148.
34. What follows is a summary of the letter in *Breve relacion*, pp. 19–27.
35. *Breve relacion*, p. 23.
36. Ibid., p. 24.
37. *Calendar of State Papers Ireland. James I 1615–1625* (London, 1880), 11 October 1617, 'Lord Deputy to Winwood', vol. 234.9, no. 373, p. 169.
38. *Breve relacion*, p. 25.
39. Ibid., pp. 28–30.
40. *Bibliotheca Lindesiana (Vol. VI): A Bibliography of Proclamations of the Tudor and Stuart Sovereigns*, no. 222, p. 22.
41. *Breve relacion*, pp. 31–3.
42. Ibid., p. 33.

43.   *Bibliotheca Lindesiana* (*Vol. VI*), no. 224, p. 22.
44.   *Breve relacion*, p. 36.
45.   Ibid., pp. 44–9.
46.   Ibid., p. 38.
47.   Ibid., p. 39.
48.   Ibid., p. 40.
49.   Ibid., p. 40.
50.   Ibid., p. 40.
51.   Ibid., pp. 40–1.
52.   Ibid., p. 49.

BIBLIOGRAPHY

Manuscripts

National Library of Ireland MS 16, 236
Royal Irish Academy MS 24G16
Trinity College Dublin MS 580
Trinity College Dublin MS 1335 (formerly T.C.D. H. 3. 16)
Trinity College Dublin MS 1399 (formerly T.C.D. H. 5. 28)

Printed Primary Sources

Arber, Edward (ed.). *The Return from Parnassus* [1602]. London, 1879.
Ariosto, Ludovico. *Orlando Furioso*. Eds. Santorre Debenedetti and Cesare Segre. Bologna: Commissione per i testi di lingua, 1960.
———. *Ludovico Ariosto's 'Orlando Furioso' translated into English heroical verse by Sir John Harington* (1591). Ed. Robert McNulty. Oxford: Clarendon Press, 1972.
Aristotle, *Politics*. Trans. Sir Ernest Barker. Oxford: Clarendon Press, 1961.
Ascham, Roger. *The Scholemaster*. London, 1570.
Beacon, Richard. *Solon His Follie, or A Politique Discourse, Touching the Reformation of common-weales conquered, declined or corrupted*. Oxford, 1594.
———. *Solon His Follie, or A Politique Discourse Touching the Reformation of common-weales conquered, declined or corrupted* (1594). Ed. Clare Carroll and Vincent Carey. Binghamton: Medieval and Renaissance Texts and Studies, 1996.
Borlase, Edmund. *The History of the Execrable Irish Rebellion*. London, 1680.
Breatnach, Pádraig A. 'Metamorphosis 1603: dán le hEochaidh Ó hEódhusa'. *Éigse* 17 (1977–8): 167–80.
Breatnach, R. (ed.) 'Donal O'Sullivan Beare to King Philip III, 20th February, 1602'. *Éigse* 11 (1964–6): 314–25.
Breve relacion de la presente persecucion de Irlanda. Sevilla, 1619.
Byrne, Matthew J. (trans.). 'Philip O'Sullivan Beare, soldier, poet, and historian'. *Cork Historical and Archaeological Society Journal*, series 2, ii (1896): 392–7, 423–8, 457–67, 516–23; iii (1897): 26–30, 182–8.
Cabala, Mysteries of State, in Letters of the Great Ministers of K. James and K. Charles. London, 1656.
Calendar of the Carew Manuscripts Preserved in the Archiepiscopal Library at Lambeth, 1515–1624. Ed. J. S. Brewer and William Bullen. 6 vols. London: Longmans, Green & Dyer, 1867–73.

Calendar of the State Papers Relating to Ireland, of the Reigns of Henry VIII, Edward VI, Mary and Elizabeth, and James I, 1547–1625. Ed. H. C. Hamilton, E. G. Atkinson, and R. P. Mahaffy. 11 vols. Nendeln: Kraus Reprint, 1974.

Carney, James (ed.). *Poems on the O'Reillys.* Dublin: Dublin Institute for Advanced Studies, 1950.

Casas, Bartolomé de las. *In Defense of the Indians.* Trans. Stafford Poole. DeKalb: Northern Illinois University Press, 1992.

——. *Brevísima relación des las destrucción de las Indias.* Ed. José María Reynes Cano. Barcelona: Planeta, 1994.

——. *The Devastation of the Indies: A Brief Account.* Trans. Herma Briffault. Baltimore: Johns Hopkins University Press, 1992.

——. *La Destruction des Indes de Bartolome de las Casas* (1552). Trans. Jacques de Miggrode (1579). Ed. Alain Milhou and Jean-Paul Duviols. Paris: Editions Chandeigne, 1995.

——. *The Spanish Colonie.* London, 1583.

——. *Tears of the Indians.* London, 1656.

Colgan, John. *The 'Acta sanctorum Hiberniae' of John Colgan*, with introduction by Brian Jennings. Dublin, 1948.

Collins, Arthur (ed.). *Letters and Memorials of State . . . written and collected by Sir Henry Sidney, Sir Philip Sidney and his brother, Sir Robert Sidney.* 2 vols. London, 1746.

Columbus, Christopher. *The Diario of Christopher Columbus 1492–1493.* Trans. Oliver Dunne and James E. Kelly Jr. Norman: University of Oklahoma Press, 1989.

Cox, Richard. *Hibernia Anglicana.* London, 1689.

Crant, Thomas. *The plott and progresse of the Irish rebellion: wherein is discovered the machavilian policie of the Earle of Straford, Sir George Ratcliffe and others, etc.* London, 1644.

Crawford, James Ludovic Lindsay, Earl of, and Robert Steele. *A Bibliography of Royal Proclamations of the Tudor and Stuart Sovereigns, 1485–1714.* 2 vols. Bibliotheca Lindesiana vols. 5–6. Oxford: Clarendon Press, 1910.

Davies, Sir John. 'A Discovery of the True Causes Why Ireland Was Never Entirely Subdued'. In *Ireland under Elizabeth and James the First.* Ed. Henry Morley. London, 1890.

——. *A Discovery of the True Causes why Ireland was never Entirely Subdued.* Shannon, 1969.

de Herrera y Tordesillas, Antonio. *Historia general de los hechos de los castellanos en las islas & terra firme del mar oceano.* Madrid, 1601–15.

——. *Primera-tercera parte de las historia general del mundo.* Madrid, 1601–12.

de Léry, Jean. *History of a Voyage to the Land of Brazil.* Trans. Janet Whatley. Berkeley: University of California Press, 1990.

de Mariana, Juan. *The General History of Spain from the first Peopling of it by Tubal, till the Death of King Ferdinand, Who United the Crowns of Castile and Aragon, To which are added Two Supplements, The First by F. Ferdinand*

Camargo y Salcedo, the other by Basil Varn de Soto, bringing it down to the present reign. Trans. John Stevens. London, 1699.

——. *De rege et regis institutione.* Toledo, 1599. *The King and the Education of the King.* Trans. George Albert Moore. Washington, D.C., 1948.

Derricke, John. *The Image of Ireland with A Discoverie of Woodkarne* (1581). Ed. David B. Quinn. Blackstaff Press, 1985.

de Vargas Machuca, Bernardo. *Apologias y discursos de las conquistas occidentales.* Ed. M. L. Martinez de Salinas Alonso. Junta de Castilla y Leon, 1993.

Draak, A. M. E. (ed.). 'Orlando agus Melora'. *Béaloideas* 16 (1946): 2–48.

Eusebius, *Ecclesiastical History.* 2 vols. Trans. Kirsopp Lake. Cambridge, Massachusetts, 1928.

Flower, Robin, and Standish Hayes O'Grady. *Catalogue of Irish Manuscripts in the British Museum.* 2 vols. London: British Museum, 1926; reprint: Dublin: Dublin Institute for Advanced Studies, 1992.

Gardiner, Stephen. *A Machiavellian Treatise by Stephen Gardiner.* Ed. Peter Samuel Donaldson. Cambridge: Cambridge University Press, 1975.

Giovio Paolo. *Descriptio Britanniae, Scotiae, Hyberniae et Orchadum.* Venice, 1548.

Giraldus Cambrensis. *Expugnatio Hibernica, The Conquest of Ireland by Giraldus Cambrensis.* Ed. and trans. A. B. Scott and F. X. Martin. Dublin: Royal Irish Academy, 1978.

——. *Topographia Hibernia* in *Giraldi Cambrensis Opera,* Vol. 5. Ed. J. F. Dimock. Rolls Series, 1867.

——. *The History and Topography of Ireland.* Trans. John J. O'Meara. London: Penguin, 1982.

——. *The Irish History.* Trans. John Hooker. In Raphael Holinshead, *Chronicles of England, Scotland and Ireland.* London: J. Johnson, 1807–8.

Harington, Sir John, et al. *Nugae Antiquae.* Ed. H. Harington, re-ed. Thomas Park. 2 vols. London, 1804.

——. 'A Short View of the State of Ireland Written in 1605 by Sir John Harington'. In *Anecdota Bodleiana* no. 1. Ed. W. Dunn Macray. Oxford: James Parker, 1879.

——. *The Letters & Epigrams of Sir John Harington.* Ed. Norman Egbert McClure. Philadelphia: University of Pennsylvania Press, 1930.

Herbert, William. *Croftus Sive de Hibernia Liber.* Ed. and trans. Arthur Keaveney and John A. Madden. Dublin, 1992.

Jonson, Ben. *Ben Jonson.* Ed. C. H. Herford, Percy Simpson, and Evelyn Simpson, 11 vols. Oxford: Oxford University Press, 1925–52.

Keating, Geoffrey. *Foras Feasa ar Éirinn. The History of Ireland.* 4 vols. Ed. and trans. David Comyn and P. S. Dineen. London: Irish Texts Society, 1902–14.

——. *History of Ireland from the earliest period to the English Invasion.* Trans. John O'Mahony. New York, 1857.

——. *Dánta amhráin is caointe Seathrúin Céitinn.* Dublin, 1900.

Lhuyd, Edward. *Archaeologica Britannica: An Account of the Languages, Histories, and Customs of Great Britain, from collections and observations in Travels through Wales, Cornwall, Bas-Bretagne, Ireland, and Scotland.* Vol. i. *Glossography.* London: Bateman, 1707.

Lombard, Peter. *Irish Historical Documents,* 1, *The Irish War of Defence 1598–1600, Extracts from 'De Hibernia Insula Commentarius' of Peter Lombard.* Ed. Matthew J. Byrne. Cork, 1930.

——. *De regno Hiberniœ sanctorvm insvla commentarivs.* Louvain, 1632.

Lynch, John. *Alithinologia.* St Malo, 1664.

——. *Cambrensis Eversus, seu potoius historica fides in rebus Hibernicis Giraldo Cambrensi abrogata.* n.p., 1662.

——. *Cambrensis Eversus.* Trans. Matthew Kelly. Dublin, 1851–2.

Macalister, R. A. Stewart (ed.). *Lebor Gabála Erenn, the Book of the Taking of Ireland.* 5 vols. Dublin: Irish Texts Society, 1956.

Machiavelli, Niccolò. *Il principe e Discorsi sopra la prima deca di Tito Livio.* Ed. Sergio Bertelli. Milan: Feltrinelli, 1983.

——. *The Discourses.* Ed. Bernard Crick and trans. Leslie J. Walker, S.J. Harmondsworth: Penguin, 1970.

——. *The Prince.* Trans. George Bull. Harmondsworth: Penguin, 1961.

McKenna, Lambert (ed. and trans.). *Dánta do chum Aonghus Fionn Ó Dalaigh.* Dublin and London: Maunsel and Company, 1919.

Mhac an tSaoi, Máire (ed.). *Dhá Sgéal Artúraíochta. Mar atá Eachtra Mhelóra agus Orlando, agus Céilidhe Iosgaide Léithe.* Dublin, 1946.

Moryson, Fynes. *An Itinerary.* 4 vols. Glasgow, 1907–8.

——. 'A Description of Ireland', in *Ireland Under Elizabeth and James the First.* Ed. Henry Morley. London, 1890.

Nicolson, William. *The Irish Historical Library.* Dublin: Aaron Rhames, for R. Owen, Bookseller, 1724.

O'Donovan, John (ed.). *Annals of the Kingdom of Ireland, by the Four Masters, from the earliest period to the year 1616.* 7 vols. Dublin, 1856.

O'Mahony, Conor. *Disputatio apologetica de Iure Regni Hiberniae pro Catholicis Hibernis adversus haereticos Anglos. Accessit eiusdem authoris ad eosdem Catholicos exhortatio.* Lisbon, 1645.

O'Rahilly, Cecile (ed. and trans.). *The Pursuit of Gruaidh Ghriansholus.* London: Irish Texts Society, 1924.

O'Rahilly, Egan. *The Poems of Egan O'Rahilly* ed. Patrick S. Dinneen. London: Irish Texts Society III, 1900.

Orrery, Roger Boyle, 1st Earl of. *The Irish Colours Displayed.* n.p., 1662.

O'Sullivan Beare, Philip. *Historiae Catholicae Hiberniae Compendium.* Ed. Matthew Kelly. Dublin, 1850.

——. *Historiae Catholicae Iberniae Compendium.* Lisbon, 1621.

——. *Ireland Under Elizabeth, being chapters towards a history of Ireland in the reign of Elizabeth being a portion of the history of Catholic Ireland by Don Philip O'Sullivan-Bear.* Trans. and ed. Matthew J. Byrne. Dublin, 1903.

——. *Selections from the Zoilomastix of Philip O'Sullivan Beare*. Ed. Thomas J. O'Donnell. Dublin, 1960.

Ovid. *Metamorphoses*. Trans. Frank Justus Miller. Cambridge, Mass.: Harvard University Press, 1958.

——. *Tristia, Ex ponto*. Trans. Arthur Leslie Wheeler, second ed. G. P. Gould. Cambridge, Mass., 1988.

Quinn, D. B. (ed.). 'Conjectures on the State of Ireland, 1552'. *Irish Historical Studies* 5 (1947): 303–22.

Riche, Barnabe. *A New Description of Ireland*. London, 1610.

——. *A True and Kinde Excuse, written in Defence of that Booke, intituled A New Description of Irelande*. London, 1612.

——. *My Ladies Looking Glasse*. London, 1615.

——. *The Irish Hubbub, or The English Hue and Crie*. London, 1617.

Spenser, Edmund. *The Works of Edmund Spenser: A Variorum Edition*, 9 vols. Ed. Edwin Greenlaw, C. G. Osgood, F. M. Padelford. Baltimore: Johns Hopkins University Press, 1932–49.

——. *A View of the Present State of Ireland*. Ed. W. L. Renwick. Oxford: Clarendon Press, 1970.

——. *The Faerie Queene*. Ed. Thomas P. Roche Jr. with C. Patrick O'Donnell Jr. New Haven: Yale University Press, 1981.

——. *Shepheardes Calender*. In *The Yale Edition of the Shorter Poems of Edmund Spenser*. Ed. William A. Oram, Einar Bjorvand, Ronald Bond, Thomas H. Cain, Alexander Dunlop, and Richard Schell. New Haven: Yale University Press, 1989.

Stafford, Thomas, Sir. *Pacata Hibernia, or, A history of the wars in Ireland during the reign of Elizabeth I.* 2 vols. Dublin: reprinted by Hibernia Press, 1810.

Stanihurst, Richard. 'A Treatise Conteining A Plaine and Perfect Description of Ireland'. In *Holinshed's Chronicles of England, Scotland, and Ireland*. Vol. 6. New York: AMS Press, 1976; reprint of 1808 edition, London: J. Johnson.

Stokes, W. (ed.). *Irische Texte* IV, pt. ii (1909).

Suárez, Francisco. *De Legibus, ac Deo Legislatore*. Coimbra, 1612.

——. *Defensio Fidei Catholicae, et Apostolicae adversus Anglicanae Sectae Errores*. Coimbra, 1613.

——. *De Fide, Spe et Caritate*. Coimbra, 1621.

——. *Selections from Three Works of Francisco Suárez, S.J. De Legibus, ac Deo Legislatore, 1612. Defensio Fidei Catholicae, Adversus Anglicanae Sectae Errores, 1613. De Triplici Virtute Theologica, Fide, Spe, et Charitate, 1621.* Trans. Gwladys L. Williams, Ammi Brown, and John Waldron, with revisions by Henry Davis. Oxford, 1944.

Thevet, André. *Cosmographie Universelle*. Paris, 1575.

Ussher, James. *The Works of the Most Rev. James Ussher*. 17 vols. Ed. C. R. Elrington. Dublin: Hodges and Smith, 1847–64.

Virgil. *Works*. 2 vols. Trans. H. Rushton Fairclough. Cambridge, Mass.: Harvard University Press, 1934.

Walsh, Sir Nicholas. *The Office and Duety in Fighting for Our Country*. London, 1545.

Walsh, Paul. *Beatha Aodha Ruaidh Uí Dhomhnaill*. 2 vols. Dublin, 1948, 1957.

Walsh, Peter. *A Prospect of the State of Ireland*. London, 1682.

White, Rowland. ' "Discourse Touching Ireland" c. 1569.' Ed. Nicholas Canny. *Irish Historical Studies* 20 (1976–77): 451–83.

Wilson, Charles. *Select Irish Poems Translated into English*. Dublin, 1782.

Yepes, Fray Antonio de. *Cronica General de la Orden de San Benito*. Ed. Fray Justo Perez de Urbel, O. S. B. Madrid: Atlas, 1959–60.

Secondary Sources

Allison, A. F. and D. M. Rogers. *The Contemporary Printed Literature of the English Counter-Reformation between 1558 and 1640*. Aldershot: Scolar Press, 1989.

Anderson, Benedict. *Imagined Communities*. London: Verso, 1983.

Andrews, K. P., N. P. Canny, and P. E. H. Andrews (eds.). *The Westward Enterprise*. Detroit: Wayne State University Press, 1979.

Anglo, Sydney. 'A Machiavellian Solution to the Irish Problem: Richard Beacon's *Solon His Follie* (1594)'. In *England and the Continental Renaissance*. Ed. Edward Chaney and Peter Mack. Woodbridge: Boydell Press, 1990.

Aptekar, Jane. *Icons of Justice*. New York: Columbia University Press, 1969.

Arnold, Mathew. *Culture and Anarchy*. Ed. J. Dover Wilson. Cambridge: Cambridge University Press, 1971.

Baldick, Chris. *The Social Mission of English Criticism*. Oxford: Clarendon Press, 1983.

Bartlett, Kenneth R. *The English in Italy, 1525–1558: A Study in Culture and Politics*. Geneve: Slatkine, 1991.

——.'The Strangeness of Strangers: English Attitudes Towards Italy in the Sixteenth Century'. *Quaderni d'Italianistica* 1 (1980): 46–63.

——.'Dangers and Delights: English Protestants in Italy in the Sixteenth Century'. In *Forestieri e Stranieri nelle Città Basso-medievali*. Firenze: Salimbeni, 1988.

Benjamin, Walter. *Schriften*. Ed. T. W. Adorno and Gretel Adorno. Frankfurt: Suhrkamp Verlag, 1955.

——. *The Origins of German Tragic Drama*. Trans. John Osborne. London: New Left Books, 1977.

Bennett, Josephine Waters. 'Did Spenser Starve?' *Modern Language Notes* 52 (1937): 400–1.

Berry, Herbert, and E. K. Timings. 'Spenser's Pension'. *Review of English Studies* 11 (1960): 254–9.

Bhabha, Homi K. 'Signs Taken for Wonders'. In *The Post-Colonial Studies Reader*. Ed. B. Ashcroft, G. Griffiths, and H. Tiffin. London: Routledge, 1995.

——. 'Sly Civility', *October* 34, 71–8.

Bossy, John. *The English Catholic Community, 1570–1850*. New York: Oxford University Press, 1976.

Bradshaw, Brendan. *The Irish Constitutional Revolution in the Sixteenth Century*. Cambridge: Cambridge University Press, 1979.

——. 'Robe and Sword in the Conquest of Ireland'. In *Law and Government under the Tudors*. Ed. Claire Cross et al. Cambridge, 1988.

——. 'Edmund Spenser on Justice and Mercy'. In *The Writer as Witness: Literature as Historical Evidence*. Ed. Tom Dunne. Cork: Cork University Press, 1987.

——. 'Geoffrey Keating: Apologist for Gaelic Ireland'. In *Representing Ireland*. Ed. B. Bradshaw, A. Hadfield, and W. Maley. Cambridge: Cambridge University Press, 1993.

——. 'The English Reformation and Identity Formation in Ireland and Wales'. In Brendan Bradshaw and Peter Roberts (eds.), *British Consciousness and Identity: The Making of Britain, 1533–1707*. Cambridge: Cambridge University Press, 1998.

Bradshaw, Brendan, and John Morrill (eds.). *The British Problem c. 1534–1707: State Formation in the Atlantic Archipelago*. London: Macmillan, 1996.

Brady, Ciaran. 'Spenser's Irish Crisis: Humanism and Experience in the 1590s'. *Past and Present* 111 (1986): 16–49.

——. 'Reply to Nicholas Canny'. *Past and Present* 120 (1988): 210–15.

Brady, Ciaran, and Raymond Gillespie (eds.). *Natives and Newcomers: Essays on the Making of Irish Colonial Society, 1534–1641*. Dublin: Irish Academic Press, 1986.

Breatnach, Caoimhín. *Patronage, Politics, and Prose: Ceasacht Inghine Guile Sgéala Muice Meic Dhá Thó Oidheadh Chuinn Chéadchathaigh*. Maynooth: An Sagart, 1996.

Breatnach, Pádraig A. 'The Chief's Poet'. *Proceedings of the Royal Irish Academy*. Vol. 83, C, no. 3 (1983): 37–79.

Breatnach, R. A.'The Lady and the King'. *Studies* XLII (1953): 321–36.

Brigden, Susan. *New Worlds, Lost Worlds: The Rule of the Tudors 1485–1603*. London: Allen Lane, 2000.

Bruford, Alan. *Gaelic Folk-Tales and Mediaeval Romances*. Dublin: The Folklore of Ireland Society, 1969.

Butler, W. F. 'The Identity of Philip O'Sullivan Beare "the Historian"'. *Royal Society of Antiquaries of Ireland Journal*, series 6, xv (1925): 95–8.

Byrne, Francis J. 'Senchas: the nature of Gaelic historical tradition' in J. G. Barry (ed.), *Historical studies* IX (Belfast, 1974), pp. 137–59, p. 138.

Caball, Marc. *Poets and Politics: Reaction and Continuity in Irish Poetry, 1558–1625*. Cork: Cork University Press, 1998.

——. 'Faith, Culture and Sovereignty: Irish Nationality and its Development, 1558–1625'. In Brendan Bradshaw and Peter Roberts (eds.) *British Consciousness and Identity*. Cambridge: Cambridge University Press, 1998.

——. 'Providence and Exile in Early Seventeenth-Century Ireland'. *Irish Historical Studies* xxix, no. 114 (Nov. 1994): 174–88.

Cairns, David, and Shaun Richards. *Writing Ireland: Colonialism, Nationalism, and Culture*. Manchester: Manchester University Press, 1988.

Canny, Nicholas. *The Elizabethan Conquest of Ireland: A Pattern Established 1565–76*. New York: Harper & Row, 1976.

——. 'Edmund Spenser and the Development of an Anglo-Irish Identity'. *Yearbook of English Studies* 13 (1983): 1–19.

——. 'Debate: Spenser's Irish Crisis: Humanism and Experience in the 1590s'. *Past and Present* 120 (1988): 201–9.

——.'Identity Formation in Ireland: The Emergence of an Anglo-Irish Identity'. In *Colonial Identity in the Atlantic World*. Ed. N. Canny and A. Pagden. Princeton: Princeton University Press, 1987.

Canny, Nicholas, and Anthony Padgen (eds.). *Colonial Identity in the Atlantic World*. Princeton: Princeton University Press, 1987.

Carey, Vincent. 'John Derricke's *Image of Ireland*, Sir Henry Sidney, and the Massacre at Mullaghmast, 1578'. *Irish Historical Studies* vol. 32, no. 123 (May 1999): 305–27.

——. 'The Irish Face of Machiavelli: Richard Beacon's *Solon His Follie* (1594) and Republican Ideology in the Conquest of Ireland'. In *Political Ideology in Ireland 1541–1641*. Ed. Hiram Morgan. Dublin: Four Courts Press, 1999.

——. ' "Neither good English nor good Irish": Bi-lingualism and Identity Formation in Sixteenth-Century Ireland'. In *Political Ideology in Ireland, 1541–1641*. Ed. Hiram Morgan. Dublin: Four Courts Press, 1999.

Carey, Vincent, and Clare Carroll, 'Factions and Fictions: Spenser's Reflections of and on Elizabethan Politics'. In *Spenser's Life and the Subject of Biography*. Ed. Judith Anderson, Donald Cheney, and David Richardson. Amherst: University of Massachusetts Press, 1996.

Carney, James. *The Irish Bardic Poet*. Dublin: Dolmen Press, 1967.

Carpenter, Andrew, and Alan Harrison. 'Swift's "O'Rourke's Feast" and Sheridan's "Letter": Early transcripts by Anthony Raymond'. In *Proceedings of the First Munster Symposium on Jonathan Swift*. Ed. Herman Real and Heinz Vienken. Munich, 1985.

Carpenter, Humphrey. *Tolkien*. New York: Ballantine, 1977.

Casey, J. G. 'Patriotism in Early Modern Valencia'. In *Spain, Europe, and the Atlantic World: Essays in Honour of John H. Elliot*. Ed. Richard L. Kagan and Geoffrey Parker. Cambridge, 1995.

Casway, Jerrold I. *Owen Roe O'Neill and the Struggle for Catholic Ireland*. Philadelphia, 1984.

Cavanagh, Sheila. *Wanton Eyes and Chaste Desires: Female Sexuality in the 'Faerie Queene'*. Bloomington: Indiana University Press, 1994.

Chakrabarty, Dipesh. 'Postcoloniality and the Artifice of History: Who Speaks for "Indian" Pasts?'. In *The Post-Colonial Studies Reader*. Ed. Bill Ashcroft, Gareth Griffiths, and Helen Tiffin. London and New York: Routledge, 1995.

Coby, J. Patrick. *Machiavelli's Romans: Liberty and Greatness in the Discourses on Livy*. Lanham, Maryland, New York, Oxford: Lexington Books, 1999.

Corish, Patrick. 'Two Contemporary Historians of the Confederation of Kilkenny: John Lynch and Richard O'Ferrall'. *Irish Historical Studies* 9 (1952–3): 271–36.

Coughlan, Patricia (ed.). *Spenser and Ireland*. Cork: Cork University Press, 1989.

Covington, F. F. 'Another View of Spenser's Linguistics'. *Studies in Philology* 19 (1922): 244–8.

Coyle, Martin (ed.). *Niccolò Machiavelli's The Prince: New Interdisciplinary Essays*. Manchester and New York: Manchester University Press, 1995.

Crapanzano, Vincent. 'Hermes' Dilemma: The Masking of Subversion in Ethnographic Description'. In *Writing Culture: The Poetics and Politics of Ethnography*. Ed. James Clifford and George E. Marcus. Berkeley: University of California Press, 1986.

——. 'Truth or Metaphor', *Res* 32 (Autumn 1997): 45–51.

Cressy, David. 'Describing the Social Order of Elizabethan and Stuart England'. *Literature and History* 3 (1976): 29–44.

Crotty, Raymond. *Ireland in Crisis: A Study in Capitalist Colonial Underdevelopment*. Dingle: Brandon, 1987.

Cunningham, Bernadette. *The World of Geoffrey Keating*. Dublin: Four Courts Press, 2000.

——. 'Representations of King, Parliament and the Irish People in Geoffrey Keating's *Foras Feasa ar Eirinn* and John Lynch's *Cambrensis Eversus* (1662)'. In *Political Thought in Seventeenth-Century Ireland*. Ed. Jane Ohlmeyer. Cambridge: Cambridge University Press, 2000.

Cunningham, Bernadette, and Raymond Gillespie. '"The most adaptable of saints": The Cult of Saint Patrick in the Seventeenth Century'. *Archivium Hibernicum* XLIX (1995): 82–104.

Davies, Gareth. 'The Irish College at Santiago de Compostella: Two Documents about Its Early Days'. In *Catholic Tastes and Times: Essays in Honour of Michael E. Williams*. Ed. Margaret A. Rees. Leeds, 1987.

Davies, Norman. *The Isles: A History*. New York: Oxford University Press, 1999.

Deane, Seamus. 'Civilians and Barbarians'. In *Ireland's Field Day*. Notre Dame: Notre Dame University Press, 1986.

de Blacam, Aodh. 'The Story of the Fight for the Southern Irish Ports and the Great Retreat of O'Sullivan Beare' (from the *Capuchin Annual* 1946/47), foreword by Donal O'Siodhachain. Cork, 1987.

de Certeau, Michel. *The Writing of History*. Trans. Tom Conley. New York: Columbia University Press, 1988.

Denoon, D. *Settler Capitalism*. Oxford: Oxford University Press, 1983.

de Scoraille, Raoul, S.J. *François Suárez de la Compagnie de Jésus*, 2 vols. Paris, 1912.

Dillon, Myles, et al. *Catalogue of Irish Manuscripts in the Franciscan Library Killiney*. Dublin: Dublin Institute for Advanced Studies, 1969.

Doan, James E. ' "An Island in the Virginian Sea": Native Americans and Irish in English Discourse, 1585–1640'. *New Hibernia Review* I, 1 (Spring, 1987): 79–99.

Donoghue, Denis. 'Fears for Irish Studies in an Age of Identity Politics'. *Chronicle of Higher Education*, November 21, 1997, B4–B5.

'Don Philip O'Sullivan; the Siege of Dunboy and the Retreat and Asassination of the O'Sullivan Beare'. *Waterford and Southeast of Ireland Archaeological Society*, 7 (1901): pp. 76–96, 103–23.

Draper, John W. 'Spenser's Linguistics in the Present State of Ireland'. *Modern Philology* 17 (1919–20): 471–86.

Duffy, Eamon. *The Stripping of the Altars*. New Haven: Yale University Press, 1992.

Dunseath, T. K. *Spenser's Allegory of Justice in Book Five of 'The Faerie Queene'*. Princeton: Princeton University Press, 1968.

Dussel, Enrique. 'Eurocentrism and Modernity'. *Boundary 2*, vol. 20, no. 3 (Fall 1993): 65–76.

——. *The Invention of the Americas: Eclipse of 'The Other' and the Myth of Modernity*. Trans. Michael D. Barber. New York: Continuum, 1995.

Edwards, David. 'Beyond Reform: Martial Law and the Tudor Reconquest of Ireland'. *History Ireland*, vol. 5, no. 2 (Summer 1997): 16–21.

——.'Ideology and Experience: Spenser's *View* and Martial Law in Ireland'. In *Political Ideology in Ireland 1541–1641*. Ed. Hiram Morgan. Dublin: Four Courts Press, 1999.

Edwards, R. Dudley. *Ireland in the Age of the Tudors: The Destruction of Hiberno-Norman Civilization*. London: Croom Helm, 1977.

Elliott, J. H. *Spain and Its World 1500–1700*. New Haven and London, 1989.

Ellis, Steven G. *Tudor Ireland: Crown, Community and the Conflict of Cultures 1470–1603*. New York: Longman, 1985.

Fabian, Johannes. *Time and the Other: How Anthropology Makes Its Object*. New York: Columbia University Press, 1983.

Falls, Cyril. *Elizabeth's Irish Wars*. London, 1950.

Fennessy, Ignatius. 'Printed Items Among the Wadding Papers', *Collectanea Hibernica*, Nos. 39–40 (1997–8), pp. 32–95.

Finegan, Francis, S. J. 'Irish Rectors at Seville 1619–1687, *Irish Ecclesiastical Record* CVI (July/Dec. 1966) 5th series, pp. 46–63,

Fletcher, Angus. *The Prophetic Moment*. Chicago: University of Chicago Press, 1971.

Fogarty, Anne (ed.). *Special Issue: Spenser in Ireland: The Faerie Queene; 1596–1996. Irish University Review*, vol. 26, no. 2 (Autumn/Winter 1996).

Foucault, Michel. *The Order of Things*. New York: Random House, 1973.

——. 'What is an Author?' in *Language, Countermemory, Practice*. Trans. Donald F. Bouchard and Sherry Simon. Ithaca: Cornell University Press, 1977.

Gellner, Ernest. *Nations and Nationalism*. Oxford: Blackwell, 1983.

Gillingham, John. 'The Beginnings of English Imperialism'. *Journal of Historical Sociology*, vol. 4, no. 4 (December 1992): 392–409.

Greenblatt, Steven. *Renaissance Self-Fashioning*. Chicago, 1980.

Greenlaw, Edwin. 'The Influence of Machiavelli on Spenser'. *Modern Philology* 7 (1909): 187–202.

——. 'Spenser and British Imperialism'. *Modern Philology* 9 (1912): 347–70.

——. *Studies in Spenser's Historical Allegory*. Baltimore: Johns Hopkins University Press, 1932.

Grennan, Eamon. 'Language and Politics: A Note on Some Metaphors in Spenser's *A View of the Present State of Ireland'. Spenser Studies* 3 (1982): 99–110.

Grosjean, Paul. 'Un Soldat de Fortune Irlandais au Service des "Acta Sanctorum": Philippe O'Sullivan Beare et Jean Bolland (1634)'. *Anal. Boll.* 81 (1963): 418–46.

Gross, Kenneth. *Spenserian Poetics*. Ithaca: Cornell University Press, 1985.

Gwynn, Aubrey. 'An Unpublished Work of Philip O'Sullivan Bear'. *Analecta Hibernica* 6 (1934): 1–11.

Hadfield, Andrew. 'Rocking the Boat: A Response to Hiram Morgan'. *Irish Review* 12 (1992): 15–19.

——. *Spenser's Irish Experience: Wilde Fruit and Savage Soyl*. Oxford: Clarendon Press, 1997.

Hammerstein, Helga. 'Aspects of the Continental Education of Irish Students in the Reign of Queen Elizabeth'. *Historical Studies* 8 (1971): 137–53.

Hankins, John Erskine. *Source and Meaning in Spenser's Allegory*. Oxford: Clarendon Press, 1971.

Hastings, Adrian. *The Construction of Nationhood: Ethnicity, Religion, and Nationalism*. Cambridge: Cambridge University Press, 1997.

Haywood, Eric G. 'Is Ireland Worth Bothering About? Classical Perceptions of Ireland Revisited in Renaissance Italy'. *International Journal of the Classical Tradition* vol. 2, no. 4 (1996): 467–86.

Henley, Pauline. *Spenser in Ireland*. Dublin and Cork: University of Cork Press, 1928.

Henry, Gráinne. *The Irish Military Community in Spanish Flanders 1586–1621*. Dublin, 1992.

Herbert, Máire. 'Goddess and King: The Sacred Marriage in Early Ireland'. In *Women and Sovereignty*. Ed. L. O. Fradenburg. Edinburgh, 1992.

Hindley, Reg. *The Death of the Irish Language*. London and New York: Routledge, 1990.

Hobsbawm, E. J. *Nations and Nationalism since 1780*. Cambridge: Cambridge University Press, 1990.

Hollo, Kaarina. 'Eachtra Ridire na Leomhan ina comhthéacs Eorpach'. In *Nua-Léamha: Gnéithe de Chultúr, Stair agus Polaitíocht na hÉireann c. 1600–c.1900*. Ed. Máirín Ní Dhonnchadha. Baile Átha Cliath: An Chló-chomhar, 1996.

Hull, Suzanne W. *Chaste, Silent & Obedient: English Books for Women 1475–1640*. San Marino: Huntington Library, 1984.

Jago, C. J. 'Taxation and Political Culture in Castile'. In *Spain, Europe and the Atlantic World*. Ed. Richard L. Kagan and Geoffrey Parker. Cambridge: Cambridge University Press, 1995.

Jameson, Fredric. *Marxism and Form*. Princeton: Princeton University Press, 1977.

Jardine, Lisa. 'Mastering the Uncouth: Gabriel Harvey, Edmund Spenser and the English Experience in Ireland'. In *New Perspectives on Renaissance Thought: Essays in the History of Science, Education and Philosophy*. Ed. John Henry and Sarah Hutton. London: Duckworth, 1990.

Javitch, Daniel. *Proclaiming a Classic: The Canonization of 'Orlando Furioso'*. Princeton: Princeton University Press, 1991.

Jenkins, Raymond. 'Spenser with Lord Grey in Ireland'. *PMLA* 52 (1937): 338–9.

Jones, Ann Rosalind, and Peter Stallybrass. 'Dismantling Irena: The Sexualizing of Ireland in Early Modern England'. In *Nationalisms and Sexualities*. Ed. Andrew Parker et. al. New York, 1992.

Judson, Alexander. *Life of Edmund Spenser*. Baltimore: Johns Hopkins University Press, 1945.

Kagan, Richard L. 'Clio and the Crown: Writing History in Habsburg Spain'. In *Spain, Europe and the Atlantic World*. Ed. Richard L. Kagan and Geoffrey Parker. Cambridge, 1995.

Kiberd, Declan *Inventing Ireland*. London, 1995.

King, John. *Tudor Royal Iconography: Literature and Art in an Age of Religious Crisis*. Princeton: Princeton University Press, 1989.

Kipling, Rudyard. *The Phantom Rickshaw*. Boston: The Greenock Press, 1903.

Kirkpatrick, Robin. *English and Italian Literature from Dante to Shakespeare: A Study of Sources, Analogy and Divergence*. London: Longman, 1995.

Knott, John Ray. *Discourses of Martyrdom in English Literature, 1563–1694*. Cambridge, 1993.

Laurence, Anne. 'The Cradle to the Grave: English Observations of Irish Social Customs in the Seventeenth Century'. *Seventeenth Century* 3.1 (1988): 63–84.

Leerssen, Joep. *Mere Irish and Fíor-Ghael: Studies in the Idea of Irish Nationality, and Its Development and Literary Expression prior to the Nineteenth Century*. Cork: Cork University Press, 1996.

Lennon, Colm. *Richard Stanihurst, the Dubliner 1547–1618*. Dublin, 1981.

Lestringant, Frank. 'Le nom des cannibales de Christophe Colomb à Michel de Montaigne'. *Bulletin de la Société des Amis de Montaigne* 17–18 (1984): 51–74.

Lewis, C. S. *The Allegory of Love*. Oxford: Oxford University Press, 1936.

Lloyd, David. *Anomalous States*. Durham: Duke University Press, 1993.

Loeber, Rolf. 'Preliminaries to the Massachusetts Bay Colony, "The Irish Ventures of Emmanuel Downing and John Winthrop, Sr."' In *'A Miracle of Learning': Studies in Manuscripts and Irish Learning*. Ed. T. Barnard, D. Ó Cróinín, and K. Simms. Aldershot, 1998.

McCarthy-Morrogh, Michael. *The Munster Plantation*. Oxford: Oxford University Press, 1986.

McCavitt, John. 'Veni, Vidi, Vici: Sir John the Conqueror'. Paper delivered at the Folger Library in September 1995.

——. *Sir Arthur Chichester*. Belfast: Institute of Irish Studies, 1998.

Mac Craith, Mícheál. 'Litríocht an 17ú hAois: Tonnbhriseadh an tSeanghnáthaimh nó Tonnchruthú an Nuaghnáthaimh'. *Léachtaí Cholm Cille* XXVI (1996): 50–82.

——. 'Gaelic Ireland and the Renaissance'. In *The Celts and the Renaissance: Tradition and Innovation*. Ed. Glenmore Williams and Robert Owen Jones. Cardiff: University of Wales Press, 1990.

——. *Lorg Na hIasachta Ar Na Dánta Grá*. (Baile Átha Cliath: An Clóchomhar, 1989.

——. 'Gaelic Courtly Love Poetry: A Window on the Renaissance'. In *Celtic Languages and Celtic Peoples: Proceedings of the Second North American Congress of Celtic Studies*. Halifax, Nova Scotia, 1989.

MacCurtain, Margaret and Mary O'Dowd, eds. *Women in Early Modern Ireland*. Dublin, 1991.

MacDonald, William, 'Irish Colleges Since the Reformation', *Irish Ecclesiastical Record* VIII (1872), pp. 465–73.

——. 'Irish Ecclesiastical Colleges Since the Reformation. Seville', *Irish Ecclesiastical Record* IX (1873), pp. 208–21.

McGee, T. Darcy. *Irish Historical Writers of the Seventeenth Century*. Dublin: James Duffy, 1846.

MacIntyre, Alasdair. 'Relativism, Power and Philosophy'. In *Proceedings of the American Philosophical Association* Vol. 59, no.1 (1985): 5–22.

McMurphy, Susannah. *Spenser's Use of Ariosto for Allegory*. Seattle: University of Washington Press, 1924.

Malavassi Vargas, Guillermo. 'Ideas Politicas de Francisco Suárez (1548–1617)'. In *Acta Academica* (October 1989 and May 1990): 14–18.

Maley, Willy. *Salvaging Spenser: Colonialism, Culture, and Identity*. New York: St Martin's Press, 1997.

——. 'Spenser's Irish English: Language and Identity in Early Modern Ireland'. *Studies in Philology* (1994): 417–31.

——. 'How Milton and Some Contemporaries Read Spenser's *View*'. In

Representing Ireland. Ed. B. Bradshaw, A. Hadfield, and W. Maley. Cambridge: Cambridge University Press, 1993.

Mazzeo, Joseph A. 'Machiavelli: The Artist as Statesman'. In *Renaissance and Seventeenth-Century Studies*. New York: Columbia University Press, 1964.

Mesnard, Pierre. *L'essor de la philosophie politique au XVIe siècle*. Paris, 1936.

Mignolo, Walter. *The Darker Side of the Renaissance: Literacy, Territoriality, and Colonization*. Ann Arbor: University of Michigan Press, 1995.

Montrose, Louis. 'The Work of Gender in the Discourse of Discovery'. *Representations* 33 (Winter 1991), pp. 1–41.

——. 'The Elizabethan Subject and the Spenserian Text'. In *Literary Theory/Renaissance Texts*. Ed. Patricia Parker and David Quint. Baltimore: Johns Hopkins University Press, 1986.

Moody, T. W., F. X. Martin, and F. J. Byrne (eds.), *A New History of Ireland: Vol. III: Early Modern Ireland 1534–1691*. Oxford, 1976.

Morgan, Hiram. 'Mid-Atlantic Blues'. *Irish Review* 11 (1991), pp. 50–1.

——. *Tyrone's Rebellion*. London: Royal Historical Society, 1993.

——. 'Faith and Fatherland in 16th Century Ireland'. *History Ireland* vol. 3, no. 2 (Summer 1995), pp. 13–20.

Morgan, Hiram (ed.). *Political Ideology in Ireland 1541–1641*. Dublin: Four Courts Press, 1999.

Murphy, Andrew. *'But the Irish Sea betwixt us': Ireland, Colonialism, and Renaissance Literature*. Lexington: University Press of Kentucky, 1999.

Murrin, Michael. *The Veil of Allegory*. Chicago: University of Chicago Press, 1969.

Nicholls, Kenneth. *Land, Law and Society in Sixteenth-Century Ireland*. O'Donnell Lecture. Dublin, 1972.

——. 'Worlds Apart? The Ellis Two-Nation Theory of Late Medieval Ireland'. *History Ireland* vol. 7, no. 2 (Summer 1999): 22–6.

Ní Dhonnchadha, Máirín. 'Review of Caoimhín Breatnach, *Patronage, Politics, and Prose*'. *Éigse* 30 (1997): 216–29.

Ó Buachalla, Breandán. '*Annála Ríoghachta Éireann* is *Foras Feasa ar Éirinn*: An Comhthéacs Comhaimseartha'. *Studia Hibernica* 22–3 (1982–3): 59–105.

——. 'Poetry and Politics in Early Modern Ireland'. *Eighteenth Century Ireland/Iris an Dá Chultúr* 7 (1992): 149–75.

——. 'James Our True King: The Ideology of Irish Royalism in the Seventeenth Century'. In G. Boyce et al., *Political Thought in Ireland*. London, 1993.

——. *Aisling Ghéíar, Na Stíobhartiagh agus an tAois Léinn 1603–1788*. Dublin, 1996.

O'Connell, Pat. 'The Irish College, Santiago de Compostella: 1605–1767'. *Archivium Hibernicum* (1996): 19–28.

O'Connor, Denis. 'The Retreat of O'Sullivan Beare to the North'. *Irish Ecclesiastical Record*, 4th series, xii (Oct. 1902): 320–34.

O'Connor, Thomas (ed.). *The Irish in Europe 1580–1815*. Dublin: Four Courts Press, 2001.

O Cuív, Brian. 'The Irish Language in the Early Modern Period'. In *A New History of Ireland*. Ed. T. W. Moody, F. X. Martin, and F. J. Byrne. 9 vols. Oxford: Clarendon Press, 1976.

———. 'An Appeal to Philip III of Spain by Ó Súlleabháin Béirre, December 1601'. *Éigse* 30 (1997): 18–26.

O'Doherty, Denis J. 'Domnaill O'Sullivan Beare and his family in Spain'. *Studies* xix (March 1930): 211–26.

O'Doherty, D. J. (ed.). 'Students of the Irish College, Salamanca'. *Archivium Hibernicum* III (1914): 87–112.

Ó Dónaill, Niall. (ed.). *Foclóir Gaelige-Béarla*. Dublin: Richview, Browne & Nolan, 1977.

O'Dowd, Mary. 'Gaelic Economy and Society'. In *Natives and Newcomers*. Ed. C. Brady and R. Gillespie. Dublin, 1986.

O'Grady, Standish. *Ulrick the Ready, A Romance of Elizabethan Ireland*. London, 1896.

Ó hAnnracháin, Tadhg. ' "Though Heretics and Politicians should misinterpret their good zeale": Political Ideology and Catholicism in Early Modern Ireland'. In *Political Thought in Seventeenth-Century Ireland*. Ed. Jane Ohlmeyer. Cambridge: Cambridge University Press, 2000.

Ohlmeyer, Jane. 'Seventeenth-Century Ireland and the New British and Atlantic Histories'. *American Historical Review* vol. 104, no.2 (April 1999): 446–62.

Ó hÓgáin, Dáithí. *Myth, Legend & Romance: An Encyclopedia of the Irish Folk Tradition*. New York: Prentice Hall, 1991.

Oliver, George. *Collections towards illustrating the Biography of the Scotch, English and Irish Members of the Society of Jesus*. London, 1880.

O'Rahilly, T. F. 'Notes, Mainly Etymological'. *Éigse* 13 (1942): 207–11.

———. 'The Names *Érainn* and *Ériu*'. *Ériu* XIV (1946): 7–28.

Pagden, Anthony. 'Dispossessing the Barbarian: The Language of Spanish Thomism and the Debate over the Property Rights of the American Indians'. In *The Languages of Political Theory in Early-Modern Europe*. Ed. Anthony Pagden. Cambridge: Cambridge University Press, 1987.

Palmer, Patricia. 'The Grafted Tongue: Linguistic Colonisation and the Native Response in Sixteenth-Century Ireland'. D.Phil. dissertation, Oxford University, 1998, forthcoming from Cambridge University Press.

Peltonen, Markku. 'Classical Republicanism in Tudor England: The Case of Richard Beacon's *Solon His Follie*'. *History of Political Thought* 15, 4 (1994): 469–503.

———. *Classical Humanism and Republicanism in English Political Thought 1570–1640*. Cambridge: Cambridge University Press, 1995.

Pitkin, Hanna Fenichel. *Fortune is a Woman: Gender and Politics in the Thought of Niccolo Machiavelli* with a New Afterword. Chicago: University of Chicago Press, 1999.

Pocock, J. G. A. *The Ancient Constitution, and the Feudal Law: A Study of English Historical Thought in the Seventeenth Century.* Cambridge, 1957.

——. *The Machiavellian Moment: Florentine Political Thought and the Atlantic Republican Tradition.* Princeton: Princeton University Press, 1975.

Praz, Mario. *Machiavelli in Inghilterra ed altri sagii.* Rome: Tumminelli, 1942.

——. 'Machiavelli and the Elizabethans'. In *The Flaming Heart.* New York, 1968.

Quinn, David B. 'Sir Thomas Smith and the Beginnings of English Colonial Theory'. *Proceedings of the American Philosophical Society* 89, 4 (1945): 543–60.

——. 'Ireland and Sixteenth-Century European Expansion'. *Historical Studies* 1.20 (1958): 20–32.

——. *The Elizabethans and the Irish.* Ithaca: Cornell University Press, 1966.

——. 'Renaissance Influences on English Colonization'. *Transactions of the Royal Historical Society* 26 (1976): 73–93.

Quint, David. *Epic and Empire: Politics and Generic Form from Virgil to Milton.* Princeton: Princeton University Press, 1993.

Raab, Felix. *The English Face of Machiavelli: A Changing Interpretation 1500–1700.* London: Routledge & Kegan Paul, 1964.

Reynolds, Susan. 'Medieval *Origines Gentium* and the Community of the Realm'. *History* 68 (1983): 375–90.

Rich, Townsend. *Harington and Ariosto: A Study in Elizabethan Verse Translation.* New Haven: Yale University Press, 1940.

Richter, Michael. *Medieval Ireland: The Enduring Tradition.* New York: St Martin's Press, 1988.

Rossi, Sergio. 'Italy and the English Renaissance: An Introduction'. In *Italy and the English Renaissance.* Ed. Sergio Rossi and Daniella Savoia. Milano: Edizioni Unicolpi, 1989.

Royal Irish Academy. *Dictionary of the Irish Language.* Compact Edition. Dublin: Royal Irish Academy, 1983.

Sabin, Joseph. *A List of the Printed Editions of Fray Bartolomé de las Casas.* New York, 1870.

Said, Edward. *Orientalism.* New York: Pantheon Books, 1978.

Sayers, George. *Jack: C. S. Lewis and His Times.* San Francisco: Harper & Row, 1988.

Scott, Joan. *Gender and the Politics of History.* New York, 1988.

Shepherd, Simon. *Spenser.* London: Harvester Wheatsheaf, 1989.

Shire, Helena. *A Preface to Spenser.* London: Longman 1978.

Silberman, Lauren. 'Singing Unsung Heroines: Androgynous Discourse in Book 3 of *The Faerie Queene*'. In *Rewriting the Renaissance.* Ed. Margaret W. Ferguson, Maureen Quilligan, and Nancy Vickers. Chicago: University of Chicago Press, 1986.

Silke, J. J. *Ireland and Europe 1559–1607.* Dublin, 1966.

————. 'The Irish College, Seville', *Archivium Hibernicum* XXIV (1961), pp. 103–47.

Simms, Katharine. *From Kings to Warlords: The Changing Political Structure of Ireland in the Later Middle Ages.* Woodbridge, Suffolk: Boydell Press, 1987.

Smith, Roland M. 'Spenser's Tale of the Two Sons of Milesio'. *MLQ* 3 (1942): 547–57.

————. 'The Irish Background of Spenser's "View"'. *JEGP* 42 (1943): 499–515.

————. 'Spenser, Holinshed, and the *Leabhar Gabhála*'. *JEGP* 43 (1944): 390–401.

————. 'Irish Names in the *Faerie Queene*'. *MLN* 61 (1946): 27–38.

————. 'Spenser's Scholarly Script and "Right Writing"'. In *Studies in Honor of T. W. Baldwin.* Ed. Don Cameron Allen. Urbana: University of Illinois Press, 1958.

Sommerville, J. P. 'From Suarez to Filmer: A Reappraisal'. *Historical Journal* 25, 3 (1982): 525–40.

Stradling, R. A. *Philip IV and the Government of Spain, 1621–1665.* Cambridge: Cambridge University Press, 1988.

————. *The Spanish Monarchy and Irish Mercenaries: The Wilde Geese in Spain 1618–68.* Dublin, 1994.

Strong, Roy. *The Cult of Elizabeth.* Berkeley: University of California Press, 1977.

Thomas, Henry. *Spanish and Portuguese Romances of Chivalry.* Cambridge: Cambridge University Press, 1920.

Todd, Jennifer. 'The Limits of Britishness'. *Irish Review* 5 (1988): 11–16.

Trumpener, Katie. *Bardic Nationalism: The Romantic Novel and the British Empire.* Princeton: Princeton University Press, 1997.

Waller, Marguerite. 'Academic Tootsie: The Denial of Difference and the Difference It Makes'. *Diacritics* 17.1 (1987): 2–20.

Walsh, Micheline Kerney (ed.). *Spanish Knights of Irish Origin: Documents from Continental Archives.* 4 vols. Dublin, 1960.

————. 'O'Sullivan Beare in Spain: Some Unpublished Documents'. *Archivium Hibernicum* 45 (1990): 46–63.

Walsh, T. J. *The Irish Continental College Movement.* Dublin: Golden Eagle Books, 1973.

Wilenius, Reijo. 'The Social and Political Thought of Francisco Suárez'. In *Acta Philosophica Fennica*, Fasc. XV (1963).

Wormald, Jenny. *Court, Kirk, and Community.* New History of Scotland 4. Toronto: University of Toronto Press, 1981.

Yeats, W. B. *The Cutting of an Agate.* London: Macmillan, 1919.

Zimmermann, T. C. Price. Paolo Giovio: *The Historian and the Crisis of Sixteenth-Century Italy.* Princeton: Princeton University Press, 1995.

INDEX